Process

LUCY SPRAGGAN

Process

FINDING MY WAY THROUGH

BLINK
bringing you closer

First published in the UK by Blink Publishing
An imprint of Bonnier Books UK
4th Floor, Victoria House,
Bloomsbury Square,
London, WC1B 4DA

Owned by Bonnier Books
Sveavägen 56, Stockholm, Sweden

Hardback – 9781788709095
Trade Paperback – 9781788709125
Ebook – 9781788709118
Audio Digital Download – 9781788709132

A CIP catalogue of this book is available from the British Library.

Designed by Envy Design Ltd
Printed and bound by Clays Ltd, Elcograf S.p.A.

1 3 5 7 9 10 8 6 4 2

Blink Publishing is an imprint of Bonnier Books UK
www.bonnierbooks.co.uk

For anyone who has ever shown me kindness.

Trigger warning: sexual assault; substance abuse; violence.

Contents

Prologue

'Are you that girl off *X Factor*?' the man asks as he shuffles customers along the self-service checkout queue at WHSmith in Euston Station. 'I voted for you!'

It's been ten years and he still remembers my audition. He's being kind.

It's not even the first time I've been asked that question today. It's actually the question I have been asked the most over the last decade.

In 2012, when I was twenty years old, I was a contestant on the UK version of *The X Factor*. That year, my audition was the fourth most watched video on YouTube – in the world! – and I became the most googled artist in the UK. I was the first contestant in the show's history to sing their own songs and play an instrument. When I performed a funny ditty about getting drunk in a northern accent, I became an overnight phenomenon and was the bookies' favourite to win the whole show.

I'd been gigging since I was twelve and had already released several EPs plus a pretty well-received album. Up until that point, it had kept me in beer money, but the day after my audition aired, my track 'Last Night' overtook Little Mix, *X Factor* winners from the previous year, on the iTunes chart. Which was almost exactly the moment I received a call from a lawyer from Simon Cowell's Syco, one of companies that produce *The X Factor*, asking me to take down my music from iTunes.

I could see that my album was heading for the top – it eventually climbed to number five and 'Last Night' was at number eleven in the singles chart – but what did I do? I took the advice of the lawyer that had been appointed by the show to 'act on behalf' of the contestants and did what Syco had asked me to do. The next email I got was from the distributor I used, asking if I was sure I wanted to remove the record. In their opinion, 'Last Night', and my album, were both headed for number one.

As the show progressed, I won support from viewers for refusing to change my style, not ditching my guitar and for declining – quite publicly – the advice of the show's make-up artists and hair stylists. I also remained very much on brand for someone best known for a song about getting drunk and was often photographed falling out of clubs totally obliterated. The viewers voted for me and the tabloids loved me.

I rode the wave of positivity through the pre-recorded boot camp stage and onto the 'Judges' Houses' stage, where you get flown to a very posh hotel abroad that's made to look like your mentor's home. From there, I made it to the live shows and performed every Saturday night, hoping the public would vote to keep me in the competition. I survived the first live show. I sang the following Saturday night and was voted through again. And then, after being watched by 11 million people every week, I disappeared.

The public was told I was ill.

I wasn't ill.

That wouldn't have required the producers to hire countless privacy specialists and cyber experts to remove any leaked information about what *had* happened to me from the internet. They bleached the truth from sites like Reddit, Digital Spy, Twitter, Facebook and the comments sections of online newspapers after the truth had been leaked to the press, allegedly, by a member of the Metropolitan Police.

Consequently, I have a number of emotions when I'm asked if I'm 'that girl'. Ultimately and unquestionably, the answer is 'Yes, I am,' but it always reminds me of what could have happened. It also reminds me of what *did* happen.

If I had spoken openly about the reason I 'disappeared', about why a man was sentenced to ten years in prison, about the events that altered the course of my life so greatly, I don't think I'd have truly had the space to recover from them. The question I would have been asked at train stations would be 'Are you the girl *that* happened to?'

Sadly, the answer to that question is also: 'Yes, I am.'

I'm in a strong enough place now to talk publicly about what really happened for the first time and I'm going to relinquish my legal right to anonymity – something I've clung onto for more than a decade – to do so. But I don't just want to write about the fact I was raped – I can't express how hard it is to put that into black and white – I also want to talk about everything that happened afterwards, how the press, the police, *The X Factor* and the music industry treated me, because that's also left me with scars which have caused some pretty big issues. Issues that I have worked very hard to overcome. I want to tell you about that part too.

I had long-standing problems with drugs and alcohol before I appeared on the programme – let me tell you, 'Last Night' was based on extremely detailed and thorough research – but what happened when I was on the show made getting sober so much harder. But I did get sober and sobriety has allowed me to see plenty of things differently, just as therapy has helped me gain insights which I think other people will find useful if they have been through significant, life-altering experiences too.

I look back at the girl I was on the show with a mix of disbelief and pride, but mostly with compassion. I'm still not sure how she survived. There are things I want to tell her and hugs I want to give her. Every time I see other young women – especially in the music industry – struggling with the same shit and hitting the same barriers, I want to help them too.

I started writing 'Dear Lucy' letters to my earlier self and, because I know she's not the only one who needed support, I'm sharing them now with you. But that isn't the only reason I am writing this book. I also want to tell these stories to show the kind people at checkouts that I'm not *just* that girl. I have a story to share.

This is going to be quite a ride.

Is This How It Ends?

I was twenty-eight when I stopped drinking. If I hadn't, there were two possible outcomes: I would go to prison or I would die.

I realise that sounds extreme but they were genuinely the only ways in which I could see my life playing out. If you asked the people who were closest to me at the time, I'm sure they'd agree, without hesitation, because I was so careless – with my belongings, my friends, other people's feelings, my organs and, ultimately, with my life – that there really were no other options.

I know memory is supposed to be impaired by alcohol but there's something about near-death levels of adrenaline which has cemented the events that follow into my hippocampus.

I was twenty-two and my friend Lloyd and I were on a bender. I have no idea how long we had been on that particular bender, only that we were deep into it and that it was a heavy one. How do I know it was heavy? Because the last place we'd been drinking was a strip club. If I ever tell a story that involves a strip club or a casino, it's a sure sign I was on a wild one and probably did something illegal. Or stupid. Or gross. Or, quite possibly, all three.

I'd met Lloyd, pre–X *Factor*, behind the scenes of one of those national 'talent competitions', otherwise known as complete rackets for exploiting young and impressionable singer-songwriters (and their families) by relieving them of hundreds of pounds via pay-to-vote systems. Lloyd, a young, blond-haired, blue-eyed, handsome Yorkshireman, was a stage hand, or 'artist herder', at one of them and we became party friends and regular fixtures in each other's lives.

When Lloyd was high on coke, his eyes would be so wide he looked like an owl. Eyebrows raised, a permanent surprised expression, as if someone had just told him an outrageous secret. My own coke quirk was to straighten my arm by my side and bend my hand at the wrist, palm facing backwards and upwards, fingers curled, giving myself what Lloyd called my 'claw'. I've seen other people do it too but I have no idea why it happens. It's a dead giveaway though, and if we ever wanted to go about our benders without being clocked as clearly off our tits, I'd have to tell him to tone down his eyes and he'd have to tell me to uncurl my claw.

It was 5.30 a.m. on a Monday morning and I was lying next to Lloyd in a hotel room in Doncaster, though I have absolutely no idea where we had been for the preceding weekend. This wasn't unusual. When I wasn't touring, Lloyd and I would often set off on an adventure that ended in a hotel like this. As I stared at the outdated, wood-panelled ceiling, I thought: 'I cannot believe I am going to die in a hotel called the Earl of Doncaster. What the fuck has my life come to?'

We had done a lot of cocaine, potentially a few days' worth, and I was convinced my heart couldn't cope. It was beating so fast and hard that I was certain it was about to explode. Death was imminent.

Thirty minutes beforehand, we had realised that not only were we out of coke but also that the dealer was no longer picking up the phone. There's a very particular feeling when coke starts to wear off and the euphoria leaks away to be replaced – slowly but surely – by unwavering doom. A drip-feed of anxiety starts to build about the things you said or did, or about when you're supposed to be at work, or what time checkout is, or why you continue to do this despite the visceral, harrowing feeling that you're ruining your life. Neither of us could face the reality that was pouring back into our bodies. We had to find more.

All of a sudden, a thought flashed into my mind. A few weeks earlier, I'd flown to LA to hang out with friends and I'd met a girl at a party. She had given me a pill that I'd left in my make-up bag. Not the kind of pink pill with a Nike tick made in someone's bedroom in Birmingham. It was a small, orange capsule. What had she said it was? 'A' something? I wracked my brain . . . Adderall. It was called Adderall.

I tore into my make-up bag and rummaged around for this loose pill; a single dose of an amphetamine Americans call 'the study drug' because it's prescribed to help students focus. It was our last-ditch effort to stay high.

I felt it between my fingers and held it in the air as if I'd found the final puzzle piece on *The Crystal Maze*. The next problem? How do two people share one capsule?

We hurried over to the desk and carefully pulled it apart, emptying the contents over the surface, assuming we would cut up the drug with a credit card and get it into our noses via a rolled-up tenner. But Big Pharma was one step ahead of us. They had designed the contents of the capsule to be unsniffable. Its amphetamine-based innards were not a fine powder but lots of small, hard, uncrushable, slow-release balls.

Lloyd and I looked at each other and silently decided that anything was better than nothing. We rolled up a note and snorted our divided ball bearings.

The pain was instant and extreme. I turned to Lloyd and his eyes, like mine, were bloodshot and tears streamed down his face. My nostrils were on fire; my sinuses rattled. My head felt like, well, it felt like it was full of tiny, little, hard ball bearings, as if a mini shotgun had blasted two barrels up my nose. The pain stretched across my forehead and over my skull towards the top of my spine. It took around three seconds to realise our most recent decision, as well as several previous ones we had made that weekend, was an extremely stupid one. We both started to panic.

The combination of the coke, the alcohol, the Xanax I'd taken earlier in the day and the unbearable nasal and cranial pain caused my heart to race in a way it hadn't before. Like something fatal was happening. I could tell by looking at Lloyd he felt exactly the same.

And then we both collapsed backwards onto the bed and waited to die.

Obviously, we didn't die but the tragic thing is, I bet we did it all again, minus the Adderall, the following weekend. That's how careless I was. Unable or unwilling to learn from, or respond to, these red flashing warnings that, whatever I told myself, I wasn't actually having fun.

Perhaps I didn't see it because I didn't drink every day and I didn't drink alone. Nor did I drink in secret or pour Special Brew on my breakfast cereal, or any of the other things on the standard 'you have a problem if you do at least one of these things' list. But that didn't mean I didn't have a problem.

I'd always thought alcohol brought out the 'real' me. My best self. It made me carefree, funnier (to me, at least) and conversation seemed to be easier. And when there wasn't any conversation, I could always offer another drink or encourage the person sitting with me to finish theirs. When I was drunk, I could share my feelings without concern; it allowed me to open up about things I didn't talk about otherwise.

It never dawned on me how much of a mental health red flag I was vigorously waving. If you only open up about the things that make you sad, angry or afraid when you're pissed or high, it's a sure sign you're using intoxicants for a reason. I see now that alcohol let the trauma out. There were thoughts – dark, painful, complicated, jagged – I never shared with anyone unless I was steaming. The alcohol opened the gate to the bit of my brain where I kept bad memories and it also removed the emotions that were attached to them. There was usually a point on every night out where I would matter-of-factly tell a friend, or sometimes a total stranger, my deepest, darkest secrets without the spiralling thoughts or earth-shattering panic that prevented me from saying those things whilst I was sober. I told myself the alcohol was helping me deal with the memories. It wasn't.

I've since learnt that the part of the brain which regulates fear, shame and guilt, the hypothalamus, is incapacitated by alcohol. I clearly did want to deal with things but my conscious, sober self couldn't bear to. It wanted to protect me from the emotions that were connected to my trauma. Yet my drunk self, my 'best self' as I saw it, was willing to divulge my traumatic information to practically anyone: a girl in the toilets, a man in the pub, my new best friend in the smoking area. And fuck me, the anxiety that came from waking up and knowing I'd divulged huge, looming pieces of my life to a stranger didn't feel good.

I've learnt that I was using alcohol to numb parts of my reality. I can see now that the traumas that made me cry to my friends in the early hours were the things I needed to deal with most. But when I woke up hungover, confused and unsure, I told myself that by speaking about them, I had dealt with them. All I can say is, I was wrong.

Dear Lucy,

I want to start by saying: I get it. You were in a lot of pain.

For a long time, there wasn't anything more painful to the inside of your skull than thinking about how you were feeling and about what had happened to you. I know that the drugs felt so helpful in that respect. When you were high it was like you were closer to the people around you, like you could open up and thrive. You felt alive and interesting. It made talking easier.

The words you couldn't even think about in the sober daytime became as smooth as crushed-up cocaine as soon as it went up your nose. And you did talk. You did try. You thought you were being brave, wearing an oversized shirt and jeans, picking up the tab everywhere you went. You always wanted to be in charge. You wanted to feel in control of what happened to you, and that's understandable. Though, your idea of being in control was very different to actually being in control and, most of the time, it actually looked like putting yourself in real danger.

When I recall those memories, I can see why it was all so appealing: you didn't want to be alive. That's why the drugs, the alcohol and the risks always came in such large numbers. Underneath the guise of having fun, there was always a chance that after one of those weekends, you might just not wake up.

So, you kept doing it.

Looking back, I actually feel guilty for not protecting you then. Isn't that weird?

I wish I could go back in time and scoop you up off that bed in the hotel in Doncaster and take you somewhere safe. I wish you'd have been surrounded by people who did that. I wish I could have been your friend. I'm not sure you'd have listened to me but I'd have tried.

Lloyd was a great friend. I can see now he was trying to protect you in his own way. He figured if he could stay by your side, he could keep you safe. We'd both grown up around drinking culture, and neither of us really knew any different. I'm very grateful to Lloyd for sitting in the dark with you so you didn't have to be alone.

He's still your friend now, you know? Last year he got married to the girl he met not long after the Doncaster night. He has a little girl and boy, a great job and a wonderful life.

What I want to tell you, more than anything, is that the drugs and the alcohol never helped. All they did was turn off the lights. In the years to come, you won't hide from the light. In fact, you'll actively seek it out and you'll spend your life trying to make your light as contagious as possible, so that other people don't have to sit in those same dark rooms.

I know, it seems impossible, right? Hang in there. It gets better.

Love,

Lucy x

How It All Started

My issues with alcohol did not develop as an adult. I had been surrounded by the stuff since I was born, which isn't uncommon in the UK. When babies are brought home from the hospital, we wet their heads. When birthdays come around, we buy champagne. We go to pubs to talk, where we lubricate the conversation with beer and when we turn eighteen, we drink so much we throw up. It's just how it is.

The first time I got drunk, I was around seven years old. I know, the 1990s were wild, right? My older two brothers, sister and I were brought up on a friendly little cul-de-sac in Canterbury by my mum. My parents divorced when I was very young and I saw my father every other weekend or so.

There were a lot of parties at our house and many weird and wonderful grown-ups graced our home. My mum has a knack for attracting the most bizarre and extraordinary people into her life, probably because she is also bizarre and extraordinary. We were surrounded by poets, actors, artists, writers, show-jumpers, filmmakers – you name it, she knew one, and our parties were loud and frequent. I don't think I've ever used the word rambunctious before, but they were exactly that. Our neighbours hated us.

All of our family friends loved to drink and my memory is that when the booze flowed, everyone had a great time, dancing on tables, telling stories and eating party food. There was usually some kind of theme or fancy dress, and everyone always made an effort. As kids, we watched these wild parties, observing the adults dancing and laughing at jokes which made the whole room erupt. Drinking looked like so much fucking fun.

My elder brother, James, had always been as muscular and kind as a superhero. He was an incredibly promising gymnast but he wasn't quite making the grades he needed to go for the big time, so instead he – quite literally – ran away to join the circus. When the ring he was part of toured our hometown, the circus came to stay. It was one of the many wonderful, magical days of my childhood, but it came to an end when my mum announced it was my bedtime. I was, quite understandably, livid: I was a small child and there were circus folk in my house.

To ease my evident devastation, a petite girl wearing a white, full-body leotard with a blue glitter lightning bolt on it said in an eastern European accent, 'Don't worry, Lucy, we're all going to bed now too. Look, I'm sleeping here in the cupboard!' She then folded herself up into the smallest shape I've ever seen a human make and inserted her whole body, unassisted, into a kitchen cupboard. My mouth agape, I was turned around by my shoulders and walked up the stairs to bed.

It was the morning after one of those rambunctious parties when I first tried alcohol. Sleeping adults were scattered about the house and, on this occasion, there were other kids there too. Whilst our parents were cradling what must have been horrific, nine-out-of-ten hangovers, me and a younger boy I'll call Billy discovered a litre bottle of Coca-Cola in the garden. I opened the cap and took a swig. I knew straight away it wasn't just Coke.

It was a jackpot moment as we knew we'd found something we weren't allowed to have. We took it and hid in the garage where we wouldn't be seen. It didn't taste very nice, sort of sharp and muddy in fruity kind of way, but we knew what would happen if we drank it. Billy and I had seen what happened to adults when they partook and we thought we were about to have a great time.

The next thing I remember is sitting on one of those blue rope and orange plastic swings in the garden, struggling to keep my balance whilst just sitting, then falling off and lying on my back as the sky spun above me. I thought it was fucking hilarious. I thought everything was fucking hilarious.

We could barely walk. Again, hilarious. We knew it would not go down well with our parents if they saw us but I remember just belly laughing and not caring about getting caught. I don't think I cared about anything in that moment.

We got back into the garage and laid on our backs, laughing and rolling around whilst the ceiling spun. I have no recollection of the time – was it fifteen minutes, an hour? – and everything being so damn funny until Billy said he didn't feel well. And then I realised that he was not well. At all.

I don't know whether someone caught a glimpse of two

quite clearly inebriated children through the garage window or whether I had to grass us both up because he became so unwell so quickly, but my next memory is of my mum and his parents being there and the mood had quickly changed. I knew we were in big trouble but that didn't matter right then because Billy was alarmingly lifeless on the concrete floor. His dad scooped him up and a blur of adults carried him indoors and up to the bathroom. Everyone was in a state of utter panic.

I hovered in the doorway of the bathroom and watched as they lay the unresponsive child in a cold bath and splashed him with water. Because I was oldest, though still in single figures, I was screamed at. What the fuck was I thinking? How the fuck could I let this happen? I was completely full of shame. My face felt prickly and my mouth tasted rancid. I thought he was going to die. I think they did too.

That was the first time shock ever sobered me up and every time it's happened since it's been accompanied by the same shame, the same prickly face and that rancid taste. I thought: 'I've fucked up BIG time.' But I had also experienced the glow of being drunk and the glee of not giving a shit. I knew I really liked it.

Billy was fine, by the way. He sobered up eventually and got back to doing regular five-year-old things. I know now that nothing those adults shouted at me in that bathroom was meant for me. With hindsight, I see their anger masked their guilt, but for years I carried their guilt and thought I was to blame. It was decades before I understood how much trauma each of those adults brought to that bathroom that day.

When we're small, we place our parents on a pedestal but, as we become adults ourselves, we start to understand that they are just flawed humans too. Sometimes their stories are more traumatic than our own and they are terrified of fucking *you* up as much as they were fucked up by the people who raised them.

I was in my thirties when my mum told me her story because, as she was an adoptee, it was only then that she was able to learn about her own history. Her trauma spans generations too – her biological mother had been put into an unmarried mother and baby unit when she became pregnant with my mum. Twenty-one days after my mum was born, she was forced to hand her over to social services against her will. Five years later, my mum's biological mother killed herself.

My mum was adopted by a couple that did not adjust well to being parents and her adopted mother, Hazel, had significant mental health issues. Her adoptive father was having an affair during her early years and as my mum acted out, she was placed on Valium from the age of five until eleven years old.

Hazel's husband went on to have other children with his lover and abandoned my mum, shutting her out of their lives and, quite literally, out of rooms in their house. When I was two years old, Hazel died of cancer and my mum lost the one constant, true example of family, and of love, that she'd ever known.

So by the time my mum met my father, she didn't know what a healthy, loving relationship really looked like, so it's not a huge surprise she found herself in a toxic relationship with him. I was the youngest of his four children, three which were with my mum, and by the time I came along, she had been long trapped and unable to escape the cycle, a cycle that – I now see – started long before I was born.

I'd heard people talk about generational trauma before but I struggled to understand what it really meant. I had this impression that it meant trauma was genetically passed down to you through DNA, like webbed feet or big ear lobes. That you were born with trauma already coursing through your veins and you'd automatically be more disposed to it by default. Though there is evidence to suggest that is biologically true, it wasn't until I learnt more about my mum's life that I understood that it isn't necessarily about biology at all.

When I was born, I was born naked, as we are. I was born naked of fear, naked of anger, naked of violence and sadness. I was born a clean slate. We are born knowing how to breathe and how to cry but from the second we arrive into the light, we start to learn from the people around us, often our families. Most of the time, those people teach us with good intention: they teach us to talk and to walk and that when we smile, they smile. Unintentionally, those people teach us everything else they know too. How to be angry, how to be violent, how to have a 'stiff upper lip', how to shut down our emotions in order to preserve an environment, how to express love for others through control or abuse . . . The list goes on. Generational trauma is the passing down of those behaviours, behaviours that we may have unknowingly inherited from our great, great grandparents. Emotional family heirlooms that go unhealed for hundreds of years.

Most of the memories I have of my father are from times of high stress because he was a very violent and angry man.

Though I have memories of playing bingo in the arcade with him, of sitting on his knee and driving his car around a field, of him making me laugh until my belly hurt and of hunting for treasure in the woods, the main memories are starkly different. I was holding my father's hand when he headbutted a street vendor to the ground who had sold me a laser pen that didn't work. I stayed sat still in the back seat of his car when he slammed on the brakes and leapt out to fight people who had cut him up. I cried quietly on the sofa when he threw his dog across the room and against the wall because it had eaten from the plastic bag he was using as a bin in his kitchen. Until my mum fled with us children and my parents divorced, I lived in active, violent, domestic abuse. I learnt that in order to be safe, I would need to study my father's expressions and read the atmosphere to try to predict the mood he was in. I also learnt that when you were feeling hurt you could hurt other people.

As an adult, I have also leapt out of my car, and got into altercations in the street, and abused alcohol. Consistently, throughout my life, I have demonstrated dysfunctional behaviours that I absorbed from both of my parents because I thought they were normal.

Unlike with my mum, I don't know what trauma my dad suffered. I don't know if it was as a result of things that happened to him or whether it was passed onto him from someone else. My understanding of generational trauma has helped me find compassion for him, and compassion for my own anger. It's clear to me that anger I've carried with me since I was a small child has spanned more than just my lifetime. It's spanned his, and maybe his parents' too. As I have grown, I have become more aware of those behaviours and I have worked desperately hard on breaking the cycles that enable them to be passed on. That is how generational trauma is healed. My awareness of familial conditioning has helped me recover and shows me that I have the power to make life easier for the younger generations in my family, whether they are my own children, grandchildren, or my nieces and nephews.

I don't speak to my father now; I last saw him in 2019. After years of being the first to initiate contact, I stopped doing it and I am still not sure if he's noticed. Lots of parts of my life have been very public and I find it hard to know that, despite the fact it's so easy to know so much about my life, he chooses not to engage. I was the last of his five children to cease reaching out to him. It took me the longest to stop trying to be loved by him; I was twenty-nine years old.

My mum says that she truly learnt to love when she had her own children. I do not have a tactile relationship with my mum; we don't hug or have much physical proximity at all. We have always had a difficult relationship. Learning that my mum spent a part of her early life alone in a metal cot in an orphanage, without her mother or father to hold or kiss or hug her, helps me understand that she shows me love in different ways. My siblings and I were a huge factor in her eventual escape from the abuse she endured. If there was a positive in any of this, it's that my mum's response to being controlled for so long was to give me the freedom she had never experienced in her life. That meant I was a wild child who made their own decisions.

One of the decisions I made early on was that I was a boy called Max. To my family, friends, teachers, doctors and acquaintances, I wasn't known as anything else.

16

When I Was a Little Boy

When I was little, I wore boxer shorts, not knickers. I used the boys' toilets, never the girls'. My hair was shaved into a short back and sides by the local barber, not the hairdresser. I didn't even answer to the name Lucy. Matter of fact, being called Lucy, or being referred to as a girl, would hurt me so much that I'd cry for hours.

Lucy was the name on my birth certificate but she didn't truly exist until I stopped being Max at around ten years old. I know a lot of women who say 'I was a real tomboy' or 'I was always climbing trees and playing football', but that wasn't me. I *was* a little boy and when I met new people, many had no idea I was biologically female.

In the early years of primary school, a group of boys heard that their friend Max's *real* name was Lucy and that, actually, he was a girl. It was so inconceivable to them that they needed proof. Without malice, and born of the purest curiosity and disbelief, Max was cornered by four or five other six-year-olds and asked to prove once and for all who they really were.

The gender litmus test. Out there in the playground.

'Pull down your trousers!'

This might sound like it's heading in a traumatic direction. You might be unconsciously tightening your jaw at the idea of poor little Max being rumbled by his innocent, yet ferocious, school-age inquisitors. You might be wincing at your own experience of navigating your own difficult early years, but for Max it wasn't stressful. You see, Max had such confidence in who he was that there was no doubt in his mind. He knew he could prove he was just the same as the other little boys because to him, that was the truth.

Max puffed out his chest, took a life-affirming breath and unbuttoned his grey school trousers. There was a palpable tension from the entire school of onlookers who had assembled, brimming with shock and genuine curiosity, as he slowly pulled them down to his ankles.

There was an audible gasp as the trousers hit the floor.

Max revealed a pair of striped navy blue and white Woolworth's boxer shorts.

'See!'

The other little boys reeled back, assured in their judgement. They were right all along. Of course Max was a boy. Boys' pants = must be a boy. Thank God for six-year-old logic.

This may be the first time I realised that knowing something, really *knowing* something, whether or not it is true, has real power. If only I had been so sure about who I was in the twenty years that followed.

We went on holiday to America and my most vivid

memory of that trip is giving all my pocket money to a homeless man. Max dug deep into his pockets and handed over all the cash he had.

'Thank you, sir,' came the reply.

Max's little brain nearly exploded with joy and that gift from a stranger was worth so much more than loose change. I ran to my mum so fast, so full of excitement and awe, and tugged on her arm. 'Did you hear that, Mum? He called me "sir"!'

I can still feel the sheets of pain in my abdomen and the jolts of breathlessness that came from hysterically crying when someone tried to tell me I was a girl, or when a burning meteorite became lodged in my throat because I wanted to use a urinal in the boys' toilets or didn't want to be a bridesmaid at a family wedding.

I sometimes feel like I have been trying to prove who I am my entire life. Granted, I never had to prove anything by pulling down my trousers again, but I've been metaphorically cornered in the playground many times since and asked to show what or *who* it is that I really am. Honestly, I haven't always had the answer. And yet Max knew. He was this fierce little person who knew exactly who he was.

Things are so different nowadays that Max would probably get the chance to stay as Max, which leads me to wonder what grown-up Max would be like. I think I would have loved to have been that man. But that doesn't mean I don't love being a woman now.

I have tried to explain this many, *many* times to people who cannot understand it, and for a long time it was hard for me to understand too. I don't resent the fact I chose to grow up as Lucy. I don't feel like I made the 'wrong' decision.

I just would not have been opposed to staying a boy. These days, I would probably have been given the option to start testosterone and that would have started to make physical changes, and maybe have led me on a path towards surgeries that would have made me 'physically male'.

But that wasn't possible for me twenty years ago and little Max inevitably started to grow breasts. Puberty flourished like unwanted ivy on the front of a house and there wasn't very much anyone could do about it. Something had been set on fire but there was no water, no fire blanket, no extinguisher, that could put it out. You just had to watch it burn down; watch Max burn. It's heartbreaking.

One day, as the little buds of boobs became more defined, Mum sat me down and asked what I wanted to do. She never said what she thought I should do. She didn't ask who I was going to be or try to persuade me that I would have an 'easier' life as Lucy. She just metaphorically guided me across a busy street, the same way a mother duck would her ducklings, with no control over whether they would walk into the oncoming traffic and under a wheel or find their way to the opposite curb, safe from harm.

I don't know why I chose to be Lucy but I think it is hugely to do with the fact that, at the turn of the millennium, there wasn't much hope for trans kids. I have no doubt that is what I was, by the way. A trans kid.

My mum tells me now that, little by little, one piece of clothing at a time (and a visit to get my ears pierced at Claire's Accessories), I shed my Max skin and started looking for my Lucy skin. I was almost thirty before I found it and in the intervening decades, I battled with my weight, my body image, aggression, my black sheepishness, my issues with authority, issues with masculine men, with feminine women. I have struggled with my identity ever since and I now have the insight as to why: I never really said goodbye to Max. And by becoming Lucy, I know I broke his heart into a million little pieces.

★

As a society, we have this horrible habit of asking children what they want to be when they grow up. I know that seems like a harmless question and for the most part it is, but it does give the impression that it's something we should actually know by any point in our lives. I still don't know what I want to be when I grow up and I'm thirty-one. And what I wanted to be when I was a child is quite far from what I am now. In my primary school years, when the class gathered in a show-and-tell style circle to ask each child what they wanted to be, I followed the more common answers of 'a fireman' and 'a nurse' with 'I want to be a transexual'. My mum got a call from a very sheepish teacher, repeating what Max had said in the classroom. My mum, unfazed by the topic of conversation, explained to the teacher that there had been recently been a very informative and eye-opening storyline on *Coronation Street* in which the woman who married the local shopkeeper had come out as trans. Max had been glued to it.

I'd been raised around trans people but I don't think I knew they were trans. Why would I? To children, all people are just people. I never wondered what my mum's friends did for work or what they got up to in their spare time, let alone what reproductive organs they were born with. They were just women called Jane and Kathy, and they were nice to me. That's all kids really care about.

The other day, my four-year-old niece told my sister, 'Some people are girls when they're little and then they are boys when they grow up,' and my sister admired the simplicity of her logic. I struggle with the fact that there are people twenty times my niece's age that can't make sense of that. So much of the simplicity of life gets lost with age.

When I was Max, to the other children my age, my gender was as simple as the underwear I wore. No one was in uproar about using he/him pronouns for me. That's why I don't have a problem calling someone by the name they have chosen for themselves or using pronouns that are different to the ones they used growing up. I know what it feels like to be called a girl when you are not a girl. Of course, I was born with a vagina, making my physiology technically female, but, in my being, I was Max and I was a boy.

If you're reading this and you're thinking, 'I still just don't get it', I get it. I don't know what it's like to live as a disabled person. I don't know what it's like to live as a person of colour. But I do try to learn about those who are different to me with an open mind. I listen to podcasts or read books by those people so that I can try to understand them better. I acknowledge that my perspective on many things in life is different to every other single person on this earth, and whilst I might not agree with everyone, I do want to have empathy towards them and their beliefs. I know what it's like to feel trapped in the wrong body and I really want to explain what that feels like.

Think about a Ferrero Rocher. Normally, Ferrero Rochers are made with a milk chocolate exterior and a brown, hazelnut interior. They also have those fancy white Ferrero Rochers, which have coconut on the outside and a delicious milk cream on the inside. They're called Raffaellos. One day at the Ferrero Rocher factory, a delicious treat comes out of the machine with a brown, milk chocolate exterior so it looks just like a Ferrero Rocher but it is filled with the delicious white, creamy interior of a Raffaello. A glitch in the matrix. Now, let's say this little sphere of anomaly is also a sentient being and it knows, due to its creamy, white insides, that it is definitely a Raffaello. Though by looking at it, no one who works in the factory would ever know it was different to any other milk chocolate Ferrero Rocher that had come out of that machine. Only that sentient little snack knows what it is on the inside. If this wonderful, joyful, delicious little oddity would like to go back into the machine and be given a white, milk-cream exterior to match it's white, milk-cream interior then why the fuck not? It's just a fucking chocolate. Instead of trying to crack it open and see what's inside for ourselves, we could just say, 'Go ahead, little Raffaello, do what makes you happy.'

Throughout life, we're told 'it's what's on the inside that matters' but we do all kinds of radical things to feel more comfortable in our outer shell. We get tattoos, pursue drastic weight loss, wear expensive clothes and get new tits. Modification is a human part of making ourselves more comfortable. It's our instinct to protect the people we love from making 'mistakes' with their shells too. My mum told me I'd regret my first tattoo and, of course, I do (don't tell her I said that), but that tattoo is now part of who I am. It's part of my identity. There are no wrong or right decisions when it comes to who we are, so we need to override the instinct to interfere and instead to help people live as authentically and comfortably as they can.

PROCESS

There's a term 'deadnaming' which is where someone addresses a trans or non-binary person with their previous name, the name that was on their birth certificate, instead of their new, chosen name. This might be done by accident – which I've done before, a few times, actually – or in malice, for example, by a parent who refuses to accept their child's new identity. I remember being 'deadnamed'.

When I was little, there were people who knew full well that I was Max and would still call me Lucy or refer to me as a girl. When that happened, I felt like I was being accused of being something that I wasn't. It used to make me so angry that I could do nothing but cry.

Being accused of being something that you're not, or being accused of doing something you haven't done, is one of the most frustrating feelings on the planet. Everyone knows that. I specifically know what it felt like to be told that I was something that, at that point in time, and in the deepest part of my soul, I knew I wasn't. It means that now, as an adult, if I can do anything that makes someone's life just that little bit more comfortable, especially that costs little-to-no effort, like addressing them by a different name or adopting different pronouns for them, or even showing compassion for other people's actions which I don't fully understand, I will. I hope that people show that compassion to me too, for all of the parts of my identity that I've wrestled with, on the inside and the outside.

★

I have struggled with body image since I was in double figures and, in 2019, I lost a significant amount of weight, thinking this would help the way I felt about my body.

Using the lockdown to my advantage, I got very lean and began building muscle, and I started to look a bit like a body builder. Throughout my life, society had taught me that the only reason I should hate my body is for being overweight, so when I had an incredibly low percentage of body fat, I couldn't work out why I still hated what I saw in the mirror.

I would study my very athletic-looking body – my shoulders rounded at the top and bulging on the bicep, my quads curved against the shape of my femur bone with veins standing out either side of my groin – but I didn't admire what I'd achieved. I wasn't able to see anything other than imperfections. I would grab at the skin on my stomach and see rolls of fat, flesh bunching between my fingers. I'd see something that wasn't there. It was exhausting.

It wasn't until I met and spoke with trans activists Charlie Craggs and Kenny Ethan Jones whilst on holiday in 2022 that I began to understand the relationship I had with my body and my gender. I sat in front of them as a feminine, bikini-clad, blonde-haired woman and showed them pictures of me as young Max as they cooed over me as a little boy, with absolutely no judgement. Both of their perspectives – their lived experience as trans people – helped me, a seemingly cis-gendered woman, align with my own identity. I had lived as a boy for so many years and one day puberty came, and I just turned my back on Max to be Lucy again. What I hadn't recognised is that there is an element of Max that lives on in me. All of the years I'd associated the resentment I had towards my body with my weight started to make more sense when I learnt to link that resentment with my gender.

I actually lost so much body fat that my breast tissue

completely depleted and I was left with grade three ptosis of the breast – basically, very empty bags of skin where a pair of Ds used to be. I thought for a while about what to do about my predicament. I spoke to multiple surgeons who told me I required surgery – more specifically, a mastopexy and augmentation (a removal of skin, uplift and implants). They were the only options the surgeons suggested, but I began to ponder some options that they didn't suggest, options that didn't stand out to me at the time as perhaps a little *alternative*.

I considered whether to have my breasts returned to the shape they were before I lost weight or whether they should be taken off completely. Yeah, I didn't know whether I wanted to keep my flat chest and remove my boobs altogether, keeping the nipples, having what's called 'top surgery' (where the breast tissue is removed and your chest is made to look more masculine) or have them augmented. I didn't consider that perhaps top surgery versus a boob job wasn't what most women weighed up when considering breast modification. Most women probably just consider the size of the implant they're putting in.

In the end, I got the surgery that the surgeons recommended; 240cc implants, the loose skin removed, returning me to a D cup. I love my boobs now and maybe I'd have loved my flat chest, had I had top surgery. What I have learnt is that as long as I embrace myself as much as possible and always try to learn more about my relationship with my brain, I understand my body a little more. My body will never stop changing.

It is incredibly clear to me now that one of the most important factors in making sure that I stay happy is surrounding myself with people who are concerned with what is on the inside, rather than my outer shell. My sister revealed that she and my mum recently had an unprompted conversation about the fact they'd be utterly unfazed and unsurprised if at some point I decided to be Max again. They said they wouldn't flinch. I'm not sure they are aware of what a privilege it is to be surrounded by people like them.

The ways in which I picked my body apart in the mirror, how I chased a six-pack and huge muscly arms and masculine angles, I think was a bit of Max showing me he's still here. Understanding that part of me is still mourning the fact that I don't look like Max whilst working to embrace the fact I look like Lucy has helped me to understand my body dysmorphia, but I still struggle with it.

In some ways, I still don't feel like a boy or a girl. On the outside, yeah, I look like a woman and my pronouns are she/her, and I'm always learning how to love and appreciate my body more, but inside, sometimes I align more with feeling like a boy, sometimes a girl, sometimes a mix of both or neither.

I know this is hard to understand for anyone who hasn't experienced it, but I hope that explaining it like this shows that, really, all that matters is that people are allowed to live as their authentic selves. *That* is what makes them fulfilled. I have been so lucky to be surrounded by people who accepted me as Max and as Lucy, and who didn't hesitate when I told them about feeling a bit like both as an adult. In some countries, they've been observing this phenomenon for thousands of years and some legally recognise a third gender. Here in the West, and I'm aware it carries some negative connotation due to its use in the media, we call it being non-binary. Which is what I am quite sure I am. I haven't ever put that on my social media or announced it in a 'coming out' fashion, that is just what I am. And I am just me.

I spent ten years as a boy, far more than a decade as troubled Lucy and ten years as 'that girl off the telly'. I thought I was going through the process of figuring out who I was, but it's obvious to me now that all those personas were aspects of the real me. Our identity is always changing, but that doesn't alter who we are.

It's taken me a long time to realise that – no matter how uncomfortable it makes you feel, you are who you are from the second you are born until the moment you die. Everything you do in between is who you are. The good, the bad and the ugly. But the beautiful thing is that we are always capable of change. I have realised that from this moment to the next, I am constantly evolving, and I always will be.

And that gives me more comfort than anything else in this world.

Dear Max,

You taught me how to prove everyone wrong, right from the off, and for that I will always be grateful. It was such a privilege to have been you, Max.

I show people pictures of you all the time. People say we look exactly the same and you were so cute they actually gasp. When I look at those photos I feel this warmth deep inside of me. I think it comes from knowing that you were living so authentically, more authentically than most of the adults I know do now. More authentically than I did for many years after you shed your skin and became Lucy.

There was a lot of stress in our house but your family gave you a great gift: freedom. In another family, an adult hand might have swiped the money out of your grasp and told you that giving it away to a homeless person was a waste. But not my family. You were allowed to make those choices and I have always thanked my lucky stars for that.

You grew up to live as a woman. A lesbian woman, who is surrounded by other lesbian, gay, bisexual and trans people. By people from so many walks of life. Being you helped me to understand the fact that our bodies, the vessels that we exist in, do not always correlate with the person living inside. You showed me the pain that comes from people not understanding that. You are the reason I feel so passionately about trans rights and why it's important those of us living as cis (or the gender we were assigned at birth) are open, supportive and empathetic to those who know that they are not what is written on their birth certificate.

You're probably still processing the news that you grew up to be Lucy. Just wait till you hear that I sometimes wear dresses. And that I have fake boobs.

Max, you have always been with me; you have always been this spark of understanding, drive, fire and identity that I have carried with me, like a locket around my neck. In many ways, I am still you.

I think you'd be so proud of everything we've achieved and I am so, so proud of you too. I always will be.

Love,
Lucy x

The ~~Worst~~ Best Coming Out Story Ever

I've heard coming out stories that are full of happiness and wholesome, familial understanding and acceptance. I particularly enjoy hearing this kind of story when it begins with an expectation of them receiving no understanding or acceptance from their family, and then hearing the beautiful plot twist. Stories where Mum, Dad or Gran is the unexpected hero that surprisingly celebrates their child. And then on the other hand, I've been told many coming out stories that made my heart hurt for the storyteller: tales of abandonment and excommunication, again, made worse when that was not the outcome they expected at all. A modern tragedy that is frequently the origin story of a lifetime of sadness thereafter. My coming out story has neither a hero nor an antagonist. I mean, I'd be lying if I said my story had an arc at all really, given the fact it doesn't have a beginning, middle or an end.

PROCESS

Where most coming out stories feature extreme reactions like pride, frustration, defiance and self-love, my story doesn't feature anything. Perhaps it does, actually – nonchalance. As you already know, throughout my life I have always tried to explode into situations like a firework into a night sky, listening out for the 'Ooohs' and 'Aaaaahs' of onlookers below as I cascaded down from my dramatic peak. But there is no gunpowder in this story. No fanfare, no banners, not even a fucking card because, in the best possible way, absolute nobody gave a shit. From when I was very little, even before living as Max, I have, for as long as I can remember, been attracted to women.

In the mid-nineties, when I was in my first year of primary school, I wanted to send my best friend, Ella, a Valentine's card because I was deeply in love with her. My mum felt that she needed to ask Ella's mum's permission for me to send it for fear another 'girl' sending her daughter a proposal of love might be ill-received. Thankfully, Ella's mum was more outraged that my mum had queried her open-mindedness than she was at a five-year-old sending a love letter. Round of applause for Ella's mum, please.

I feel incredibly lucky to have a non-coming out story. I feel a pang of guilt when I hold my experience up against those who had a much harder time. 'I wish I had a family like yours,' people in this position sometimes say, and I understand. I wish they did too. Both my mum and I found my 'coming out' so irrelevant that we actually remember two completely different stories that took place in different scenes, at different ages. My mum tells me she remembers me aged around fourteen, with black box-dye hair, wearing grey skinny jeans around my arse with a big belt buckle, and a band t-shirt skipping up the driveway shouting, 'I'm gay! I'm gay!'

I don't remember that at all, literally absolutely zero recollection of that, but it does sound a lot like me. In my version of my coming out, I remember walking into my mum's room with intention, standing at the end of her bed and telling her at spitfire speed about a girl I didn't like at school. My mum looked at me, waiting for the punchline of the story that was evidently incoming, when I proudly and flamboyantly said, 'My GIRLFRIEND is prettier than her anyway,' and turned on my heel, breezing out of the door to let that information hang suspended in the air. But my mum doesn't remember any of that. So it clearly had less of an impact than I wanted. Instead of covering her mouth with her hand and crying – which is what a lot of mums do, by the way – my mum took another sip of tea, got out of bed and went about her day. My brother and sister are more likely to remember me saying 'I'm going to the shop to buy some milk' than they would remember me announcing my sexuality. It's just never been a big deal.

Having a family that says 'Yeah . . . So?' when you announce a huge part of your identity is a privilege that so few people I know have been afforded. Even now, to have a truly accepting family and not hear 'It's just a phase, you'll grow out of it' or 'Perhaps you just haven't found the right man yet' or 'What a waste' (the last example being the first words uttered by an ex's mum when she came out to her) is uncommon. If you're straight, you might roll your eyes at this, and I get it.

I've heard many people say that we shouldn't have to have a 'coming out' anymore because it's 'just not a big deal'. It makes me want to scream with frustration. I know it's meant well and that the people who say that believe that being gay really isn't a big deal but, the truth is, not everyone shares that view. If everyone thought like that then yes, no one would ever have to come out again. If everyone truly saw being gay as 'not a big deal' then no one would ever have secret relationships for fear of losing friends, family or even jobs, for being honest about who they love. If all around the world it was safe to be LGBTQ+ – and by 'safe', I mean not at risk of being beaten, arrested or killed – we could get on board with that idea of scrapping coming out altogether. If people didn't walk into gay nightclubs and attempt to shoot everyone in there, or if religious people didn't deny the rights of same-sex couples, if there wasn't conversion therapy happening to a child somewhere in the UK right now, I'd put down my pride flag and burn all of the closets, so no one had to come out of one ever again.

But, sadly, not everyone thinks like that. I've been called a dyke in the street for holding hands with a girlfriend. I've let go of her hand in certain situations to avoid confrontation and danger. When I travel, I have to Google whether or not it's legal to be a lesbian in that country and whether or not we're likely to be targeted. I've had men get in my face and tell me I 'need some dick'. In everyday conversations I've left out the fact my partner is a woman because I've had a sense that the person I'm talking to is going to wince or say something inappropriate. Lord, there are bakers who refuse to bake cakes for gay people's weddings. So I'm very grateful that it's not a big deal to you but I can't say this enough – not everyone thinks like you.

If you've ever heard anyone ask, 'Why do you have Gay Pride festivals?' or the more offensive version, 'Why do you have to rub it in everyone's faces?', one answer is that it's because – amongst many, many other reasons – the gay community is letting everyone know that it is there. The LGBTQ+ community offers a family to those who have lost their biological family on account of their 'coming out'. Pictures of scantily clad gay men waving rainbow flags and big, butch Dykes on Bikes leading a parade on their motorcycles tells other people, those oppressed in other areas of the world, that there is hope. Sex between men in England wasn't decriminalised until 1967: there are people alive today who were arrested, in this country, for being gay. Gay Pride is a celebration of no longer being *as* oppressed; it's a celebration of identity and honesty.

Some non-queer people fear asking questions about things like Pride or being gay in case they cause offence or get it wrong. As a gay person, I'm always happy to answer those questions, so long as they are asked with genuine desire to learn and to understand, and that my answer is received with open-mindedness and observance. If you came to me defensively and asked, 'Well, why isn't there a Straight Pride?!' – a question that's asked by the same type of people who say 'All Lives Matter' – quite frankly, I'd rather you didn't approach me. If you flinched when I said 'queer', don't worry. The word has been reclaimed as positive terminology for the collective of LGBTQ+ people. Though, as always, obviously, it depends on the intention behind the use. 'Lucy's a queer woman' would be just fine, whereas 'Fucking queer bastards' clearly isn't.

In 2022 (as far as we could tell), I was the first out, British lesbian to have had a top-ten album in nearly a decade. The last out, British lesbian to have had a top-ten album before that? Also me, in 2013. Before that, it looks like that last out, British lesbian to have had a top-ten album was Alex Parks of *Fame Academy*, in 2003, who was probably the first lesbian I saw on TV.

A large part of my career was built on support from the LGBTQ+ community. Even before my TV audition catapulted me into the touring circuit, I'd been playing at Prides across the country throughout the summers, starting off at Manchester Pride at the age of sixteen. After my stint on *The X Factor*, I was booked for hundreds of club performances and meet-and-greets in gay clubs. I played the same Pride events across the UK that I'd played at years before, albeit on the bigger stages. The crowd at my smaller headline shows was normally a sea of lesbians but I was also playing festivals like T in the Park and V Festival, where I had a great hetero turnout. To a degree, playing so many LGBTQ+ shows pigeonholed me as a 'lesbian artist' but I've never viewed that as a bad thing. In 2015, I was asked in an interview if I thought that being a lesbian has had a negative effect on my career. Funnily enough, that was the first time I ever considered if it had. I've never really known my stance on that because I've only ever had the experience of being an out lesbian in the music industry. I haven't ever been a closeted gay woman in this industry, nor have I been a straight woman, so I don't know if the adversities I've come up against have been related to my sexuality or not.

I can see that change is happening but even still, if you look at the commercial UK music scene, can you name any out lesbians? Off the top of my head, I can only name a few and I'm involved in both the music world and the LGBTQ+ world. The same doesn't apply for gay, male singers. I'm sure you can name me plenty of those. So, when a lesbian does appear, it's an irregularity and I can see why it might become a focus.

It's for this same reason that I am so supported and welcomed by the majority of the lesbian community, though: because it's so unusual to see someone to relate to in the public eye. On television, the lesbians we are permitted to watch are usually quite short, rotund ladies who wear brogues and blazer jackets. They often have short, coiffed hair and would be perceived as being more masculine presenting. They are allowed to be awfully jolly and funny, but not sexy. I mean, Clare Balding *is* sexy in her own way, but you know what I mean.

When I was growing up, I don't think I ever saw a feminine presenting lesbian on my television screen. It subconsciously made me feel like there was only one way to be a lesbian and that I'd better go and buy some brogues. I presented as masc for many years, opting for beanie hats, baggy shirts and bulky suits. I was jolly and funny and that was that. It wasn't until 2019, when I got sober and took a deep dive into my identity, that I realised a part of me was pretty bloody feminine. Some days I'm in a dress and others I'm in a suit, or a tracksuit. If by being in the public eye I could achieve one thing, it would be to let people know that you can be whichever version of yourself that you want to be and you don't have to fit inside of any kind of box to be liked or accepted.

Enter Stage Right

I didn't have posters of pop stars on my wall when I was growing up but if I had, they wouldn't have been of Blue or NSYNC. That wasn't just because I wasn't interested in boys, it was because I was so captured by music that the very last thing I cared about was what the person singing it looked like. Why would I care about the clothes they wore or the colour of their eyes when I could close mine and just absorb the lyrics that they had written, the intensely special way in which they told their truth? It felt like magic, the way that their message arrived at my ears from the disc I slotted inside the hi-fi in our living room, the invisible soundwaves carrying the artist's message directly to my brain.

I obsessed over songs, playing them over and over until I knew where every inward breath was placed, the position of every vocal adlib or nuance. The first album I fell in love with was Tracy Chapman's 1988 self-titled album, the one which has 'Fast Car' and 'Baby Can I Hold You' on it. I mention those because they are the most well-known on that album but they are nowhere near the best songs on it. That album comes best as one piece listened to all the way through; it's like a melodic audiobook of adversity and observation of a world that was so unfathomably different to mine as a young, white, British child.

I didn't know what Tracy Chapman looked like because I'd found the silver CD, with a black and red ring around the outer edge and the track listing down its middle, without its case nestled in my mum's collection of partially scratched discs that lived next to the speakers. With her deep, rich voice, I didn't even know if Tracy Chapman was a man or a woman, but I did know, from the stories she told me, that she was Black and that she was American and that she'd been through some awful things. She told me about her experience of racism and segregation, about domestic abuse, about falling in love and dreaming of a better life. She told me about her views on the class system that oppressed her and sang of her aspirations for a world with less hate and more freedom in it. She took my breath away. I played that album so many times that, eventually, my mum made me wear a pair of big, over-ear headphones because, as much as she loved the record, she just couldn't hear it again. Those headphones had a short cable, so I'd have to sit on a wooden dining chair to be close to the CD player, the bottom of my back aching, but enduring the discomfort in exchange for the comfort that album gave me.

Music took me into someone else's world. I remember hearing Don McLean's *American Pie* for the first time. It was like eating food from another country or culture that you've never tried before, the combinations of flavours and colours and textures dancing on your tongue, coating the inside of your cheeks with discovery. Like 'Fast Car', 'American Pie' was a song and a story, an adventure that twisted and turned and painted pictures on the inside of my eyelids. I could see 'the good old boys drinking whiskey and rye' sitting at the bar in a saloon and I imagined the expressive face of the 'jester on the sidelines in a cast'.

For me, if lyrics didn't tell me a story, I wasn't really interested in listening. I couldn't understand the appeal of 'Oops Upside Your Head' by The Gap Band because the song wasn't telling me anything. My love of lyrics meant that I wasn't confined to just one genre of music, though I loved American artists. I was taken by the stories of Tupac Shakur, about his struggles as a young Black man and the permanent nature of death and gang culture that he was surrounded by. Dolly Parton told me about being a poor, white woman in America and being raised by a single mother. The Offspring gave me their perspective on the hypocrisy of American culture through clashing guitars and imperfect vocals. Later, hip-hop duo Blackalicious taught me about their positive outlook on life and even rapped about the periodic table. When Lily Allen burst onto the scene, singing about her own life, in her own style, with her own accent, I was in love. To me, music was like literature and HMV was a library. Listening to the stories these people told taught me how to do the same thing.

I was about ten years old when I started to play the guitar and write my own songs. The first full song I remember writing was from the perspective of a persona; it was someone else's story, not mine. The song was called 'PIY', which stood for 'Plan It Yourself'. It was about finding the body of a person who had died by suicide. It was told from the perspective of the dead person:

> *If you wake up tomorrow and I've got blood on*
>   *my wrists,*
> *Don't try and wake me up.*
> *Because my face will be pale and my eyes will be dark,*
>   *in my mind there's no more hate.*
> *My eyes are fixed to the ceiling as you gaze at my face,*
> *Your heart's in your throat you wish you weren't in*
>   *this place.*
> *My expression is angry and my lips are blue,*
> *Please remember it was never you.*

It was a very, very dark song. I don't know where I gathered the storyline from, perhaps it was from other music I'd absorbed. It suggests that my issues with my mental health started far younger than I had realised and that I have always expressed them through music. I sing down the phone to my friends; many of them remember hearing that song twenty years ago, the contents of it staying with them until now:

> *See, I never told you I loved you enough,*
> *wherever I am just know I'm looking at you*
>   *with a smile.*
> *Big decisions that lead to forever,*
> *just know that I'm with you all the while*

I don't remember learning to write songs, it was just something I did. There wasn't a moment when I decided I wanted to be a songwriter – it just ended up like that.

My sister always kept a diary but that didn't ever appeal to me. She'd have an argument with my mum, storm upstairs and write furiously in it. I didn't ever write music in fury. Music was never a place where I deposited my anger. My lyrical content varied; it could be sad, desperate, thoughtful, positive, observant and often loving, but never angry. There wasn't a process that I followed in order to write a song. Words and melodies would come at the same time and I'd use my guitar to match whatever I could hear in my head. I wrote from the perspective of other people a lot, like my song 'You're Too Young', which I wrote as a teenager, that describes the life and death of a girl that didn't exist. Doing that took me away from the parts of my own life that I didn't enjoy.

When I started writing songs, I didn't know the names of the chords I was playing and I guessed where verses and choruses and middle eights should go. To be honest, I still don't know the names of chords and I learn everything by ear because I can't read music. When I recorded my debut album, it turned out a lot of my songs, like 'Tea and Toast', changed time signature halfway through. It caused the producer and engineer a fair bit of confusion. I would nod along whilst they explained how they would work around it and set up the metronome on the track, and all the while, I still had no idea what they were talking about. Lots of my writing was quite unconventional, and that worked for me.

When I was growing up, there was music all around me. My dad played guitar and sang, as did my brothers. My mum and sister sang around the house. We weren't like the von Trapps or anything (we hit each other too much), each of us made our noise very independently. My brothers and I were first to stand up and perform at an open mic, whereas my sister would only perform in front of the mirror. When my sister and I sang songs together she was always the lead and I was the backing singer, doing the harmonies. I could always naturally find a variety of harmonies, thirds and fifths and sevenths (which are the triad of notes you might hear a barbershop trio harmonise in) came easily to me. My ability to harmonise so easily is still recognised when I'm in the studio and I can thank my sister's stage direction for that.

Though I loved singing with Ella, it taught me that I didn't want to be part of a duo or a band. I didn't want anyone telling me what to do. I loved being the lead and telling *my* stories in *my* songs. When I was 11 years old, I went to a drama club on a Saturday morning which only cemented that being part of a group performance wasn't going to be for me. Much like the dynamic with Ella, I was never selected for the lead role, so I left that drama club and set about creating my own.

In Year 7, I became good friends with a boy called Tom. Tom's mum, Marie, worked as a barmaid in a very traditional pub called The Eagle. Marie was younger than my mum, a blonde, slim woman who always chewed chewing gum and wore gold jewellery. She was very old school in the way she wouldn't hesitate to clip Tom, or me, or a regular in the pub around the ear for stepping out of line. She was fierce. I've always been inspired by fierce women. I was never inspired by the conventionally beautiful women on television who hosted breakfast TV or were featured in magazines wearing bikinis and big sunglasses, emerging from the ocean. I loved real life women. I loved landladies who threw grown men out of their pubs and told them to 'fuck off'. I loved another friend of mum's who was a defence lawyer, who eventually acted for me during police interviews in my more rebellious periods, who was unafraid of the policemen sitting opposite her with their arms folded, clearly underestimating her. I loved how quickly she could outthink them, like a fox. I loved seeing women working on building sites. I loved fearless women. I still do. But back to Marie. She overheard me singing one of my songs in the living room of her small flat. 'There's an acoustic night on in the back room of The Eagle on Wednesday. I'll tell them you're coming.' You didn't argue with Marie.

Club Acoustic is what they called the night at The Eagle. The back room had once been for men only and despite the fact women were now allowed in there, and that the smoking ban had been in force for a good few years, the air still carried the smell of stale cigarette smoke and misogyny. The bar, the tables, the seats and little raised stage area at the back of the room were all in dark, varnished wood, not dissimilar to any working men's club your grandad might have taken you to when you were little. Think Peter Kay's *Phoenix Nights*. If you ever want to see how very eclectic us British people truly can be, I suggest you attend an open mic night in the back room of any pub in the north of England.

The night was hosted by a man called Chris Rockcliffe. Chris was a giant of a man in his late fifties. He had a full head of messy white hair, a big, friendly red nose and flushed cheeks. An unassuming man who mostly wore a plain shirt tucked into his blue jeans, which helped to hold in his traditional ale-sponsored belly and a pair of leather boots on his feet. Chris sat on a table for one beside the stage with a pint of amber ale and a sheet of A4 paper in front of him. He looked up, surprised to see a young girl with a guitar standing in front of him, but made sure to quash any judgemental looks his face might give away so as not to scare me back out of the room. At twelve years old I was, after all, about a fifth of the age of most of the regulars at Club Acoustic. Many of whom swivelled their heads around to look at me as I told Chris my name and he wrote it down on the sheet of paper.

I sat down on a stool with a Diet Coke and studied the Eagle's back room clientele. Some of them had instrument cases in shapes that I'd never seen before, housing accordions or pipes. Some of them nursed their pints and peanuts, not there to perform but to listen. I would later get to know these people very well. In their own way, they would nurture my songwriting and performing. They'd teach me chords or inspire me with their old folk songs, and, most importantly, teach me the vital, international etiquette of an acoustic night.

When the room had settled, Chris stepped up onto the stage and started the evening with his own performance – as I would learn he did at every Club Acoustic. He'd pick up his walnut guitar with his huge hands, making it look like a three-quarter size, and start to play. Chris sang in his own Geordie accent for some songs but could switch to this utterly convincing southern drawl when he chose to. More Georgia than Geordie. He covered songs that dated back to the frontier times, songs about being on the Mississippi river or about working on a ranch. He sang with such emotion, almost like it felt painful to him. It was as if he transformed into the writer of the song, or like he was at least alive when it was written. He was connected to it.

I'll be honest with you: not every person that gets up on stage at an acoustic night gives such a compelling performance. But, as per the international etiquette, every person is given their two-song slot with enough time to give a brief description of the song before they sing it. Then another name is called out and they get to do their two songs. Kathy, a red-haired woman in her mid-forties who smelled like a mixture of incense and damp and wore dresses made of hemp and floaty material, would sing songs about her pet African lands snails whilst clunkily plucking her guitar. There were a pair of small, jovial men with the same red cheeks and face that Chris had, one armed with a banjo and the other an accordion. They would step up to the stage and take a seat, their bellies between their thighs. When they played, they transported everyone to the Troubles of Northern Ireland, with traditional songs from the sixties; none of us could tell if they had been there or not. It didn't really matter at Club Acoustic. It was as much a showcase of storytelling as it was a showcase of music, some people standing on stage with nothing but their foot against the floor as a drum, singing shanties of old.

I sat there, as if waiting for my name to be called at the doctor's office, full of suspense, going over what I would play, what I would say, how I would finish. I decided I'd play one of my songs because I didn't like playing covers. Then, 'Lucy Spraggan,' said that Geordie voice. All eyes were on me instantly – I don't think they often had new additions at Club Acoustic. I picked up my guitar, stepped up onto the wooden stage and sat down in the chair. 'My name is Lucy and this is one of my songs.'

When I finished playing, everyone was quiet for a fraction of a moment before the applause began. The clapping was led by a pair of hands the size of shovels, the sound of heavy palms thudding against each other. I looked at Chris, who was beaming, his eyes kind of glassy, breaking every other clap or so to wipe a tear from the side of his eye.

After that first time at Club Acoustic, Chris Rockcliffe became my biggest champion. It was the first time I'd really had my music championed by anyone. Chris believed that I had something that needed to be shared and, despite his knowledge of the music industry being small and very local, he went on to introduce me to people I formed professional relationships with that I would carry deep into my career. When I was fourteen, Chris secured me my first ever festival gig. Granted, it wasn't quite Glastonbury – it was an unplugged performance in a vintage tram carriage at Crich Tram Museum – but it was a show out of town, in the Derbyshire Dales, and I had an audience, albeit a small, tram-focused one.

Chris told me I had to make an EP, just something small, but enough to showcase my favourite of the songs I'd written so far. I did that. I recorded five songs in the basement flat of a family friend in what some might call a studio and others might call a living room. I used my mum's laptop to burn multiple copy discs and stuck on white circular CD labels with my name, the track listing and my contact details printed onto them. I then put them into clear, square, plastic wallets. Like business cards, but these ones could sing for you.

High Peak Radio was a local radio station that covered most of the Peak District. It was quite the outfit. The weird, half house, half radio studio was nestled in a housing estate in Chapel-en-le-Frith. The fact it was a radio studio and not just another bungalow belonging to a seventy-year-old was only given away by the huge antenna that was perched on top of the roof. I didn't know but Chris had gotten in his beat-up, little red Nissan Micra and driven one of my EPs directly to the studio. He called me a few days later: 'Lucy, High Peak Radio love your EP. They want to make it Record of the Week!' High Peak Radio was hardly Abbey Road but it was more exposure than I'd ever had before, and I was unbelievably excited. 'They want you to come and do an interview,' he added.

That week, Chris took me to Chapel-en-le-Frith and I did my first ever radio interview. We were welcomed into the studio/ex-council house, which smelt a bit like beans and old food cupboards, by the host, a handsome Italian-looking man in his mid-twenties with blue eyes, thick, black hair and bushy eyebrows. He shook my hand. 'My name is Ben,' he said. 'I love your music.' Ben Price was a local football pundit, crazy for Sheffield United, who absolutely loved radio and music. We got on straight away. I wasn't to know it then but years later I would move to Sheffield to live in a house share with Ben, and he would become not only my best friend but my manager, eventually my tour manager and best man at my wedding.

I loved performing and I loved being at Club Acoustic, with all those quirky older people from different back-grounds, but I was constantly flip-flopping between my own personas, just like I was in my songs. The only time I really felt comfortable was when I was performing but, other than that, I never really felt like I belonged.

Dear Lucy,

Chris died of prostate cancer in 2008 and you never did get an opportunity to truly thank him.

He nurtured the development of your talent when it was just a seedling. He saw not only it's potential to flower, but its need for nourishment and care. Your need for nourishment and care. The part he played in our life was pivotal to who, and what, we became and I wish he could see us now.

Chris, and all the Club Acoustic crowd, sowed the seeds of the self-belief that ended up transporting you to so many places. He inspired you to help new and emerging talent too, because without Chris our story doesn't even get started.

I am eternally grateful for him and for the kindness he showed you. He was one of the first people to give you a piece of themselves without expecting anything in return; he taught you to trust the people that do that.

God, you were young then but always so willing. I have always loved that about you. If there was a stage, there was a song. If there was an opportunity, there was a strategy.

Blind ambition.

I hope that wherever Chris is, he can see the difference he made. I can see it and maybe that's enough.

Love,

Lucy x

The Black Sheep

'Hey look, Lil, it's you!'

My sister pointed out the window of our mum's moving car to a field of white Derbyshire sheep grazing alongside a single lonely black one. I knew what she meant, and it wasn't even a shady comment, just an observation. I was a black sheep, a lone wolf, the odd one out since, well, forever, really. My family call me Lillian, by the way. I wish there was an interesting story that explains why but I asked around for one and there isn't. No one really calls me Lucy. A lot of my friends call me Sprags or Luce, though you can call me whatever you like.

For the majority of my life, it felt natural to travel at a hundred miles per hour. I didn't rush through life with the intention of not existing in the present moment but for fear that I might miss something from the next. If life gave me lemons it didn't really matter – I'd just drop them on the floor and see what other fruit was on offer. Rather than feel one experience very intensely, I would spread myself across several experiences so that I could feel all of them. Often a blessing but it was sometimes a curse.

Though it was something I honed as I grew up, I was actually born in the same kind of hurry. I was so keen on getting out of my mum's womb that I didn't engage (which is the word for babies getting into the right position before they are born) and went for a record-breakingly quick labour. During my troubled entry into this world, I went into shock and my heart began to slow to a stop. My very quiet and worryingly blue body was snatched from my mum and out of the room to be resuscitated. As the midwives sprinted out of the room another nurse was sent in to make small talk with my parents.

'Two boys and two girls then, eh? How great is that?!' My parents said nothing. 'Let's have a look at the time, shall we?' A sidestep from my parents' questions about my welfare. The nurse made more time-filling observations about the room until they heard a newborn shrieking from down the hall. At that point, she gave up the act. 'Thank fucking God,' she said, as they brought me in. My first ever performance. My first taste of a reaction, to arrive with a gasp. When most people say this, they mean since they could talk, but I mean it literally: I've been a performer since I was born.

Since I can remember, I could perform my way out of situations. Not just out of trouble (though I was good at that), I could perform my way out of sadness, I could perform my way into friendship and into most adults' good books. I could really put on a show. I was always very good at it. Early in life, I realised I could make people laugh and as soon as I knew how to do that my world changed forever. There isn't much weight behind a scolding from a superior who is suppressing a laugh. I mastered the art of watching, from the side of my eye, how the eyes in the room were watching me and I gave more or less of a performance based on that.

★

I was born, and went to primary school, in Canterbury, Kent. From the start, it was clear I had some behavioural problems. As many children are, I was a terrible bullshitter and made things up for absolutely no reason. One of my favourite lies was telling my family I'd seen one of my school-teachers wherever we were in the world: out the window of the car on a camping trip in France, a glimpse of her walking down Oxford Street from the open top bus we were on in London. I'd say, 'Oh my God, I just saw Mrs Barrett!' I don't remember if I genuinely thought I'd seen her or if I pathologically made stuff up. I'd go into school and create elaborate tales about what I'd been up to at the weekend: racing motorbikes through the woods with my supportive dad, winning a boxing tournament or spending quality time with my Swedish twin sister, none of which even remotely happened. I definitely don't have a twin sister. I suspect, like poor Tracy Beaker, I was probably trying to carve out a life that was far removed from the life I was living. I carried this story-making it right into my teens, when most kids had grown out of it.

I was also an excellent tantrum thrower, well past the age with which you'd associate tantrum throwing. I thoroughly enjoyed running away from home after a tantrum. When I deemed myself old enough to make the five-minute walk around the block on my own, I would abscond to my mum's friend Pauline's house. Pauline was a very calm and very softly spoken woman who moved very slowly around me and always consoled me with a hug, a cup of tea and a biscuit. Though the triggers of my extreme behaviours weren't predictable, I was. The way I soothed myself was with rage. When things didn't go the way I anticipated, I struggled to understand why and could be very quickly overwhelmed by the sense of disorganisation, which would lead into an all-consuming, explosive meltdown.

Today, in my thirties, after extended periods of stress, or when I'm faced with a personal problem that I cannot fix, or when too many of my senses are being stimulated at once, or if my plans backfire without time to reorganise, or even when doing something as simple as trying to pick an outfit, I can melt down into that same horrible downward spiral that I felt so intensely as a child. The older I get, the easier it is to catch myself before committing to the kind of tantrums I threw then, and I spend a lot of time making my life as predictable and routine as it possibly can be to prevent them, but when the stars align incorrectly and I am unable to calm myself, I can still experience the feelings of total desperation and inability to use my brain properly. I feel the exact same completely inconsolable, white-hot rage and decreased ability to process sensory information that I did as a toddler.

It isn't 'normal', I know that. My brothers and sister didn't have the same traits and, due to the frenzied similarities between me and the Looney Tunes' Tasmanian devil, my mum suspected, pretty much since I could walk, that I had ADHD. I had suspected that I was neurodiverse for as long as I knew it was a thing. As the awareness of neurodiversity has spread, along with the understanding that girls often present differently to boys, and that actually, you can be creative and extroverted and social as well as being neurodiverse, my suspicions increased.

As well as always being in a hurry, I was obsessive and hyper focused. Something that has always stood out for me is that I have been an imitator since I can remember. I have always believed, and still do, that I can do absolutely anything if I'm shown how to do it once. I can mirror techniques, behaviours, accents, emotions. I imitate what I've seen and repeat it over and over until I can do it. It's a superpower. I am quite sure that I have been able to write this book because I have read so many: I am copying what I've seen.

I even learnt music, the thing I made a career out of, by mimicry. Because I was so jealous of my brother's guitar playing, I watched him and taught myself to play too. I wrote moody, angsty songs about being in love or being depressed, like you do, but music wasn't the only kind of expressive art I discovered as a young person. I had also had a keen interest in magic. Yeah, magic – like Harry Houdini or David Copperfield (stop laughing). A family friend ran a magic shop and explained some of the secrets behind the basic coin tricks and showed me how to use a Svengali deck. I spent every bit of pocket money on growing my collection. My obsessive side latched onto mastering sleight of hand and quickly moved onto complex card tricks that were advanced for most adults. I could make things disappear, have the air in front of me burst into flames and, more importantly, I could impress people without even opening my mouth. I spent hours in front of the mirror repeating the same tricks over and over, fixated on perfecting them. Once perfected, each trick was appointed an elaborate patter to go with it.

But there were some things I couldn't copy. One of my earliest memories is from primary school, sitting on my teacher's knee hysterically crying and hyperventilating whilst she tried to calm me down because I couldn't work out a maths equation. I have always struggled to cope when I cannot do something and, like I said, that can trigger unusual amounts of frustration and a lack of emotional control. I have learnt that working some things out, like mental arithmetic, you can't imitate. Unless I could copy someone's actual work, I could not do maths. I still can't. You see, there's a big difference between imitating and learning. That's why by the time I was twelve, I could drive a manual car, roll a cigarette and change a tyre. I watched and imitated. And yet I still struggle to count loose change or read the time from an analogue clock.

Whilst I was writing this book, I decided to do an official autism assessment. I got a working diagnosis of OCD last year and, despite having some traits of OCD, I didn't feel like that was an accurate diagnosis. The autism assessment felt a lot like a one-size-fits-all box ticking exercise for traits of autism that seemed very old-fashioned. I sat in on a Zoom call that they'd asked my mum to be present on and she was asked questions like 'did Lucy make eye contact as a child?', 'did Lucy hit herself in the head when she was stressed?' and 'did Lucy go through long periods of time without talking?'. When my mum brought up my obsession with magic, I got the idea that because it was performance based and that I was quite extroverted, it didn't fit the bill. I noticed that this kind of assessment doesn't consider whether the participant is a boy or a girl (as girls are more likely to mask or imitate others), whether or not they had siblings, or the dynamic of their household. It was interesting to say the least. My ability to communicate well as a child and my lack of interest in collecting stamps or train spotting scored me low on their scale and, at the end of the assessment, I was diagnosed as not autistic. They did suggest forking out another £1,700 to confirm their suspicion that I have ADHD, but I think we already know that.

In a really positive way, doing that assessment confirmed to me that I don't really care to know what kind of neurodiversity I have, especially when the diagnosis is based on a scoresheet. I know what my non-neurotypical traits are and the things that I struggle with. The older I get, the more I accept that this is part of who I am. Though it's not easy. The people I surround myself with, the team I work alongside and my family all know my traits too, because I don't hide them. On public transport I wear earplugs AND noise-cancelling headphones that play white noise. When I voiced my suspicions that I was neurodiverse to the people closest to me, none of them flinched. I guess I'd like to be part of spreading the awareness that neurodiversity doesn't look the same on everyone. It's a part of who I am and for all of the things I find challenging that other people might not, I quite like me. Growing up, my extended family called me 'lawless' because I was fearful of absolutely nothing and no one, and a lack of fear is associated with the ADHD brain. But despite being a burly, funny and fearless child,

I was also incredibly sensitive. I was also called Captain Fair by my close family because, as a black-and-white thinker who processed the facts and formed expectations based on them, I could never get my head around unfairness. And life can be pretty unfair.

*

When I was ten years old, my mum, my brother and sister and I moved 230-ish miles away from Kent up to Buxton, in Derbyshire. My mum had found a job as a teacher and, I suppose, had been yearning for a new start. It meant I joined Year 6, the last year of primary school, in a town I'd never even heard of, let alone visited before, into a class full of kids that had known each other since they were toddlers. My behaviour throughout early childhood had already been problematic but this cross-country upheaval definitely fanned the flames of my troublemaking.

Moving to a new life when you are ten is traumatic. I found Buxton terribly boring: it was a tiny town with very little to do and we moved in the first week of the summer holidays, so I didn't know anyone. My wider family and friends were so far away. I was desperate to impress others and make friends but I struggled. And I was so angry. All of the time. Angrier than before. Angry that my life had changed so much, at the fact I had no control over it. Angry that I had been taken so far from everything I had previously known. Angry like I'd learnt to be from my dad. My relationship with my mum started to fray.

I was a difficult child. I had been a difficult child since I could make decisions.

I started to imitate, looking for a way to fit in, and, within a year, my strong Kent accent started to head north. My pronunciation of the word bath, which had been baarth, was no longer the same as the Queen's. Arse was now pronounced ass.

Though my behaviour had been bad before, it took a real turn when I went from primary to secondary school. I started getting into fights. I started drinking.

In my first year at Buxton Community School there was a teacher training day. A day off, basically. But as my mum was a single parent who worked full-time, had very little money and didn't know any other parents, a random school day off meant that I would be left to my own devices. That was bad news. I know this would have filled my mum with dread but she didn't really have any other option.

At 7.30 a.m., my mum set off for her work as a teacher at a college a couple of towns over. By 8.30 a.m., I had already gained access to any available alcohol in our house and made myself a 'shit mix'. I was about to say 'We've all made one of these' (and I *think* most of us have?) but probably not when we were twelve.

A shit mix is where you combine several different spirits and liqueurs, generally ones that belong to your parents, in a plastic container and drink it straight from said container, despite it tasting like something you'd put into a car engine, being sure to top up the bottles you took it from with tap water. Like no one will ever notice.

I took it to the park to meet my friends. I was showing off. I drank some, then I drank some more. These kids must have thought I was fucking mental. I wonder if they'd seen anything like that before.

I already told you the story of when I first got drunk and

how I was introduced to that feeling of not caring. Looking back, it makes me feel extremely uncomfortable to know that I was doing this at this age. I always felt so much older than I was. It's strange to look back on where the coping mechanism that damaged so much of my life really began.

Needless to say, that day didn't go well for anyone. Mum got a call at work from one of my sister's friend's mums to say I'd been spotted absolutely paralytic in the park. She had to come back from work and find me, then load me into the car and take me home.

I have so many stories like that one. Being paralytic. Or being drunk and in trouble. There are so many explanations I could suggest for my uncontrollable desire to be absolutely shit-faced since I was a young child, but I suspect it was because I was exposed to quite a lot of violence from my father during my childhood. From that very first time I got drunk, I knew what it felt like to escape. I grew up around a lot of adventure, excitement, happiness and love, but I also witnessed and experienced a lot of rage, sadness, anger and loneliness. Pulled between two poles of emotional extremes. I always felt like an outsider, that I didn't fit in and wasn't fully welcome, both in my family life and my social surroundings. For as long as I can remember, I felt like I was swimming in a different direction to the rest of the shoal.

Despite it being evident that I had behavioural issues, and despite the fact we weren't getting on, my mum disagreed with the suggestion of medicating me with Ritalin, which is something that I am incredibly grateful for because – as emotional, uncontrollable, misunderstood, wild, strange and savage as I was as a child and teenager –

I was also kind, funny, talented, passionate, imaginative and described as 'bright' by my school (which is what teachers call intelligent kids who are also little shits). She didn't want to change me, which I know took a lot of effort to nurture.

If I had to choose whether I have negative or positive memories of high school, I'd say they were mostly positive. If you asked my teachers if they had negative or positive memories of me at high school, they would definitely say the opposite. My favourite ever school memory is of my German teacher, Frau Gordon, sending me out of the classroom for disrupting the class, a regular occurrence. About five minutes after she'd sent me out, she joined me outside. She shut the door quietly behind her and silently looked up and down the corridor, checking for any bystanders. Once she knew the coast was clear, she paused, then looked me dead in the eyes and said plainly, 'You are a twat.'

I really liked her after that.

★

The magic tricks helped to break down barriers. I got so good that at twelve years old I was being hired for children's parties under the extremely imaginative pseudonym 'Magic Lucy'. I ventured out to the local print shop and had little business cards made. I was a short, chubby, little, strange and somewhat androgynous kid who wore an oversized black suit blazer and, at times, a top hat. Before the David Blaine and Dynamo street magicians of the world, magic really wasn't very cool. It was all toothy grins and jazz hands. Despite looking like an absolute sausage, I turned out to be really quite good at performing magic in front of an audience and later that summer ended being hired at a Rolls-Royce event as an actual table magician.

I have a tattoo on my right wrist that says 'pick a card', which often brings me onto the topic of nearly becoming a magician by trade. People ask, 'If you were as good as you say you were, then why did you stop doing magic?' The truth is, there are only so many times you can hear a white, middle-aged man say 'I know how you did that' when you know he definitely doesn't without punching him in the throat. With fewer people to challenge my songs, music soon took over from magic, but if we're ever in the same room with a deck of cards, I can still bust out a trick for you.

In high school, I made friends with a lot of the other kids but didn't belong to one group. I was versatile, sometimes spending lunchtime at the chess club, other times smoking with the naughtier bunch on the bottom steps. I would shapeshift into whoever I needed to be to fit in. Though I much preferred the excitement of being one of the naughtier kids, naturally. Classmates would stop me as I walked by so that I could entertain them with magic tricks during our lunch break, which is quite wholesome. It's a strange contrast because outside of school I had slowly become the kind of kid that other kids' parents didn't want them to hang around with. I was still going to Club Acoustic and I started playing these funny songs in assembly to my whole year group, but they were songs I'd written about teachers. Some of them laughed along, but others, like my music teacher who never really liked me at all, didn't find them funny and put a stop to the assembly performances. There were so many versions of me: Magic Lucy, Singing Lucy, Bright

Lucy, Naughty Lucy . . . Who I was, was always dependent on the environment I found myself in.

I was in Year 8 when I smoked weed for the first time, about thirteen years old. I told my mum that I was staying at a friend's house but was actually in a flat with two or three older girls my brother's age, four years above me. We sat in this dark, typically teenage bedroom that belonged to a pale, sickly-looking girl called Lily, whose dad either wasn't at home or didn't care about teenagers smoking weed in his flat. There was a single bed in one corner and grubby Nirvana posters Blu-Tacked to the walls. For some reason, one of those mini exercise trampolines was sitting in the other corner. They were all passing around a joint and eventually it came to me, sitting on the bed. I inspected it for a second, took a little puff and breathed it out. I didn't feel anything; it just tasted a bit ashy. Lily, the girl who had passed it to me, said, 'You didn't inhale it!' and took the spliff off me.

She came and sat next to me on the edge of the bed and, as if putting on a performance, took a toke, held it in her mouth and then took a big deep inhale, paused for a few seconds, and exhaled. She passed it back to me. Ah, I got it. I put it to my lips, took a drag, held it, then took a big deep inhale – or tried to, at least. The smoke caught the back of my throat immediately and I felt I was choking. I was coughing and spluttering with my body bent over, my right hand in the air, still holding the joint between my thumb and middle finger so as not to harm it, despite the fact I felt like I couldn't breathe. Lily and the couple of other kids in the room cracked up. I laughed too, my eyes brimming with tears – not because I had the giggles but from the pain at the back of my throat.

Within minutes of my first hit, I was on that mini-trampoline, bouncing up and down, chanting and singing, whilst Lily and co. watched me through their heavy eyelids, laughing incurably. I didn't love being high. Once I'd stepped down from the trampoline, I had this weird paranoid feeling, a feeling that I needed to escape the room. Weed never mellowed me out like it seemed to other people.

I started taking ecstasy pills at the weekends not long after this, a drug that increases your sense of love and makes you want to party all night. But I don't believe that weed is a gateway drug. I believe the gateway to all drugs is curiosity. Natural curiosity. The thing that keeps you going back to them? Trauma. Something I'll talk more about later in this book.

★

Later that year, 2005, my mum met Colin, who she has been married to ever since. Colin had two kids, a couple of years younger than me. My older brother had left for university, so my mum, Colin, my sister, Ella, and Colin's kids, Charlie and Ruby, all moved into the same house in 2006, just a year after they met. Colin's kids had been raised in a very different way to us and they were very quiet and reserved. When our two single-parent families collided, it was clear that my mum and Colin had immeasurably different parenting styles.

To be honest, I hadn't really been parented very much. My mum had been focused on getting her life on track and, though she was my parent, I always felt very far away from her. I was very independent and the youngest of four, so I was a bit feral. Colin's parenting was the opposite: he and his kids were very close to each other and the kids were very obedient. They looked at me and my sister like we were aliens. I found being in a house with a male parent figure that wasn't *my* parent unbearable. I had been the youngest in my family for my entire life but that dynamic changed. I was wild child and noticeably, even at this point, I was quite damaged. Tensions were very, very high. For some reason, no one could understand why I was so angry and frustrated. I felt like an outsider, so I acted like one.

I was fourteen when I got arrested for the first time. I got into a scrap with another girl and the police came to arrest me at our family home. Because I was underage, my mum had to come with me. To be honest, I'd expected being arrestedto be scarier than it was. I thought I'd be sharing a holding cell with hardened criminals like you see in films, them smoking and staring at you, asking, 'What you in for?' It wasn't like that. I got interviewed and cautioned and let go.

Mum and Colin got married and when they went on their honeymoon, I threw the world's biggest house party. I invited basically everyone from my high school. I did try pretty hard to keep it under wraps, but it got out of control and the police were called, and they both had to come home early from their trip. Apparently, it was the party of the century but I wouldn't know – I was paralytic and throwing up in bed from 7 p.m. onwards.

That same year, I had my first diagnosable mental health crisis. I'd been out the whole weekend, having told my mum I was somewhere safe but actually taking pills somewhere quite the opposite. I hadn't slept since the Friday and by the Sunday night, I felt really strange. On Monday morning, when I was cleaning my teeth, the water that was running from the tap was making this unusual sound. When I put my ear closer, I was convinced that I could hear someone shouting. I turned off the tap and it stopped. I put it back on and it happened again. I was hallucinating. I was fucking terrified. I went downstairs and told my mum what was happening. I told her I'd taken one pill, for the first time ever that weekend, and she took me to the GP. On my medical record it says 'drug induced psychosis'.

Colin was a violin maker and his twelve-year-old daughter had recently started playing the violin. As with any child that learns any instrument, it sounded horrendous, like someone throwing a bag of knives down the stairs, but both Colin and my mum were outwardly proud and supportive of her new hobby. One day, my mum told me that she was driving my stepsister to Derbyshire's prestigious private school, Repton, because they'd secured her a place on a week-long violin-playing course there. Were they fucking joking? I was full of envy. I'd been writing songs since I was a child. Good songs. Why wasn't I on a week-long music course at a private school? I'd taught myself the guitar and everyone who heard me play would observe how young I was and how advanced the songs were. Plus, she was shit! I went with them in the car that day and I sat outside this school that looked like Hogwarts, wondering what the tutors in there would think about my songs and my style. I thought about how I'd fit into a school where the kids wore ties and pleated skirts and played Vivaldi. She stayed for two days because she didn't want to stay for the rest.

★

At the end of high school, just before I turned sixteen, I moved out of the blended family home. My behaviour was getting worse and, despite the scare, I'd continued drinking and taking drugs. I felt like absolutely no one understood me. The tension between my mum and me was at its peak. One day, she and I were having a huge argument in the house, her at the top of the stairs and me at the bottom, screaming back and forth at each other. All of a sudden, I felt this thud into my right side, just above my hip height. I was now on the floor. The thud was Colin's shoulder. He had come hurtling through from the living room and rugby tackled me to the ground.

I don't know whether Colin's action was born of frustration or panic or just not knowing what to do in that situation. Even though at that time I was doing very adult things, and using adult words, I was still a child, and I had never had a physical altercation with any of them. I was hysterical, and winded. I felt disgusted, actually. Later down the line, after another argument where Colin had been involved, I called my dad, even though I hadn't seen him much at all since we had moved, and I told him what had happened. My dad called Colin and told him he was on his way to Buxton from Kent to collect me, and that he would kick the shit out of him when he got there. Even though that is not the right way to respond, it was the first time I'd felt supported in a long time. My dad didn't know how to show many emotions other than anger, even when he was trying to show love.

For a short time, I lived with my dad in our old family home in Canterbury. He worked in the building trade, so he spent very little time there. When he was at home, I would listen to him and his girlfriend have huge, violent fights from the same room I used to hear the same bangs and shouts as a young child.

When I'd settled in, I reconnected with some teenage friends that I'd gone to primary school with and got invited to a party one weekend. We were drinking cheap cider out of dark blue, two-litre bottles. At the party, my northern accent cut through all of the Kentish twangs and attracted a bit of attention. Two girls, a pair of lesbians, approached me and accused me of flirting with one of their girlfriends. One of them got right up into my face and I warned her that I'd hit her if she didn't fuck off. She didn't fuck off and, true to my word, I punched her in the face. She fell to the ground and I made a run for it, out the door and down the road.

I thought I'd got away but when I got to the bus stop, I realised that there wasn't another bus for twenty minutes. I saw a big group of people from the party marching down the road, led by the two lesbians. Shit. As they got closer, I noticed that I'd broken the nose of the one I'd hit, quite badly. They both wanted revenge and I knew there wasn't much point in trying to win a fight against two people. I put my hands either side of my face as they started laying into me, punches and kicks flying. The group of teenagers they'd walked down with were gathered around us as if spectating a bare-knuckle brawl, though there was no referee to intervene. I figured they'd stop eventually if I wasn't throwing punches back but I was wrong. The flurries just carried on, minute after minute. It felt like a lifetime. Some of the faces in the crowd started to look a bit sorry for me but no one tried to stop it; I was the outsider. My eyes and cheeks were so swollen I could barely see out of them, but I stayed standing up on my feet no matter how hard they tried to get me on the floor.

Eventually, I felt this rush of adrenaline combined with a clarity that simple defence was not going to end this altercation, and I changed tack. I pushed them both backwards and turned to a garden fence on my right just next to the bus stop, putting my foot against it and yanking off a plank of two-by-four wood. I held it with both hands, above my shoulder like a baseball bat, making it clear that I'd use it if they came any closer. One of the girls advanced towards me. 'You wouldn't d . . .' she began, as the wood connected with the side of her face.

All three of us were arrested for affray. I was taken to hospital; I had a fractured eye socket and two broken ribs. My face was a swollen mess of purple and black.

In Canterbury police station, whilst I was being interviewed, my lawyer protested that I should not be there, having acted in defence. When the police officer, using both hands, lifted a clear evidence bag containing a large piece of wood onto the table and pushed one end of it forward, the lawyer's face dropped: there was a six-inch nail hanging out the end of it, covered in blood. Without knowing the nail was there, when I'd swung, I had punctured the girl's shoulder – luckily not her neck or head, as I could have killed her.

We both agreed to drop the charges against each other and I left with a reprimand.

★

Over the next few weeks, I made friends with some of the faces that I'd seen in the crowd at the fight. They'd given me the nickname 'Northern Tank' because I'd taken such a battering and stayed on my feet. I liked the tough-guy persona. I wasn't speaking to my mum but my sister had started university in Brighton and over the summer, she came to visit us at my dad's house. She'd been experimenting with drugs too and, like me, the experiments had gone very well. Because there were never any adults at my dad's house I became very popular and would regularly throw parties. That time in my life was like a real-life version of the British TV show *Skins* and we all started taking a lot of Class A drugs. Even in the midst of this chaos, I'd still get the guitar out at house parties and play my songs to everyone.

I knew that I needed to buck my ideas up. Trying to figure out what to do next, I applied to join the Navy but failed the medical, so didn't make the cut. That day, I took so much ketamine that I went into a massive K-hole and sat slumped unconscious against a tree in my dad's back garden for an unknown amount of time.

After getting involved in some more serious fights and knowing my drug taking was getting out of hand, I soon realised that staying in Canterbury wasn't going to lead anywhere positive. I headed back north and moved back in with Mum and Colin very briefly, but that dynamic unsurprisingly still wasn't functional. I asked my dad to help with the rent on a place back in Buxton. He agreed. I ended up in a cheap little place behind the town's only nightclub and, being the only one of my teenage peers who had their own gaff, my house became the place for reckless abandon. The parties were quite something. I flunked a year of my A-levels and then I went to college to study Public Services with the intention of becoming a firefighter. I hate to ruin the ending for you but I didn't become a firefighter.

Dear Lucy,

When you moved out of that little flat behind the club, the landlady kept the entire tenancy deposit. When you got a rundown of the charges it all made complete sense, but up until then, you had no idea what you were being held responsible for.

At the beginning of my tenancy, you noticed this tiny droplet of water on the living room ceiling, just below the bathroom upstairs. You went to investigate the bathtub but couldn't see any holes or visible compromised seals, so you figured it must have been condensation or something and stopped thinking about it. Over time, that droplet dripped more frequently and the droplet itself became larger. Eventually, a dark patch began to spread on the ceiling behind it.

As it turns out, there was a tiny little hole in the base of that bath and whenever it was used, a little bit of water escaped and came through to the living-room ceiling. Over time, that leak caused hundreds of pounds worth of damage, costing the entire deposit.

That leak developed so slowly that you didn't notice how bad it got, meaning you didn't consider the implications it would have further down the line. The leak just became part of your normality.

This is how your drinking habits developed, you know. I bet you would read the above and think, 'Why the fuck didn't I just get a plumber in?!'

But, really, there are a few reasons.

I've learnt that, like that leak, habits form very slowly, so they are very hard to notice. I didn't notice that since I was a child, I always trying to source alcohol. Drip, drip.

I didn't realise that other people didn't get as angry and violent as I did. Drip, drip.

I didn't feel the sadness or the habits developing. Drip, drip.

Our drinking got out of hand pretty subtly and over the years, it has cost us far more than a tenancy deposit.

You didn't have anyone showing you how to navigate any of it.

Throughout life, when problems appeared, rather than burying our head in the sand, we buried it in about eight pints of beer and vodka shots.

Now I own my own home, if the ceiling started leaking, I have the resources to call a workman out; I can afford to hire a plumber. When my brain starts to tell me that I should run away, that I should be violent, or that I should drink, I have the resources to deal with that too, but it took an awfully long time.

My problems used to sneak up on me. They were covert. But I'm vigilant now, always looking for the drips, because I know how much damage can happen without even noticing it.

It wasn't easy being you and none of the adults around you ever told you that. There wasn't much compassion for your behaviour but I want you to know that I understand why you were the way you were. In your heart, you wanted someone to take you in their arms and tell you it was OK to be angry, that they understood, and that you'd work it out together.

Mum was trying to improve her own situation in

those years, understandably, because she'd had a shit time for most of her life. She moved all that way for a job and to be happier, and you felt like you were a burden. That move wasn't just for a job, though; she does that every few years. For some reason or another, she ups sticks and moves hundreds of miles away, leaving her old life behind for a fresh start.

You learnt that from her because you did the same for years.

Recently, she told me that she did understand you, so much that it hurt, because she was always a black sheep too. She said she didn't know what to do to help you.

I wish you could see the life I live now; you'd never have believed it.

I love you very much and I'm sorry it was so hard.

Love,

Lucy x

PS. Ella describes that time in Canterbury as 'Like Lord of the Flies but with lots of ketamine' – well done for getting out of there.

Fuck Mickey

In 2008, I played Manchester Pride for the first time.
My thirty-minute set was in a car park behind Canal Street,
in Manchester's Gay Village, underneath a tarpaulin that
was disguised as a marquee. That first year, I was watched
by about ten or fifteen people, most of whom I'd brought
with me. By then, I'd played a lot of gigs basically wherever
I could blag the opportunity to do so. Manchester Pride had
a portal on their website where you could apply to be a
performer, so I did, and there I was. Performing at Pride
would help me start to build my fanbase and, even early on,
the majority of the audience was lesbians. I, of course, loved
it. That guy, Ben, who I'd met at High Peak Radio, was
helping me to get gigs all across the north of England too.

In 2009, I returned to play a second time. My mum and
my sister had come along to watch with a couple of their
friends and my then girlfriend, Sophie. This performance
was in the same car park as the year before, but the stage set-
up had advanced slightly and the speakers were configured

in a way so that people could hear me from a little further away. I stood on the little riser, which was about a foot off the ground, played my guitar and sang my songs. A crowd started to form. I loved that feeling. If you've ever been at a gig and wondered what the performer can see from the stage, the answer is – you. When I'm performing I love studying the audience. Witnessing two people turn to each other and sing my lyrics whilst eye to eye makes me want to cry. Seeing people try their very best to contain whatever emotion it is they are feeling, whilst their face scrunches up and an involuntarily tear rolls down their cheek – I have to look away because it makes me emotional. Seeing people get so lost in the lyric or story that they forget they are there or that anyone can see them, or watching parents watch their own children get lost in my show, is amazing.

Here at Pride, I was watching people arrive at my set, enticed whilst passing by. I could see them give me a minute or two to weigh up whether or not they liked what I had to offer and then they'd decide to stay or not. That day in Manchester, quite a few people did decide they liked what I had to offer and that feeling filled up my soul, as it always has.

After the set, whilst trying to flog my CDs to members of the audience, I was approached by a short, tanned man in his late forties. He spoke in a fast-paced American accent. Americans have an uncanny knack of being so excited about things. This man was no exception. 'I heard that song, the one about butterflies. I thought it was from a CD, I thought they were playing a CD through the speakers. I turned the corner and there you were, playing it live! I LOVE it!' He was a million miles a minute. 'My name is Chris, by the way. Listen, I run a festival in Orlando, it's called GayDays. We'd love to have you play there. I can't pay you, but if you can get yourself out there, I can put you up for a week on the resort.' He spoke with this convincing energy. I knew he was the real deal.

'Holy shit,' I thought and, without missing a beat, I said, 'Absolutely. I would LOVE to play at GayDays!'

GayDays was in June 2010, so I had nine months to figure out how the fuck I was going to be able to afford to travel to the United States. I was eighteen and just finishing my two-year college course at the University of Derby, which was in Buxton. My dad had been covering the rent on the flat behind the nightclub up until I had turned eighteen, and the plan was that when I became eligible for housing benefits, I'd do that. During college, I got £30 a week Education Maintenance Allowance and I worked part-time at Poole's Cavern. Poole's Cavern is a local cave and huge tourist attraction. I initially worked in the café until I pestered the manager long enough to become a tour guide in there. I loved that job. I'd lead large groups of people into the cave and perform my carefully rehearsed routine. When a tourist asked me a question that I didn't know the answer to, I just riffed. I made it all up. There's probably someone out there who's still quoting my fake cave facts. Sorry about that.

I bounced between a few other jobs too: I washed pots at Pizza Express and I pulled pints in The Eagle, the pub that Club Acoustic was in, for a bit of cash in hand. So I was hardly in a position to save any money but I absolutely did not care. I was going to America to play at GayDays. I moved back into my mum and stepdad's house for the last few months before I left. Sophie and I split up. My most

Derbyshire experience happened when Sophie and I broke up. She came to collect her belongings from my parents' house . . . on her horse.

I saved and saved. I tapped up every living member of my family for last-minute contributions to replace birthday and Christmas gifts for the next three years. When I was booking my flights, I realised that I needed an ESTA visa, so I applied for it. It was granted. I read that meant I could stay in America for three months. Well, that changed everything. I decided then and there that I was going to stay in the US for three months and try to make it big out there. Why wouldn't I?! I'd start at GayDays in Orlando and then I'd work out what to do. How hard could it be?

I held a fundraiser in The Eagle. That same incredible Club Acoustic community, along with my friends, my family and some fans who had already started to follow my career, raised a whopping £1,000. About $1,500 in those days. I graduated from college and June came along quickly.

I got off the flight in Orlando and the humid heat hit me. What sheer joy. Eighteen years old, a backpack and a guitar and the opportunity of a lifetime. I walked from the plane, following signs for the baggage claim and arrivals hall. I'd arranged to meet Chris, the American, in the airport but realised very quickly that Orlando International Airport is fucking huge. Somehow, on the way to arrivals, I got lost. I hadn't navigated my way around an airport before and before I knew it, I was in an area that looked like a departure gate. I turned on my mobile. I'd organised to meet him but didn't have the foresight to save his number, and this is before your emails were on your phone. Shit. I went over to one of those airport computer lounges and put a couple of dollars in. I was sure I could find his number online. I used Bing to search 'GayDays Orlando'. As soon as I pressed enter, the computer kicked me out of the search engine and ended my session 'INAPROPRIATE LANGUAGE/ PROFANITY'. You've got to be kidding me. A kind lady at the help desk used the tannoy to help me find him. It was my first lesson in how insignificant I really was when my surroundings got bigger.

Chris drove me from Orlando to the hotel where GayDays, the mecca for gay Americans, was held. It was just outside Disney World Florida. It was surreal. The hotel was huge. It was all marble and air-conditioned, it felt so high-brow. There were fountains everywhere and concierges in posh outfits were walking around with big smiles. I was shown to my room in the outdoor complex. The block was nestled amongst palm trees and green, tropical landscaping. I put on some clothes more suited to the beautiful weather – some baggy shorts and a t-shirt – and went to scope out my surroundings.

I looked at a pamphlet that had a listing of what was on over the next week. A communal trip to Disney World, a cocktail making class and, oh my God, there I was! My name and a little description of me, in an actual pamphlet, at a festival in America. What the hell?! I spotted something else on the little map on the back of the pamphlet . . . 'Lesbian Pool', it read – I knew where I was going first. I'm not joking when I say that there was a pool quite literally full of lesbians. Fuck Mickey Mouse, I was there for the ladies.

Before I left, I had joined a website called 'Couch Surfers', where you could connect with complete strangers from across the globe and arrange to sleep on their sofa. Would I do this now? No. However, in my search for cheap/free places to stay on my travels, by huge coincidence, I had found a gay couple on the site who lived in downtown Orlando, right by Disney World, who were also attending GayDays. Whilst in the lesbian pool, my shorts and t-shirt still on, with a couple of women either side of me who had been intrigued by my accent, I saw two men (who stuck out like a sore thumb) walking past the outdoor bar, scanning the pool. One of them spotted me and put his hands out excitedly. 'Lucy?!' he asked. 'Phil!' I said, recognising him from their pictures online.

Phil and Kevin were a similar height and had big frames. They were both wearing baseball caps. Phil looked around thirty; he was half-Mexican with kind, brown eyes and the friendliest smile I'd ever seen. He had a beautifully kempt short beard that faded up to his sideburns. Kevin was a fairer-skinned Floridian man, a few years older than Phil. He had blue eyes and another wide, welcoming smile. We spoke for a little while before Phil laughed. 'I gotta get out of here, the lesbians are staring at me!' I was glad to meet them and confirm that my second week in the States would not be spent with a pair of potential murderers. Phew.

The shows went down so well. In my spare time, I wandered around trying to make friends. I was eighteen, so it wasn't legal for me to drink in America, but I found ways around it and I always had a margarita in my hand. After my first show, I met a couple, Liz and Jill. The two women lived in Florida and were at GayDays for the week.

They were both in their late twenties and I was unbelievably excited when they invited me out for drinks that evening. We got on like a house on fire. We spent the whole night sitting at an outdoor table, the Floridian warmth against my skin, drinking cold Bud Light and playing cards. How was I there? How was this my life? I was so lucky. I had a crush on one of the women, Liz. She was a twenty-seven-year-old writer with blonde hair, strikingly blue eyes and one of those perfect, all-American smiles. I mean, come on, I was eighteen.

After a lot of drinks, all three of us ended up sharing the double bed in my hotel room (platonically, to my dismay). For some reason, I ended up lying between them, as if I was the filling of a sandwich and they were the bread. I lay there, holding my breath, wondering if I'd died and gone to heaven. I heard Jill's breath soften and knew she was asleep but, somehow, I knew that Liz wasn't. I found her so, so attractive. I quietly turned onto my side to face her back. My heart felt like it stopped beating when I could have sworn that she had just moved her body a little closer to mine. I lay there in disbelief with my eyes wide open, my body physically buzzing, as her hand came and found mine. I fell asleep holding it.

As the week went by, the three of us spent more time together at the lesbian pool and at the bar. Phil and Kevin came to my shows, but neither party really desired to stray from our gay and lesbian areas, segregated by free choice. I loved the fact that Liz and Jill wanted to spend time with me. I hadn't mentioned the handholding thing. Maybe that was just an American thing – they are all so friendly, after all. Every so often, mine and Liz's eyes would meet, and I would get a jolt of energy and have to look away. She was married, so I was definitely imagining it. When she'd walk towards us from the pool bar, laughing whilst spilling the strawberry daquiris she was carrying, her black sundress outlining her body, the pink Floridian sky behind her, with her dark sunglasses and that bright white smile, the world around me would slip into slow motion. I had it bad.

The end of the week rolled around and it was time to part ways. I was catching a ride with Phil and Kevin to their house in downtown Orlando to stay for the week. Liz and Jill invited me to stay at their place in Jacksonville, Florida, where there were a few open mic nights in local bars. How could I say no?!

Phil and Kevin, and their friend Bubba, introduced me to true southern hospitality. My lord, did those guys know how to have a good time. We would sit on their porch smoking cigarettes and drinking beers out of a cool box, the conversations would go on all night and, between the laughter, I'd play them songs on my guitar. They took me to eat burgers in downtown Orlando and snuck me into gay bars that their friends worked in. Phil was like a big brother to me. Neither of them could get their heads around the fact that I was an eighteen-year-old girl, about to embark on some pretty loose travel plans around the States, on my own. When it was time to leave Orlando and head to see the girls in Jacksonville, Phil drove me to the Greyhound bus station and told me that wherever I went and whatever I got myself into, he was only a phone call away. He waited until I'd got onto the bus and sat down before he left.

On the way to Jacksonville, I had butterflies about seeing Liz again. She pulled up at the bus stop in a black Jeep; down went the window and there were those dark sunglasses and that huge smile. I swooned. Jill worked away, so Liz and I were left with a lot of time alone together. She showed me around the city and told me about her life. She was so smart and so funny. There was a voltage of electricity that coursed every time we spoke. Over that week, it became clear that what I was feeling was mutual. I hadn't imagined it. She said that I came in like lightning. I said that I should probably leave. We talked for hours and hours about how we had to be realistic and reasonable, and how we both knew it wasn't OK. Liz and I kissed on the day I left Jacksonville, just before boarding a Greyhound bus to New Orleans. It was emotional. I wasn't sure I'd ever see her again.

It was July and I was on a bus headed for my uncle's friend's girlfriend's house in New Orleans. Before I had left for the States, whilst hunting for potential places to stay during my trip, her offer of a little shack in a courtyard had come in and I couldn't pass up going to play some shows in the birthplace of jazz. It was already late afternoon and the bus took eleven hours but I'd need to change after the first five hours, just outside Mobile, Alabama, a.k.a. the butt-fuck-middle-of-nowhere. Phil had warned me that Greyhound buses have a pretty murky reputation. Due to the cheap tickets and long distances, the clientele can be sketchy, stinky and sometimes a little dangerous. I learnt this the hard way.

The first bus I boarded was practically empty; there was only two other people on the whole thing, right at the front. What a win. I took a seat towards the back of the bus, next to the window, with empty seats all around me. There was one more stop in Florida before the bus set off on its first long leg to Mobile.

I spotted him before he even got on the bus. He was throwing a large suitcase into the hold. He was very large man, tall and wide, whose belly was still disproportionately large in comparison to the rest of his body. He was wearing a white t-shirt, covered in stains, and, despite the heat, a big, green, waxy coat. He wore a trucker hat and had long, greasy, mousy-coloured hair underneath it. I watched him board the bus and something in my stomach lurched. He looked up the aisle and for the briefest second, we made eye contact. I quickly looked out the window. His footsteps made the bus sway and, as he made his way up towards the back of the empty bus, I knew he was going to sit beside me.

He stank of sweat, alcohol, cooking oil and clothes that hadn't been washed in a very long time. He started talking at me almost as soon as he sat down and his breath was horrific. I kept my responses short and tried not to engage with him. It didn't work. He rambled and rambled: he was a truck driver, on his way to pick up his truck to drive it cross country. He hated his ex-wife, the fuckin' bitch, she was keeping his kids away from him. He ranted about farming prized animals, how people wanted to steal his goats. He told me how many guns he had. I was absolutely petrified. The rambling went on for hours until he turned to look at me, paused for a really long time, barely blinking once, and asked, 'Do you have a friend in Jesus?'

That day, I learnt that the best way to answer that question, whenever you are in the world, is to say, 'Yes, I do.' But I was eighteen, I was panicking and I was incredibly naïve. I told him the truth: 'No, I don't believe in God.'

I genuinely thought he was going to hit me. His cheeks were crimson and the whites around his pale, green eyes were bulging. He started to ramble louder than before. One of the people at the front of the bus took a glance around but knew better than to get involved and faced forward again. He spat that I was a heathen and that God had told him it was his duty to correct the sinners in this world. He said that he could easily take me anywhere in his truck and that no one would ever even know I was gone. After he'd finished, he went silent and just stared ahead. When the bus was pulling into Mobile bus station, he stood up and walked into the small toilet at the back of the bus.

I already knew I was going to make a run for it. As soon as he locked the door, I ran down the aisle. The bus came to a stop. A man walked over to the bus and opened the door to the hold, where my guitar and backpack was. I flew off the bus, grabbed both and ran into the bus station. I didn't anticipate how small it would be. As soon as I ran in, I locked eyes with the woman standing behind the counter. She was Black and looked to be in her fifties, and she didn't even flinch as I dipped underneath the 'employees only' sign and under the counter, right behind her legs. The place was empty, it was the middle of the night.

Moments later, the man from the bus, sweating and breathing heavily, flew in the door I'd just run in, searching the room. From the ground, I could see the woman, whose legs I was hiding behind, shuffling paper and pretending I wasn't there. I tried not to breathe. A couple of minutes later, I heard the door slam shut and tried to guess whether or not he'd gone. 'Don't worry, baby,' the woman said in a strong Southern accent, without even looking at me, moving things around on the countertop. 'You stay there as long as you need to, ain't nothin' gonna happen to you.' I waited with her until the sun rose and my connecting bus showed up.

I arrived at Jennifer's house in New Orleans in the end. Along the front of property was a cracked, wonky wall, too tall to climb. There was a wooden door nestled well into the wall that needed a bit of shoulder effort to get it open. Through the door was a small, quirky, concrete courtyard. On the right-hand side was a door to the property she lived in; on the back wall was a set of fire escape stairs leading up to an apartment that she rented to a local musician. She showed me to my room on the left of the courtyard: a rectangular storage room that was painted green, with a camp bed in its corner. It was perfect. I didn't know how long I'd stay there, or what my plan would be for the next ten weeks, all I knew was that I now had a muse to write songs about.

For days, I barely left the courtyard. I'd sit on a wooden dining chair in the middle of the space with my guitar and a notepad and write songs about falling in love with a twenty-seven-year-old woman, about the age gap between us and the pain of walking away. Jennifer's black and white cat would often lay at my feet to listen to what I'd written.

I don't care if it's 83, or 91,
All I care about the secret, the smiles,
And the setting sun.
Just don't leave me,
When we've just begun.
'91' (Join the Club, 2013)

Jennifer had set up a gig for me at a small venue called Bank Street Bar & Grill. 'Lucy Spraggan 7pm' was written in chalk on a blackboard outside the front of the building. I took a photo of it. My name in lights (or chalk) in New Orleans. I couldn't believe it. Jennifer had invited enough friends along for the show to be a success and some of the audience had come just to see the girl from the UK play.

The musician who lived across the courtyard was called Andrew Duhon. He was a charmingly handsome, rugged-looking man. He had very dark brown curly hair and wide, trustful, brown eyes. He had the most wonderfully thick and immaculate beard that matched the colour of the hair on his head. His skin was sun-kissed and he was wearing dark blue jeans and a plaid shirt rolled up to his elbows, looking more like a ranch man than a singer. I was back out on my chair on the courtyard. I didn't see him standing up there on the fire escape staircase listening to my new material. It wasn't ready to be listened to yet.

'You sound great!' he shouted down. My hand stopped strumming. 'Want to come and play a show tonight?!'

All of a sudden I wasn't bothered him hearing the unfinished songs.

'Absolutely!' I shouted back.

Andrew was the epitome of musicianship. He and his band invited me down to play before them at a bar near Frenchman Street. We set up in the corner of the bar – no stage, no riser, just a little PA system and a hat on the floor for people to put tips into. The music scene in New Orleans is incredible: there are hundreds of musicians playing across the city at any given time and everyone is keen to discover new music. The saturation means that most of them don't get paid in these bars, so they rely on the tips to get by.

Andrew and his band had quite a crowd there to see them and their audience loved me. After I'd played, I (illegally) got myself a beer and watched them perform. I was mind blown. Andrew was a master of the guitar and harmonica, playing them at the same time, the harmonica on a brace around his neck, his beard effortlessly sliding along the metal. His voice was perfect. His accent poked through the melodies of the songs he'd written, which were without a doubt some of the best songs I'd ever heard in my life. The double bassist stood next to him with shoulder-length hair and a long beard, bobbing his head forward and back as he played. The drummer, with just a snare, kick drum and high hat, made it sound like he was playing a full kit. I'd never heard anything like it. I sat and drank it all in – more inspiration for my notepad in the courtyard. After the show, Andrew and his band presented me with the hat full of tips, not keeping a cent back for themselves.

I'd bought an American pay-as-you-go phone and had been texting back and forth with Liz for the week and a half I'd been in New Orleans. The pull I felt towards her was so intense. She said she was really confused and that, in meeting me, her whole life had been turned upside down. She told me that she was considering leaving Jill.

They say love makes you do stupid things but I think it's actually a lack of coping strategies, rather than the love itself, that tends to fuck things up. Days later, Liz did leave Jill. She packed up clothes, her dogs and anything else she could fit into her Jeep, and drove from Jacksonville to New Orleans, leaving her life to come and find me.

For the next four weeks, we drove 10,000 miles across the country, with her clothes, her dogs, my guitar and my backpack. We slept at motels, at the side of the road, on her friends' sofas, at campsites, all kinds of places. I played in bars and we ran away from anything that was real to us. It was one of the highlights of my life. I wrote a song about that time, which I think explains enough for your imagination to do the rest.

I was stung by the sting of the worst of bees in
   New Orleans,
I was scared and unprepared but right there I was
   happy.
The one sunset I won't forget, you took my breath
   it was so perfect,
The journey of you and me started in New Orleans.

We got our rest, quality for less in Texas,
Two sunsets straight, we learned it's a state you
   don't mess with,
Papa John's with the TV on,
Back when summer just begun,
My few but favourite memories of Texas.

I wore a cowboy hat, reading a country map in
   New Mexico,
We had 'I think we're lost' silence, but I'm the co-pilot,
That's the best for you, you know,
Halfway down the interstate,
You left your phone at that picnic place,
I kept a cool face, while you were irate in New Mexico.

PROCESS

I saw the world behind the wheel,
I learnt how to feel in Arizona.
I saw the stars, felt the change,
You fell hard, I felt the same and I showed ya,
The campsite, or maybe the inn,
I don't know where this one begins,
I just know my heart lies beneath the stars in Arizona.

I guess I can't sing about all the states,
but in your country they abbreviate,
I went to FL and GA and LA and TX and NM and AZ,
    or should I say Zee.
CO and KS and MO and IL and IN, Ohio and WV,
I went to VA and NC and MD and DE and PA and
    MA and NYC.

I last saw you by the lake,
Was good to see your face in Pennsylvania,
Was such a beautiful day when you tried to explain all
    the truth and that y'know.
I told you, I'd never miss the chance, under any single
    circumstance,
Again I'd see your face in the United States of America.
– 'In a State' (Top Room at the Zoo, 2011/
    Join the Club, *2013*)

I can see quite clearly now that Liz was going through a quarter-life crisis of sorts and me, the nomadic, doe-eyed, travelling musician, was a pretty good escape from her life. I can sympathise, now that I'm old enough to have had my own premature mid-life crisis.

On the road, she'd sometimes have a little freak-out and drive that Jeep away from me, leaving me in a random state in the US. When travelling, moving around a lot will cost more than staying in one place and, on our endless getaway mission, we had driven from the East Coast to the West Coast and then back across the country to Pennsylvania. I was running low on funds. Very low, in fact.

After the last freak-out, Liz left me in Philadelphia. I was kindly welcomed into the home of a woman called Miranda, a friend of Liz's, who let me crash on her sofa for a few days, but I knew I couldn't intrude on this stranger's life for too long. I'd been told that Rehoboth Beach in Delaware had a great live music scene and a thriving gay community. It could be a great place to play some shows and make some tips. I had enough money for a train ticket there and, at a push, a night in a very cheap motel. It sounded like a plan.

I paced down the boardwalk in Rehoboth Beach, nipping in and out of motels and guest houses to find the cheapest deal. My guitar was so heavy. I lugged it around, swapping it from hand to hand. It wasn't looking good. I'd underestimated the cost of a place to stay in July, peak tourist time, in a surfing town. I walked up and down the side roads of the main strip, trying to come up with a plan. Then, hanging from a pole off the side of a pink and white, wooden building, with a bar/restaurant sign with a crab outside it, as if a sign from God, I saw a big rainbow flag. A symbol of sanctuary.

The door was propped open and, ignoring the 'closed' sign that was turned outwards in the window, I knocked and poked my head in. A stocky woman with short, spikey hair popped up from behind the bar, where she was restocking a fridge. She was wearing reflective sporty sunglasses and a tank top that showed off her muscular arms. 'A lesbian!' I thought, 'Thank God.' It turned out that Michelle was the more butch half of the couple and ran the restaurant. Her wife, Cindy, was a smaller-framed, blonde, athletic-looking woman. They were both absolutely lovely. Sitting at a table in the empty bar area, they listened to my story so far and revelled in the sheer lesbian predictability of it all. I asked them if there was any way they'd let me play in the bar for tips, so that I could find somewhere to stay in town. They looked at each other and Cindy said, 'I think we could do you one better than that.'

It turned out that the tenant in the one-bedroom furn-ished apartment above the bar had just moved out and it was going to be empty for the next week. Out of a mixture of sheer kindness, maternal instincts and good, old-fashioned queer solidarity, they let me stay in that apartment for free, for the whole week. I saved up the tips from playing in their bar and many of the bars that belonged to their friends. Enough for me to bid my farewells and head back up the East Coast.

In late August 2010, I flew back to Manchester from JFK. My ridiculous, life-changing trip had come to an end in the Empire State. My mum and my sister were waiting for me at the arrivals gate. 'Oh my God, you are SO TANNED!' they exclaimed. If only they knew. I didn't just look different, I felt like I'd lived one hundred years in the last three months. I was newly nineteen and I'd had more than a taste of what the world outside the small town I lived in had to offer. I knew that, once I got home, staying in Buxton wasn't going to be an option.

On my travels, there had been so many ropey situations, just like the trucker on the bus, that taught me how to be more vigilant, who not to trust and what not to do when travelling alone. They taught me the privilege of surviving to say, 'Fucking hell, that was close!' But despite the brushes with the unfavourable, what that trip taught me about most was the kindness of others. So many beautiful people welcomed me, a teenage stranger, into their homes and lives, for no other reason but to be kind. They saw someone trying to pursue a dream and they wanted to help. Every single one of them, including the people that I didn't mention, taught me how to trust the good people and how to be kind.

Dear Lucy,

Sorry to say it, kid, but when you came home and tried to make a long-distance relationship work with Liz, it wasn't a success. It was 2010 and unstable internet connections and expensive calls from phone boxes had a lot to answer for. You even tried to apply for a six-month visa to return to Liz and to the United States, but the American Embassy suspected that you wouldn't come back and stamped a big fat 'DENIED' on the application. 'Insufficient Ties to the UK' was the reason and . . . I suppose they were right.

You never really had sufficient ties to anything, which is why you were so good at being on the road. Since this trip, your need to constantly be moving around has never ceased and you learnt to embrace it. Your lack of roots is a part of who you are.

PROCESS

More than ten years on, you and Liz still speak. She lives in New Jersey and is married with two children.

Phil and Kevin have been two of your best friends for more than a decade and now live in Vegas, where you visit them regularly. Andrew Duhon came to support you on tour in the UK and continues to be incredibly handsome and talented.

The irony is that, later in life, you're going to almost re-enact the USA affair, but this time you will be the partner that runs away from home with a younger (but not quite as young . . .) woman. It's funny how life does that – comes full circle.

I don't know if you were brave or if you were stupid, but going on that trip was the making of you and, somehow, you made it back. Well done, you moron.

Love,

Lucy x

The Top Room
at the Zoo

I jumped back into the small pond that was Buxton, with its population of only 22,000, with a very anti-climactic splash. I had expanded, like the legend of the fairground goldfish dumped in a large body of water that grew to a ridiculous size. I'd been released into the ocean and swum deep, but now I was back. Whilst I was in the States, my anger had quietened for the first time in my life. I was free and I wasn't trapped; I was where I wanted to be. But as soon as I found myself back in town, my sadness settled right back in. I was angry again.

I hadn't given much thought to what I'd do when I got home. Before I left for the States I'd graduated with a BTEC National in Public Services, so I figured that maybe I could get fit and apply to be a fire-fighter. It was one option, at least – I kept it in the back of my mind.

I tried living with my mum and stepdad, and my two step-siblings, but I struggled with the dynamic. There were rules and I wasn't used to having them. Not just since being in America, though that had made these feelings more pronounced; I hadn't been parented like that. I had been on my own, doing my own thing, for a long time. I went out and drank, a lot. I went back to work in The Eagle and rented one of the rooms upstairs. The Eagle had a bar/club attached to it that opened on the weekend and, without a chance of sleeping through the noise of it, I'd work shifts there too.

Over the road from The Eagle there was a pub called The New Inn. If you asked someone local what it was like, they'd probably tell you not to go in because of its rough reputation. It was a three-storey building, built in the early nineteenth century of millstone grit, the locally quarried grey sandstone. From the outside, it looked quite quaint but on the inside, there wasn't much quaintness about it at all. When I asked one of The Eagle's older, white-haired regulars about it, he said, 'They call it The Zoo Inn, you know?' I waited for the rest. 'Because it's full of fucking animals.' It sounded right up my street.

I wandered into The New Inn one afternoon, not only in search of more shifts but to make my own mind up about the place. Something drew me to it. It was an old-fashioned pub, with netted, cigarette-smoke-stained curtains, burgundy wallpaper and dark wood furniture. There was a big pillar as you walked in that obscured the view of the bar, which wrapped around the back of the room. Behind it, amongst disorderly placed bottles and glasses, packets of pork scratchings and dry roasted peanuts, was a tall woman with curly dyed-blonde hair, just longer than a bob, wearing a stripey, long-sleeved jumper. She was smiling. There are people you meet in life who are unlike anyone else you have ever encountered. Marlies was her name and she was one of those.

It turned out that everything I had heard about The New Inn was wrong. Marlies was more than happy to poach me from The Eagle and from my first shift, I got why so many people didn't understand that pub: everybody in there was a black sheep. The Zoo, as everyone called it, was a church for misfits. For the rootless. Contractors and convicts, runaways and strays, all looking for a place to be themselves. The leader of the church was Marlies. She had created a space where everybody was allowed to be exactly who they were. She was a deceptively hardy woman. To Marlies, there was no such thing as trauma, only 'character building'.

As a single woman, there wasn't much she could do when a fight broke out, which was a regular occurrence, because she was no match for the physicality of drunk, angry men. So she created her own way of dealing with violence. At the first indication of aggression, she would become a circus ringleader, a showman, and, rather than trying to stop the conflict, she would draw attention to the spectacle of it. 'Roll up, roll up, everyone! Come and see what's happening for us!' she would shout across the pub, drawing the clientele's notice. The people involved in the argument wouldn't know what to do and it would sort of fizzle out.

For absolutely no reason, Marlies would wear fancy dress to serve behind the bar. One day, she wore a bikini to work, with a brown wig poking out of the bikini bottoms as part of the look. I saw her dressed a jockey, as a pin-up girl and once in her wedding dress – despite the fact that she was in the middle of a divorce – serving the regulars. They didn't even flinch.

She lived above the pub, on the second floor, with her two children, Dexter and Tilly. The third floor of the pub was disused. It was a bit damp and cold, but it was liveable and Marlies had let a lot of people stay there. I asked if I could rent that top room. It was magnolia, maybe it had been white at some point, and there was a double bed that faced a single glazed window with a view across the marketplace, and The Eagle. Marlies said yes. Knowing that I played guitar and was good at magic she asked that, in place of rent, I would give Dexter guitar lessons and teach Tilly how to do magic.

After my America trip, I was trying to play as many gigs as I could, wherever I could. Marl loved hearing me play and encouraged me to do it all the time. Whilst we were working, she'd tell me to go and get my guitar and to sit behind the bar on a stool and make up funny songs about people who came in, in between serving drinks. One day, a girl called Cassandra came in the pub and ordered a pint. Everyone knew Cassandra because she'd recently done a stint on *Jeremy Kyle*. I'd been entertaining the locals that afternoon and I couldn't turn down the opportunity to improvise about such a great topic. I sang away: 'Jeremy, Jeremy, Jeremy, Jeremy, *Jeremy Kyle*, can you help me out with the paternity of my first-born child? Because my mother, I detest her, I need a lie detector! From Jeremy, Jeremy, Jeremy, Jeremy, Jeremy Kyle.' Cassandra didn't react, I think she was resigned to having the piss taken out of her a long time before she'd even walked into the pub. That ditty later became the skeleton of a song called 'Jeremy Kyle' that in 2013, after my *X Factor* audition, I played on the actual *The Jeremy Kyle Show*. The first and only live music performance on the show.

Not long after moving into the New Inn, I was busking on Buxton high street and an elderly couple walked past right in front of me holding hands. Moments later, as if in slow motion, the old lady kind of froze and her eyes glazed over as she collapsed to the floor. Her husband tried to soften her fall. He looked petrified. She lay there, him kneeling beside her, willing her to wake up, as everyone gathered around to help. An ambulance arrived and took them both away, the old lady still unconscious, laying on a stretcher. That image and the desperate look on the man's face etched into my brain.

I quickly packed up my guitar and walked up the hill towards the pub. I ran straight up the two flights of stairs and into my room, picked up my notepad and started to write a song about what I'd just seen. That song was called 'Tea and Toast' and it took less than an hour to write. I walked into the living room and asked Marl if I could show it to her and she clapped her hands in front of her and sat down on a stool, excited to hear it. When I finished, she was sobbing but smiling: 'Lucy Spraggan, that song is incredible.'

The last time I was arrested was on 31st December, 2010, four months after I'd got back from America. A few months before the arrest, in the September, I knew I needed a plan to escape Buxton but I didn't know what it was going to be. My plan to move back to the US to be with Liz had now fallen through thanks to the rejected visa application but that only made me more desperate to get out. The cloud above me darkened as I started to drink more and more.

Due to the trouble I'd already been in with the police, my

solicitor had previously made it very clear that I didn't have many chances left. My next run-in with the law would be taken far more seriously. The last time I had walked out of the police station, the sergeant had warned me, 'Do not end up back here again, Lucy. You're about to ruin your life.'

I can't remember the details of that New Year's Eve party, just the basics of the fight that resulted in my arrest. We were at my friend's flat when an argument broke out between me and a guy we knew. We'd all been drinking, a lot, and it got physical straight away. He and I exchanged punches, crashing into the hallway. We shoved each other through an open door that led to the top of a staircase. As we both reached the top step, he fell backwards, landing at the bottom of the steps. His face was bleeding.

The next thing I knew, I was being handcuffed and thrown into the back of a riot van. I recognised one of the policemen in the front seat as he read me my rights through the black metal caging. 'It may harm your defence if you do not mention when questioned something which you later rely on in court,' he finished. 'You've had so many chances, Lucy.' The dread sobered me up very quickly.

The journey to Buxton police station was short and quiet, apart from the intermittent sound of the officer's radio. I knew the drill: I'd be held in the cells here overnight until I was deemed sober enough to be interviewed. Only this time, I didn't know what I would be charged with or what kind of sentence I'd face. I might get sent to prison. I'd fucked up so badly.

When we arrived, the gates took a little while to open. We passed into the area where they take you from the van and into the custody suite. The officers got out. Normally, as soon as you were parked, they would get you out and walk you straight in, but there was a bit of commotion outside. I was bobbing my head, trying to see what was going on. Ten minutes felt like ten years.

The back door opened.

'You are the luckiest person I have ever known,' said the officer in a tone of voice that suggested he found something funny, but his face was stoic and straight. 'Because it's New Year's Eve, the cells are full and the custody suite is rammed. We've called Chesterfield and they're the same. We have no more holding space.' He locked his eyes onto mine. 'I am de-arresting you.' I didn't understand what was happening. 'You are free to go.'

He warned me: 'Go straight home and do not go back out. I have never seen this happen before. Start using your head.'

And I did. That night, life shook me so hard by my shoulders.

A month later, during a Saturday night shift at The Eagle, I went to check the toilets and walked in on a woman kicking another woman, who was on the floor. As I went to separate them, the standing one lunged at me and twisted my hair around her fist, trying to hit me in the face with her free hand. Everything slowed down. I kept my face shielded with my hands and bent my body forwards to protect my head. For the first time, I wasn't going to fight. I knew what would happen if I did and how close I'd been to fucking it all up. Eventually, the bouncers dragged her out of the club.

It was time to figure out what my new escape-the-small-town plan would be. I'd kept in touch with Ben, the bushy-eyebrowed presenter from High Peak Radio. We'd been for a few beers together and he'd even been sorting out some gigs for me here and there. He lived in Sheffield, home of the Arctic Monkeys, the Human League and Pulp, a pretty legendary city when it came to music. Maybe I could find a way to get there.

One of the semi-regulars at the New Inn was a plumber called Paul. He was an ex-Marine in his early thirties, a very straight-forward man, tall and strange, with sandy-coloured hair. I'd always fancied myself as quite handy. One day, handing him a pint over the bar, I asked him if there was any chance he wanted an apprentice. He looked thoughtfully at the beer tap and said he'd consider it. He didn't even flinch about the fact I was a girl.

I started working for Paul a few days later. I got suited and booted with a company jumper, protective trousers and steel toe-capped shoes. I loved it. He'd pick me up in the early morning and take me to a job. We'd smoke rollies in the van and drink lots of tea. He sent me into the building supply shops, down small passages, under people's houses, and taught me quite a lot about toilets, boilers, taps and pipes. A few weeks in, on one of our cigarette breaks, I played him some of my music on the van's CD player. The Marine in him rarely showed emotion but I could see he was surprised. He stared his thousand-yard stare pensively at the dashboard, 'My friend Will knows loads about music. You should meet him.'

During one of my evening shifts at the pub, I overheard the tail end of a conversation between two contractors about women working on building sites. 'They wouldn't be able to carry as much as the men do anyway,' the younger, smaller of the two said. I couldn't resist.

'I could outlift you any day!' I challenged him, interrupting their conversation.

'Could you fuck!' he smiled back, and the three of us entered a heated debate.

'I tell you what,' said the other one. 'Prove it. Come down tomorrow morning at 7.30 a.m. and work on our site for the day, see how long you last.'

They were demolition operatives on a contract, pulling down a dilapidated Victorian hotel in town.

'Don't say things you don't mean!' I laughed. 'Because I'll be there at 7.30 a.m.!'

The conversation moved on but I meant business. The next morning, in my steel toe-capped boots and protective work trousers, I walked onto their site. The younger man caught sight of me and laughed in disbelief. 'Fuck off!' he said, in hysterics.

By the end of that first day, I had proved them completely wrong. I lifted bags of rubble up and onto my shoulder, carrying them across the site. I climbed up onto rafters to retrieve wiring. I did everything that they did. We all went back to The New Inn for a drink at the end of the day and the older contractor invited me to work on site until the whole contract was finished.

It was a reclamation project, meaning that lots of the parts of the building were to be salvaged and used on other old buildings, so it wasn't what you'd imagine typical demolition work to be. Sadly, I wasn't going to bulldoze or blow anything up.

In a twist of events, the only thing that would be dramatically destroyed during that time would be my right knee. A few weeks into the job, I was standing in the basket of a cherry picker, working 30 feet up in the air, when it collapsed. The younger contractor and I were in the basket collecting slates from the window of the third storey when the machine became overloaded and we hurtled towards the floor.

It was all very quick. Just before we hit the ground, I observed, very calmly and rationally, that I was going to die. I wasn't scared, just accepting. That's what happens when you fall from that height, after all.

Then I was on the ground. I was no longer in the basket, but lying on my back, my hardhat still on, and sheets of slate all over my body. I was fucking alive! No way. I looked over and saw the young guy from the pub who had been in the basket next to me was looking at me. It seemed impossible but we'd both survived. At the exact same time, we both went to stand up and, as if a mirror of each other, we buckled at the knee and fell back down. We realised at the same moment that our right legs were no longer functional. An ambulance arrived and took me to hospital, where it was confirmed that I had fractured my tibial plateau. Some of the 1.4 tonne of stacked slate had fallen onto my leg as the basket hit the floor and crushed the top of my knee. Fuck.

The consultant at the hospital put me in a leg brace and told me that it would be a twelve weeks before we would review if I needed surgery. No walking on it for that time. He said that this kind of fracture often leads to long-term suffering, sometimes trouble with weight bearing, and that it can result in a limp.

Though I'd been focused on music, my back-up plan was to be a firefighter. Long-term suffering? Weightbearing issues? That's firefighting out the window. Demolition was obviously out of the question now and plumbing required functional legs, as did working behind the bar. Plus, I lived up two flights of stairs in The New Inn. I moved out of the pub and in with a friend, in a house with fewer stairs. I signed on and I started to drink a lot more. My escape plan was almost definitely foiled once more and I felt helpless. I couldn't go back to America, I couldn't walk, I couldn't work. I needed something to change.

It turns out that Paul's friend Will did actually know a lot about music. During my recovery, Paul picked me up and took me to meet Will in his bungalow just on the edge of Combs Reservoir, fifteen minutes out of Buxton. He looked like he knew a lot about music too. He was a cool-looking guy who dressed in a youthfully fashionable way, a bit like a character from *Tony Hawk's Pro Skater*, punky but in his early thirties. He had black spikey hair, a bit of five o'clock shadow and wore band t-shirts.

Paul and Will had grown up together and, in their twenties, one of the bands that Will was in had taken off a bit and toured very successfully in Japan and across Europe. He'd travelled the world playing the guitar and, as he and his band members had got older and settled down, he became a dab hand at music production. After hearing some demos I'd previously recorded, Will told me he wanted to produce my first album. I said that I would love that but I didn't have any money.

'That's OK, I don't want money.' He shook his head. 'In return, I only have one request.'

I was ready to hear whatever it was.

'The only one thing I ask is that if you ever get to go on *This Morning*, you have to take me with you.' I looked at him, waiting for the punchline, but there wasn't one. That was genuinely all he wanted.

'It's a deal,' I said, thinking he was mad.

Will lived for music. I admired him a lot. He believed in the punk way of doing things, which is basically sticking it to the man and doing things for love, not cash. He would come and pick me up from the pub and drive me to his house to record my songs on a collection of vintage microphones in his kitchen. The view out of the kitchen window onto the reservoir was idyllic and calm and his partner, Kerry, would make us soups, sandwiches or leftover stew for lunch. I felt so lucky, so looked after by them both.

When we didn't have the right drum, we'd slap wooden spoons against a bowl, or record the sound of us stomping our feet on the creaky, wooden floor. We recorded our own gang vocals, recording take after take and laying them over each other. It was so DIY. It was 'punk' as Will would say. We had such a great time making it.

It wasn't hard to pick the songs to put on that album, even though there were plenty to choose from. Will and I had sat down and filtered through them, and I told him which ones had been going down well at gigs. As well as the heartfelt, love-struck, storytelling songs, I'd started writing funny songs again, observational ones, like I had done at school. Earlier in the year, I'd written this song 'Last Night' at my friend Joe's house. Joe and I had been talking about my experiences of going out and getting absolutely wasted, and I started to list them on a notepad. I put together this little three-chord riff and, all of a sudden, it was a song.

It was supposed to be a joke. I didn't think anyone would ever pay much attention to it. We put together this ska version of it and it went on the album.

Once we'd finished recording the eleven songs, we designed and handprinted the album sleeve on Will's kitchen worktops, putting them into clear, plastic sleeves. It was done. My first ever album: *Top Room at the Zoo*.

I don't think it was only my leg that healed when that album was created. I'd sit behind Will at his laptop as the songs came together and took their shape; I'd really listen to them. I wrote those songs. I'd always written songs. People liked to hear them and I loved playing live. Now I really thought about it, I came to the conclusion that I was good at it. All the while I'd been a magician, a pot-wash, a waitress, a tour guide, a barmaid, a plumber's apprentice and a demolition operative, I'd still been a musician and songwriter. I kept pointing my life in different directions and it always circled back around to music. I had to fall 30 feet to realise that I wasn't actually built for anything else. Finally taking note of all of the signs the universe had sent me, I knew it was music from now on.

In summer 2011, Ben texted me out of the blue: 'My lesbians are moving out. You should replace them!' The female couple that had rented one of the rooms in his house share in Sheffield were leaving. It wasn't like I had a job keeping me in Buxton; it had been a rough few months and I was in a rut, using drugs and drinking quite a lot. My leg was still in its brace but that didn't matter. 'When can I move in?' I replied.

PROCESS

Ben came to collect me in his Ford Ka. There was just about enough room for my guitar and my bag of clothes. It was time to leave behind the town that I'd never wanted to move to in the first place.

We lived on Carlby Road in Stannington, in a three-bedroomed terraced house that belonged to Ben's uncle. I was getting paid for gigs here and there, and if I could find some part-time work, this was going to work out perfectly. Ben loved music almost as much as he loved Sheffield United and without us really discussing it, he started booking more and more gigs for me, sourcing local festival opportunities here and there, slowly taking on the role of being my best friend and my unofficial manager.

Ben got a job working for a national singing competition called Live and Unsigned and suggested that I should enter it. I didn't know it at the time, but this competition was one of those rackets that generated huge profit because each contestant would have to sell X amount of tickets to qualify for the next round and their families would need to send £1 texts to vote for them. I was sure I could rally some troops.

The way that competition was set up worked in my favour because it meant that the audiences were generally quite large, even if they were there to support someone else. After each round, my Facebook page was getting more and more followers, and people were coming up to me asking where they could hear more. I came second in Live and Unsigned 2011, and Ben was helping me get gigs in all kinds of places. Then Live and Unsigned started another competition called Open Mic UK. In the autumn, they needed a 'guest act' to fill the empty space between the rounds of competitions whilst the judges totted up their scores. It'd mean playing three shows a day, Saturday and Sunday, all around the UK. They offered £100 a day for fifteen-hour days. I was in.

I started playing in London a lot more and the momentum really picked up. For the whole of 2011, I kept seeing and hearing this name at every gig or showcase I went to. Everywhere I was playing, this guy had been on the night before. I turned up at The Good Ship, a pub in Kilburn, ready for my show and they were changing the names on the blackboard outside from last night's act to tonight's act. There it was again. They wiped out the scribbled name 'Ed Sheeran' and replaced it with mine. 'Who the fuck is that guy?!' I asked the promoter. 'He's playing as many gigs as I am!'

Dear Lucy,

The council and the police worked together to push Marlies out of The New Inn not long after we took a horse in there. Sophie's horse, actually, the same horse she'd ridden to pick up her stuff from my house after we broke up. The locals barely even noticed it was there.

Just before Marlies was forced out, she commissioned a huge painting of her arse and displayed it on the wall in the front room of the pub.

Marlies works in care now. She says she loves it and that some of the people she cares for used to come into the pub. A weird full circle where she gets to look after them again. Some of them are the old men who refused to come in when she hung a rainbow flag outside the pub. What a funny town. Her son Dexter

*plays guitar in a band, so maybe the lessons paid off!
She says The Zoo days feel like a nostalgic dream.
They do to me too.*

*The New Inn was like a world of its own, a world
where people who were deemed 'bad' by society
showed their virtues (I mean, not always, sometimes
it was mental) and it really taught you to look past
the labels that are given to people and to make those
judgements for yourself.*

*Marlies saw you at a time when you felt no one
really did and she mothered you in a way that only
another black sheep could know how.*

*You have always had this way of squeezing through
the door just before it closed, of being the last one
to make it on board the lifeboat. You have this great
curse of being in the wrong place at the wrong time,
but every now and again you are rewarded with a
huge stroke of luck. Right place, right time – like being
de-arrested on New Year's Eve.*

You lucky little bastard.

*You were also lucky that you didn't require surgery
on your leg in the end. There was an official investigation
into the accident by the Health and Safety Executive,
who said they had never seen an accident like it that
hadn't resulted in loss of life or limb. The site manager
was prosecuted.*

*Small towns like Buxton can be a bit lawless, a bit
Wild West. It's because everyone knows each other,
so there isn't much threat or consequence, unlike in
big cities. Moving to Sheffield taught you about all of
that. Eventually, you got to travel to so many parts*

of the world and the world taught you more than Sheffield did.

There's nothing like this planet to remind you how very small you are.

I'm still not sure how you blagged it, but you did it, you got out of Dodge by the skin of your teeth.

It's funny, that time in Sheffield – living with Ben, travelling around the country, playing gigs in random places and being skint – it's one of my favourite times to reminisce about. It was all so simple and so optimistic. You were growing.

I've never regretted anything in life because I don't see the point, the past can't be changed, but if I could I'd go back to that house share on Carlby Road. I'd knock on the door and when you opened it, I'd tell you not to do what we did next. Yeah, I'd tell you not to audition for The X Factor. *I'd have told you to carry on playing in the bars and the clubs.*

I could have kept you safer that way.

I'm sorry.

Love,

Lucy x

Tell Us Your Name

I don't want to shatter the magic but I was scouted for *The X Factor*.

I always thought it sounded quite contrived when someone was suspected of being 'scouted' for a talent show, like they were a plant, a double agent. I imagined the scouts quietly hurried well-connected BRIT School students out of their classes, told them to put on their best normal person's clothes (and their best working-class accent), snuck them in the back door of *The X Factor* auditions where the clued-up producers were and whisked them through to the finals. But it's not like that. Firstly, because well-connected BRIT School students don't need *The X Factor*, and the reason *TXF* was such a desperately innovative and well-received show from the beginning was because reality TV is one of the only ways that working-class people, or just normal people without connections, can find their way into the music industry. If your mum didn't have a healthy and ground-breaking career in the 1980s, such as Neneh Cherry, and your dad wasn't the frontman of Spandau Ballet, it's genuinely very hard to find yourself rubbing shoulders with the kind of people who can get your music on the radio or into the hands of people who can make waves.

That's not to say that the sons and daughters of superstars are not talented – they often very much are. The bloodline of genetic talent and creativity is strong, you can hear and see that for yourself, but there are often a few quiet privileges that are overlooked when we talk about 'ways into the music industry'. There's even privilege in being raised around people who generate their wealth from music and grow successful careers from it. To actually see it first-hand emphasises the idea that it's possible. For the rest of us, who only see those who prosper through our TVs and are told to get a 'real job' by parents who work in banks or schools, for people who have to pick up every penny and throw it into every well to make a wish that, one day, someone who could set their career flying might hear them, a TV talent show is one of the few ways to get noticed by people other than those throwing pennies into your hat when you're busking on the high street.

It's a solid struggle for any artist in the industry; let's be real about that. The likelihood of making it is slim to none, even if you do have famous parents or a family friend at the BBC. The music industry, like most other industries, does not lean in favour of those outside of the south of England, especially those from impoverished areas. Being scouted for a TV show could mean a ticket out of Dodge for those people. People like me.

I'm sure things are different now there are new ways to get noticed, with TikTok and YouTube and viral videos, but in an industry that releases 100,000 singles a day[1], that just means the competition is greater than it's ever been.

Being scouted, as with most things in this business, was far less glamorous in reality.

★

In 2011, since moving to Sheffield, being Open Mic's guest act, trapsing up and down the country trying to get people to buy my CD, for the first time, I'd started to attract a bit of attention other than from people in the pubs in my home town. As 2012 rolled in, I'd really upped the ante. I had sent *Top Room at the Zoo* into BBC Introducing and was being championed by Dean Jackson, a BBC radio presenter from Derby. I was invited to a BBC masterclass at Abbey Road, where Newton Faulkner and Maverick Sabre told us what it was like to be popstars. I had taken part in a competition and had won a support slot for Joan Armatrading. I had met a few promotors and was regularly a support act at a few venues across the UK, including the well-known Dingwalls in Camden. I had recorded some live sessions with an artist called DJ Ironik, who I had listened to as a teenager. There was a real energy, a buzz.

At this point, I had 3,500 followers on Facebook, which, back then, was pretty impressive. I was playing around five gigs a week, of all different calibres; some supporting bigger acts in cooler venues, some still in the back room of a pub. Life was exciting.

I was scouted by a very beautiful girl called Layla. She had been at the Open Mic competition looking for singers

---

1   https://variety.com/2022/music/news/new-songs-100000-being-released-every-day-dsps-1235395788/

and bands that she thought had something and saw me performing as the guest act. Layla, with her deep brown eyes and caramel-coloured skin, approached me after my set and we started talking. She told me she worked for Syco as a talent scout. I thought, 'Holy shit, this could be it.' Even better than the potential of a career-changing opportunity, I could have sworn this girl was flirting with me too. (I now envisage my former self as a Looney Toons' cartoon character with love hearts for eyes and my tongue laid out on the carpet in front of me.) Layla sensed the power she now possessed over me and nonchalantly asked, 'Have you ever thought about auditioning for *The X Factor*?'

I mention that she was beautiful because had it not been for the fact that I fancied her, I'd have ridiculed the idea of auditioning for a show like *that*.

The X Factor, Britain's Got Talent, Pop Idol do not have the best reputation amongst open mic night musicians and gigging singers, often these people see themselves as musical purists and have a total disdain for reality TV contestants. The narrative amongst these purists went (for some reason) that having your big break on a TV show would put you on a far lower rung of the respectability ladder than those who didn't. Perhaps it comes from a belief that reality TV contestants haven't 'earned their dues' or developed their craft like those who have plugged away on the local open mic circuit. It could be jealousy. It could be deeply engrained, subconscious classicism: 'Who do they think they are? Getting a ticket out of Dodge whilst the rest of us have to stay here and strum!'

I think contestants are not judged on their capability or talent, but by the mere fact they came to the public attention via a reality TV show. Perhaps they were chasing fame and notoriety, rather than a career in music? Well, see my point above about privilege. It's not that easy for your average Joe. That disdain is something I have come across a lot, from musicians and non-musicians alike, and the more I think about it, the stranger I find it. A contestant who has only one top-ten album before slowly drifting away from the limelight after a stint on reality TV is called 'an *X-Factor* reject'. An eighties rocker with one top-ten album under their belt, whose career suffered the same fading fate, can be a rock legend. This is what I have realised since then, but back in 2012, I took part in the disdain. I had unknowingly inherited it not because I was a purist but because that was the general consensus. I followed the crowd . . . all the way up until I was a contestant myself.

Layla noticed I was unimpressed by the suggestion and made up for it by batting her lashes at me. I shrugged and said, 'I wouldn't go on a show like that unless I could play my own songs.'

'No one has ever done that before, so I'm not sure you could. But here ...' She held out a piece of paper. 'Look at the list of songs you could cover.'

I studied it for a second, wincing at the idea of me singing 'True Colours' by Cyndi Lauper or 'Get This Party Started' by P!nk.

'Not my cup of tea, that,' I said, believing that would be the end of that conversation. After all, I was a woman of integrity! Nothing was more important to me than the retention of creative control and staying true to my art. There wasn't a career carrot that could be dangled that I might be tempted to lean forward and snatch.

'Well, I can see what the producers say . . . And I'll let you take me out.'

'Deal,' I said.

And that's how I made the decision that changed the entire course of my life.

The worst part? I never did get to take Layla out on a date.

★

At the time of my audition I was twenty years old. I lived in Sheffield, in a house share with Ben, who was very much now my closest friend, and a very irritating American woman whose name I can't remember. She would Skype her family at 3 a.m. in a shrill, Midwestern accent and wore bandanas, and I hated her very much. I played a lot of shows at this point, all over the country. At this point, most of my gigs were paid in beer tokens and 'exposure', which I didn't mind too much. I made £520 a month from my 'proper' job, which covered my rent and the costs I incurred playing gigs that didn't pay. I worked as a 'portrait seller'. I got the job after seeing it advertised in the paper. I didn't know or care what a 'portrait seller' was, only that the hours were 10 a.m. to 3 p.m., Monday to Thursday, and that meant I could subsist and have enough time to travel to shows on Friday/Saturday/Sunday wherever they were in the country. I called the photography studio immediately but the lady on the phone told me the role had already been filled. Fuck! I asked if they needed another 'portrait seller'. She said no. I needed that job. Well, I needed those hours. Instead of taking no for an answer, I turned up the following week on Monday at 10 a.m. to start a job that had already been filled by someone else. When I announced myself, the lady who ran the place looked at me like I was fucking nuts. Then she laughed. This is how you get people on your side.

The role of a 'portrait seller' was to stand in the street in Sheffield city centre with a clipboard and flog expensive studio baby photo packages to young mums with prams. I told her that if she gave me the chance, I'd sell more packages than the person she'd already hired. She laughed again – and I have no idea why – then said, 'Go on then, see you tomorrow.' On the Tuesday, I turned up, sold more packages and I got the job.

A couple of weekends before my audition, I pulled off the grand effort of a show in Taunton in the West Country on the Friday, the Midlands on the Saturday and London on the Sunday. Every weekend, I drove miles and miles, sometimes to play to very few people in working men's clubs, sometimes to a healthy crowd at an open wic night or to an entire village fete on a stage that was actually a flatbed truck. I got an encore whilst supporting The Blanks at Dingwalls. Ben had got me a few slots at Sheffield's Tramlines Festival. I played to healthy crowds at Beat-Herder, in Lancaster, and Osfest, in Shrewsbury, and at Prides all over the country. In early June, Dean Jackson got me a slot at Y Not, a festival in Derbyshire, where I'd packed out the whole tent. Despite the long drives and the fact I sometimes had to take my belongings to my local Cash Converters to subsidise my rent, I loved doing it with all my heart.

I can't tell you exactly when it started, but somewhere along this process I developed this surreal, anticipating feeling. When you put a pan of cold water on the stove and turn on the heat, you start to see these tiny bubbles forming on the base of the pan. The surreal feeling I had was just like that. The heat was on and the bubbles were starting to multiply, but it was still nowhere near boiling. It was tepid. But I had this undercurrent of anticipation and excitement that, within weeks, it could be ferociously overboiling, the lid rattling and spitting, the water spilling over the edges and into the flames. It felt amazing.

I'd imagined that those who are scouted for reality TV are given a pass to the front of the queue. The VIP lane, right? To skip out on the early parts of the process and cut straight to the stage. Wrong. I found out on the day of my first producer audition in Derry Street, London, that I'd be going through the same process as everyone else who had signed up of their own free will. I joined a queue that reached around several blocks. There were no cameras, no fanfare. This was the kind of audition that actors do all the time, like a casting call. After waiting for four or five hours, I was ushered into a wide, white conference room where three or four (I can't remember how many as they were so non-descript) people sat behind a row of tables. I played 'Last Night' and was ushered back out. The experience reminded me of the process that sheep farmers use to vaccinate their sheep. One by one through the gate, a quick shot, then back out into the field. There wasn't any verbal feedback from the people behind the desk, but I did make them laugh. That was it.

I heard nothing until few weeks later, I received an email or a phone call (I'm not sure which, now), where a runner told me I had made it through the preliminary round. I was informed that my next time to shine would be in Event City, Manchester, in front of not only a live audience, but TV cameras and four celebrity judges.

Well, shit the bed.

On a bright and unassuming day in June 2012, I turned up at the dauntingly large Event City in Manchester with my guitar case in my hand and a somewhat optimistic view in my head. I figured that if the judges didn't like me and I didn't get through to the next round, at the very least, some of the 3,000-strong audience in the arena might enjoy my performance and give me a 'like' on Facebook. Always trying to seek out a silver lining whilst the sun is still shining, but prepared in case a dark cloud appears and rains on my parade.

My memory of this day is pretty hazy. In the weeks leading up to my audition, the tiny bubbles at the bottom of the pan had started to let go of their holding position and fire up towards the surface. The temperature was on its way to a gentle simmer. The nerves had started to form.

I arrived at the lobby area at the entrance to the arena to find a table with four frantic runners sitting behind it, all with masses of paperwork. I exchanged my name for a piece of paper with the number '197915' across it and some safety pins for me to attach it to my front, like a marathon runner. All of the people with numbers were directed the same way and asked to join the big, snaking line of other contestants. Again, the sheep farming simile holds true: we all followed each other, one by one, through the metal barriers, and some people were quite literally bleating with excitement.

I spent another six or seven hours queuing up again,

happily this time. It felt different to the casting call at Derry Street; this felt *real*. For the first time, there was an actual TV production crew, and they were interviewing and filming people in the queue waiting for their audition slot. There were big flag-banners that had *The X Factor's* logo on them. It was the first time the process looked like the show I'd seen on TV. The camera crew approached me in the line and took me away to film some bits. I had a suspicious feeling that this alone was a good sign. Or maybe I was reading too much into it.

All of the acts waiting to perform were gathered together in the vast backstage area. The space was huge, framed on each side by black, floor-to-ceiling curtains. There were flight cases dotted about and a buzz vibrating through the air. The nervous energy surging around the space came from muscly men in tight tops practising their scales and young, gorgeous girls in small dresses and cowboy boots holding their finger to their ear like Mariah Carey and warbling a tune out of their nose. Every so often, you'd hear the raucous applause of a successful audition filter through from the main auditorium and the whole place would go quiet. I saw shifty eyes swapping glances with visible concern that the procurer of the applause may have just taken the place of one of the hopefuls waiting backstage.

I didn't feel like that. A lot of the old people who I'd served in the pubs would say 'What's meant for you won't pass you by' and I've always felt like there's substance to that. If you create your own destiny, no one can ever take it away from you. Though, to be honest, waiting for a moment that had the potential to change my life was a little muted by the intense feeling that I did not belong there, sitting as I was on a riser in my Asda George white t-shirt, open black cardigan and blue chinos (bless my fucking soul!), looking at all these ready-made poster-popstars who could give Ariana Grande a run for her money. Still, I had gotten all the way there, to the same point as them, and I was going to give it my best shot.

I think my pessimistic optimism was actually one of my strongest superpowers that day. Because I'd convinced myself that I wouldn't get through, all I had on my mind was that I needed to entertain that crowd. The judges were actually the last thing I was worried about and I had quiet confidence in the fact that I knew I could handle a crowd. OK, I'd never won over a crowd as big as the one waiting for me behind those curtains, but if you can play to a pub full of strangers on a Saturday night in the north-west of England, an arena is child's play.

I watched runners and black-clad camera crew wearing headphones with mouthpieces rush around, approaching singers and telling them it was their time to come to stage. The contestants would take a deep breath and exhale, have one final group hug from their families, a dad leaving a lingering hand on their shoulder as they walked away with the crew. I was glad I was on my own. Fewer people to let down. If I left there with a 'NO' then at least it would stay between me and the 3,000 people in that room. I'd just carry on driving up and down the country, wearing my t-shirts and cardigans, playing my songs to anyone who would listen, selling baby portrait photos and cashing in my belongings at Cash Converters in order to pay my rent. Life was sweet. Life was an adventure. I wasn't just lucky to be there, I was lucky to have this life.

PROCESS

The pan was audibly bubbling; the tiny bubbles weren't tiny now and the water was definitely not tepid anymore. It was getting hot.

I felt like I'd been at Event City for an eternity. As the day went on, fewer and fewer people were left in the backstage area until, actually, looking around, I was one of the *only* people left back here. What did it mean? Had I been forgotten? Maybe I should . . .

'Lucy?' A runner locked eyes with me and then paused to listen to an instruction in her headset. 'Are you ready?' She smiled.

I felt like I'd just grabbed an electric fence. No, of course I wasn't ready. Maybe, actually, I had no idea why I was there, and it'd be better if I just left now. I could feel the adrenaline surging around my body. My hands started sweating so badly they felt cold and damp, like they were no longer attached to the rest of me. Despite my deafening internal heavy metal-style screaming, I calmly followed her towards the front of the room. We walked through a big black curtain, then another and another. I could hear the hum of people waiting in their seats. As we walked towards the final black curtain which separated me and the stage that was about to change my life, the runner sensed my nervousness and tried to soothe it.

'So, what are you singing today?' She had short, red hair and kind eyes.

'I'm actually singing my own song today,' I said, wiping my hands on my thighs.

She raised her eyebrows at me. 'I've not seen anyone do that before!'

'It's a song about going out and getting pissed, doing

loads of stupid stuff and waking up in the morning with *all* of the anxiety.'

She laughed, 'Like, beer fear?'

'Beer fear?!' I laughed a genuine laugh back at her. 'I've never heard it called that!' And I hadn't. I had no idea that in about two months' time, and for a lifetime after that, my name would be synonymous with those two words, that #BeerFear would have trended worldwide, on most platforms, and ten years later still would be a viral song used by over 26 million people on TikTok, or that I'd end up getting the phrase tattooed on my left ankle. Here I was, side of stage, about to embark on that moment.

If this were a film, the director would now hit rewind and go backwards through time, from me sitting here typing this into a reversed showreel of everything I have done between this moment and that one, stopping just before the red-haired girl parted the curtain. A huge camera wheeled over to my left and a man with a headset appeared. He put his hand up, palm in front of my face, with five fingers spread out and grinned at me as he folded his thumb in, then his first finger, middle, third and little finger. I walked onto the stage.

They say every time you remember something your brain changes it a little, adding its own spice and flare to the story, recalling things in a more preferable way. Interestingly, I don't think I authentically remember much of my actual audition, but I've watched it enough times to tell you what happened. The spice and flare, and dramatic backing track, were all added for me by the post-edit team, and what a bloody good job they did. Better than my brain could have ever done.

PROCESS

When I walked onto the stage, I was guitar-less, clunky, hunched over and lacking the self-confidence to stand up fully straight. There were four judges sitting at a podium in front of me, above their heads four red Xs. Tulisa Contostavlos, lead singer in the iconic urban noughties band N-Dubz, Gary Barlow of Take That, Louis Walsh of, well, no one truly knows, and Mel B. Yep, an actual Spice Girl. Tulisa asked me my name, where I was from, what I did for work. I happily told them that I was the person with a clipboard in the street that you try to avoid and that I sold baby photos for 99p. I added that if anyone had any babies and wanted some photos, I could sort them out. I got a laugh from the arena. My first taste of what I wanted so badly – that reaction from the crowd. I stood a little taller. Tulisa asked me what the song was about, and I replied as I had to the red-haired runner, this time using my newly acquired phrase. 'It's about going out and getting drunk, waking up the next day with "beer fear",' with added air quotes over it. 'I'm sure some of you can relate.' Another mass giggle. 'Holy shit,' I thought. Tulisa told me they wanted to hear the song and a man appeared from side of stage with a mic stand and my guitar. Thank God for that. As soon as I put my guitar strap around me, my insecurities were shielded by the guitar's presence and I had the tool I needed to seal the deal with this audience.

The opening four-bar riff was followed by the first line: 'Last night I told ya I loved ya, woke up blamed it on the vodka.' And I set off into the song. A huge outburst of laughter filtered like a Mexican wave through the area.

What the fuck?

With every line, the audience laughed more. I'd played

this song hundreds of times and I'd had great reactions, but this? This was something else. The judges were beaming. The audience were hooting and clapping and cheering, waiting for every punchline and then jumping out of their seats when it hit. The longer the song went on, the more I could see what was happening and I couldn't believe it. All four judges' eyes were fixed on me with huge grins across their faces. They were cackling along with the crowd. I kept playing and the roars got louder and I was swallowed up by a complete joy that I'd never felt before. This golden, vibrating, indescribable high had me on top of the actual world. It was like the laughs and the applause carried a visceral magic that went directly from them to me, like a barrage of Cupid's arrows.

All of a sudden, I realised that I was coming to the end of the song. I delivered the last line – 'And never miss a day again' – and for the briefest, almost unnoticeable, fraction of a moment, there was complete silence throughout the entire arena. And then it erupted. Every single person rose to their feet. I looked at the judges and all four of them were standing too. Just then, every single show I'd ever played, from my very first, when I was twelve years old, to the three gigs I played the week before my audition, became part of that single moment. I was standing on stage with 3,000 people on their feet in front of me. For me.

I burst into tears, covering my face with my hands. It encouraged them even more. The noise reverberated against my skull and my ear drums started to vibrate. The noise became so loud that it distorted and became more of a physical sensation than a sound. I stood there sobbing. Speechless. Completely overwhelmed. With my hands flat against my cheeks and tears streaming down my face, I thought, 'I've done it.'

Once the crowd finally calmed and sat back down in their seats, it was time for the judges to give their feedback. Had I not been able to watch the audition back I couldn't have told you what they said. I tried so hard to listen and to focus on the shapes their mouths were making, the tone of the feedback they were giving, but my brain was buzzing. It was time for them to cast their vote on whether or not I'd make it through to the next stage. It was a 'yes' from all four. The crowd started again. The roof was on fire. A chant started: 'We want more, we want more!' I couldn't believe this was happening. Was I getting an encore at my *X Factor* audition?! I was. Tulisa gestured for me to play again and I knew exactly what to do.

In the generic email I'd received about my audition (when to turn up, what to expect) there was a list of songs that they had clearance for contestants to cover. I'd made a little mash-up of almost every single song on that list – ironically starting with 'True Colours', the song I'd balked at the idea of covering when I met Layla – cutting and chopping into another, then another song. The audience got louder and louder with each song that was introduced into the medley. When I strummed the final strum of the eleven-song mash-up, the crowd lost it again. The smack, smack, smack of applause bounced off the walls of Event City Arena and rained down on me.

Pure joy.

I can't tell you what happened in the immediate after-math. I was taken off stage, several people came over and patted me on the back, my ears were ringing and I felt like I was wearing those joke glasses that give you tunnel vision. A man got me a chair to sit on. I suppose I was in shock. Strangers high-fived me; people took photos with me; I smiled for them without knowing I was even smiling. I was on top of the world. I'd just had the single most exhilarating experience of my life. I wandered back to my guitar case and packed up, unable to truly comprehend what had just happened.

Eventually, it was time to go, so I followed the signs that said EXIT and, head held the highest it had ever been, I left the arena out of the back doors. As fast as the fresh north-western air hit me in the face, it was all over. The water in the pan was back to tap water temperature, possibly even colder, and there was no evidence that it had ever boiled at all.

When I left Event City, I must have taken a wrong turn because I ended up in the middle of an industrial estate in Trafford and got completely lost. There was no one around apart from the odd car driving past. It gave me this pulled-right-back-down-to-earth feeling, reminding me that outside of that arena, I was the same girl I walked in as. To everyone else in the world, nothing had just happened. Three thousand people, four judges and a production company had witnessed what had taken place but I was going to have a very hard time explaining it to anyone else. If the cameramen had just forgotten to press record, everything that had happened would be a moment in time that stayed between us in that room. But I knew that it had all been recorded. I made my way home to Sheffield, the world's quietest journey, replaying the day over and over again in my mind.

I'd have to wait two very long months until that audition made it onto television. And when it did, *everything* changed.

Dear Lucy,

Always a sucker for a beautiful woman. That never changed. You dumbass.

I have absolutely no idea how you grew balls as big as the ones you had when you were in this phase of your life. Like, what the actual hell? It's like you weren't scared of anything. Travel to America for three months at the age of eighteen? Go on then. Being a guest act for a national talent competition? Sure! Rocking up to an X Factor audition – wait, rocking up to an X Factor audition ALONE?! All in your stride.

The world really was your oyster. I think someone would have to hold my hand now, for any of those things. Actually, I think you'd die if you saw that Morgan, my wonderful guitar tech, tunes and executes my guitar changes between songs for me now. You'd say I was being a lazy bastard. You were your own guitar tech, sound engineer, tour manager, roadie, agent AND manager back then, so unfazed by the next big mountain to climb.

Being so scared to fail, though, that's why you went alone to that audition, isn't it?

'If a tree falls in the woods' and all that jazz. If a contestant gets a NO at an X Factor audition and no family or friends are there to see it, did it happen?

If I had the magical power to approach you as a stranger in the street in mid-2012 when you were told to turn up to Manchester for your audition, I'd say something similar to a gem I heard a priest say at a wedding recently:

The reason we have companions in this life is because when we experience positive things like joy, the more of us that are there, the greater the joy multiplies. If you experience joy with ten friends, the joy is multiplied by ten. When you suffer feelings like sadness or grief, it does the opposite. When you share your sadness with your partner, you halve the sadness. You share it with the people you love and it breaks it up into smaller, more manageable fractions. Sharing experiences with people you love enhances the experience, for better or for worse.

You always told yourself that you're a lone wolf. A strong-willed predator who'd always rather brave it alone, subscribing to the belief that the only person you can truly trust is yourself. At open mic nights or pub gigs, a lot of the other aspiring singers you'd bump into were often flanked by a doting parent who acted as their driver, tour manager and #1 fan. That's not how it was for you, and you always felt a little envious about that kind of relationship. I know you were trying to protect yourself, but by racing up and down the country to play a show here, there or anywhere and by dropping everything to jump two-footed into every opportunity that arose, you missed out on quite a lot of building the kind of connections that priest was talking about. By spending all your time pursuing a career, you never really got to know who your pack was, or if you had a pack at all. Sadly, that ended up making you feel very alone.

Well, the plus side is, now we're older, every day our pack grows stronger. It took a little time. I had to realise I didn't always need to be on the hunt for that next career accomplishment and that I needed to dedicate time to actually living – to making new friends, holding my nephew, walking up a mountain with my dog and acquiring hobbies that I get joy from, which is very different to finding validation in work.

I'm proud of how you handled yourself and I'm proud of how independent you were, even though you didn't always want to be.

I will say this, though: hold onto your socks, kid. The next couple of chapters are tough.

I wish I could have been there to warn you.

Love,

Lucy x

Beer Fear

On 17th July, 2012, a few weeks after my first audition, but more than a month before it was to air on television, I found myself in the Echo Arena at the docks in Liverpool for the Bootcamp stage of the competition. This is where hundreds of contestants are whittled down to the twenty-four who get taken through to the 'Judges' Houses'.

I had received an email outlining vital information about this part of the competition:

CHALLENGE 1:
You will perform a song from a list of the judges' choosing, to a backing track provided by us. This song and the backing track will be given to you at Bootcamp not before. This challenge is designed to showcase your vocal ability so you will perform to backing track only. Guitar accompaniment is not allowed.

I didn't sing without my guitar. I never had. That really just wasn't an option. The producers had emailed a list of songs they had cleared the rights to for us to sing, but I was still very certain about the fact that I was going to be singing my own songs, with my guitar. It was clear that they'd intended for *most* contestants to play covers but after the reaction 'Last Night' got at my audition, surely they would let me do it again? They didn't.

For the first challenge, I was grouped with two other girls who I'd have to beat to get through, who picked to sing the song 'Moves Like Jagger'. The producers said I would have to abide by the rules alongside everyone else and do it without my guitar. They said that if I did this and got through, I would have an opportunity to play one of my own songs further down the line.

I'm still not sure why I agreed to it. There was a lot of subtle pressure in that situation. If I said no, then my opportunity would be snatched away and it would be my own fault. One of the runners suggested it would be a great opportunity to impress, that maybe I'd be better than I thought without my guitar. In Bootcamp, when the production team began ushering all of the contestants along, making sure they played ball, it was the first time it felt a bit like we were losing control of our choices.

They convinced me to do it and there I was, on stage in this huge room, back in front of the celebrity judges – this time Gary Barlow, Louis Walsh, Tulisa and Nicole-fucking-Scherzinger (who had been prevalent in my gay awakening) – with two very pretty, very dolled-up girls who looked much more like fledgling pop stars than me in my jeans and trainers. The backing music started and we began taking it in turns to sing some of Maroon 5's lyrics. It was horrendous. They were both waving their arms about and strutting over the stage – mostly in front of me – whilst I was standing with one arm across my body, looking like I was in physical pain, with my other hand holding the microphone to my mouth. I felt so awkward I couldn't even look up. I forgot the lyrics. I was shaking my head in disbelief at what I was doing. Gary Barlow raised a hand to stop the car crash.

My performance was so bad, there is no way I should have made it through, but I think – for whatever reason – someone behind the scenes had already decided that I was going to be a bigger part of this show. Before I'd walked on stage with those girls, the producers already knew how excellently awkward me singing a rendition of 'Moves Like Jagger' without my guitar would be. How endearing that would be. How perfect that would be for television.

I got through to the next round.

CHALLENGE 2:
To reiterate, should you make it to challenge two during Bootcamp, you have two choices. For the first time ever on The X Factor, *you can take a risk and showcase your talents by performing an original song for the judge. Alternatively, you can choose to perform a cover from the list.*

This round wasn't just in front of the judges, they were opening up Liverpool's Echo Arena. We'd be performing in front of an arena full of people. Just as before, I wasn't nervous about the audience; I knew how to get people's attention and perform in front of them, that was the easy bit. The cameras, the judges, suspense, the being pushed out of my comfort zone – that was what made me nervous. For this round, I had my guitar – both my shield and my Excalibur – and I knew what I was going to sing. In my first audition, 'Last Night' had made everyone laugh. This time, I wanted to provoke something else.

I sang 'Tea and Toast', the track I'd written about the couple in the high street when I'd lived in The New Inn. The one that had made Marlies so emotional. 'Last Night' and 'Tea and Toast' were the two songs that went down best at my gigs in pubs and when I was the guest act at open mic. I walked onto the stage, explained what the song was about, and got to work.

'. . .With some tea and toast.' I finished the final lyric of the song and, just like at my first audition, the entire arena was silent for a moment. Thousands of people, totally silent. And then they erupted. I swung my guitar onto my side and covered my eyes with my hands because I knew that if everyone in that place was on their feet, like it felt and sounded like they were, it was because of a song that *I'd* written, a song that came from me. I knew I would start crying and wouldn't be able to stop. Not just that, if everyone was on their feet, it meant that I was through to the next stage and everything in my life from then on had the potential to change.

When I opened my eyes, everyone was on their feet. The judges too. Mascara poured down my face as I walked through the audience and into Dermot O'Leary's arms. I couldn't speak. On the last day of the four-day Bootcamp, twelve girls were left standing on the stage in front of the judges ready to be told their fate. I was told I was through to the Judges' Houses.

Though having an entire arena (plus a Pussycat Doll) on their feet cheering you on is pretty momentous, one of my most memorable moments at Bootcamp didn't even happen in the arena. It happened in the lift at the hotel next door, where we were all put up. I walked into the lift and another contestant, a very tall, slim, quite beautiful and audibly gay man with bleached blond, shoulder-length hair and a beard so perfect and dark it looked like it must have been dyed, crashed in behind me. His energy was so loud. Ladies and gentlemen, meet the unforgettable Rylan Clark. Within moments, this mystical creature opened his mouth and told me, in his broad Essex twang, 'I know I ain't gonna win this competition, but one day, mark my words, I'll have my own show on Radio 2, I'll present *Strictly Come Dancing* and I will host Eurovision.' I liked him from the word go. He was one of those people, like Marlies, unlike anyone else I'd ever met. Authentic and incredibly likeable.

So was Caroline Flack, who co-presented ITV2's *The Xtra Factor*, which covered the behind-the-scenes antics of the show. Of all the people I met at Bootcamp, I felt Caroline's emotion and integrity were most authentic. She was genuinely invested in the journey of us contestants and always offered a smile, a cheeky wink or a comforting conversation when the cameras were off.

I can see now that the production team had a plan for some of us before Bootcamp had even begun – that's just how TV is. It's not a 'fix', it's a storyline and we are the characters whilst the producers write the script. When I talk to people about the intense process of reality TV shows they often say 'well, you knew what you were getting into when you auditioned' and, actually, I completely disagree. Until you are a part of that process you have absolutely no idea what you are getting into. I learnt as I went. In 2012, the production team were not just looking for talent. They'd learnt that viewers like their music with a side serving of story too, and they were determined to give the audience what they wanted. James Arthur, who went on to win, had been homeless. Jahméne Douglas was a shelf stacker in Asda and was the kind of underdog whose life would be turned around by winning. Then there was Ella Henderson, the remarkable sixteen-year old, talented beyond her years. What was my story? I didn't think I had one. Or if I did, it was that I was always up for a beer and a laugh. Alcohol was such a huge part of my identity. During the early stages of production, I had been asked by a runner if anything bad had ever happened to me or if I was auditioning for anyone else. They were fishing for storylines right from the get-go. Yeah, I'd had grown up in a violent household, I'd been to America to pursue my dream, I'd fallen 30 feet at work, but I didn't fancy telling them any of that. My story was that I loved music, and beer, and it worked.

On the last day of Bootcamp, the remaining contestants were casually ushered into a conference room and introduced to two lawyers from competing practices who each pitched for our business. One at a time, they stood at the front of the room and told us why they'd be the better choice. We were going to be presented with a whole lot of legal paperwork – for example, contracts that demanded percentages of live income and merchandise after the show, ensured our commitment to *The X Factor* tour when the winner had been picked – and we were going to need 'help' making the right choices. The only legal advice I'd had up until this point was in an interview room in a police station. I knew one criminal defence lawyer, who was also my friend's mum; I didn't even really know music lawyers were a thing.

The reason they did this is that, legally, to sign our contracts, we needed independent advice. When Syco presented us with the two firms they'd picked and asked us, collectively, to select one, to them, that meant we had chosen our own legal representation. Smart, really. I wanted to go with Adam Van Straten, but almost everyone else wanted the other lawyer and so that's who got our business. Crucially, it's important to acknowledge that we didn't pay their bills, *The X Factor* did and with hindsight, I do wonder how independent that arrangement really could have been. Ultimately, we were given the choice to sign the contracts, or leave the competition.

We also had management appointed to us. If we made it through to the live shows, our careers would fall into the hands of these people. This year's highest bidder for the contract was Quest Management. We didn't really get to choose anything about what was happening; again, it was sign the contracts or lose the opportunity. It was a copy-and-paste, one-size-fits-all for every contestant. The machine was operating at top speed, carrying out a process which the show had been through over seasons and seasons of production, but we were totally new to it. We were being appointed the people who would run our lives from here on out. We were blindsided.

You're not supposed to tell anyone how you're getting

on with the show but I obviously did. After Bootcamp had finished, I went straight back to the baby photography place and I said I was quitting because I was going on *The X Factor*. My boss took one look at me and said, 'Well, my nephew went on it and it was a disaster. They promised him the world and none of it worked out.'

For some reason, I knew my experience would be different. I thanked her for her advice and walked out of the studio, never to return.

It was August and I got an email from the production team telling me to, 'Keep an eye out on *X Factor* this weekend!' I knew what that meant. It was time for everyone to see what had happened at my first audition. I had no idea what to expect. Would it be a small segment? A feature? I'd seen Ella Henderson's audition the week before: it was exceptional. I'd met her at Bootcamp and we'd taken to each other right away. I was glad she got such a great chunk of prime time.

That Saturday night, 25th August, 2012, my friends and I gathered around a TV in an apartment in Sheffield and, at the end of the segment that contained my audition, we turned to each other with our mouths wide open. I had tears running down my cheeks as the adverts casually rolled in. I hadn't just had a small segment at all. My audition had been the main feature of the whole episode. My phone started pinging. All of a sudden, we were all jumping around the room. I was being patted on the head, the back, and lifted into the air. What the fuck just happened?! My friend's phone screen was thrust into my face. 'Fucking hell, dude, #BeerFear is trending worldwide on Twitter!' Then, five minutes later, 'Your album is number one on iTunes!'

In the weeks leading up to this, I had been working on the high street. Ninety-five per cent of my job was basically being professionally ignored. I held my clipboard to my chest whilst being dodged by passers-by, so desperate for engagement that my opening gambit was, 'Don't worry, I'm not from a charity!' For most of my working day, I was invisible, screaming into the street-salesperson void, exchanging glances of solidarity with the other clipboard clingers, sign holders and the men in the Sky TV vans. In one moment, it all changed.

That night, we went out to bars and clubs in Sheffield city centre and I quickly realised, after one ten-minute segment of a TV show, that I was now pretty fucking famous. People rushed over to me, asking for pictures and for hugs, saying how much they loved my song. I had not anticipated how many people watch that show. The next morning, the neighbour's child bounced on a trampoline in their garden. I'd never spoken to any of them before. 'Last night I told ya I loved ya!' she sang at me over the fence, not taking her eyes off me as she bobbed up and down. What the fuck?

My experience of fame was sensationally overnight. The contrast of my life was literally inverted the moment my audition aired. It was like flicking a light switch.

My phone didn't stop ringing, I had messages of congratulations from people I hadn't spoken to in years. That same Sunday, an unknown London number flashed up on my phone. I picked it up. It was a lawyer, the woman who we'd met at Bootcamp. She was calling with news from Syco. A call from a lawyer on a Sunday? It must be serious. She told me that they needed me to remove my album from sale with immediate effect. What?! My album, my own album that I wrote and recorded in Will's kitchen, the album that was currently at number one, bringing all my dreams to life . . . They needed me to remove *that*?

Syco had nothing to gain from my album doing well. Matter of fact, my album shooting to number one after just one ten-minute segment put a spanner in the whole point of the show. Did contestants really need to compete against each other, sing covers, get dolled up and be voted for every week to be successful, or did talented people actually just need a little bit of exposure? Did record labels need to sign artists for them to have a career or could they record and distribute their own music? This was an anomaly that they hadn't encountered before and it put far more power than they'd like into my hands.

'It's in your best interests to take it down,' the lawyer said. 'The recordings aren't great quality; if you leave it then you might be upset with the way it sounds in the future and you can't get rid of it then. You'll have the opportunity to record a studio album at some point and get yourself a record deal.' She continued, 'If you want to proceed in the competition it really is in your best interest to remove it with immediate effect.' I agreed to do it. What other choice did I have? It seemed like none, actually.

Days later, someone re-recorded my whole album, beat for beat, strum for strum, hired a horrible vocalist to impersonate me and uploaded it for sale. I was completely devastated. It started to climb the charts. I'd never seen anything like it. People were buying that album thinking it was mine. They were getting an income from *my* music and I wasn't. I begged the lawyer to get Syco to help me make them remove it but they didn't care. They said I could speak to the show's PR person and go to the press with it but the story that ended up in the newspapers was that I didn't like people doing covers of my songs and that I was being a diva. It felt like I was being punished. That wasn't what I'd said at all.

From just twenty-four hours of sales, 'Last Night' (the real one) had charted at number eleven and my album charted at number twenty-two in the UK top-forty charts. It would have, undoubtedly, been a number-one album had it stayed up. Unbelievably, in that time, my TuneCore account had racked up an astonishing £56,000. I was rich! Though it was stuck in the online distribution portal and would take days to withdraw. I asked my mum to transfer me £30 to go out that night, knowing, for the first time, that I would genuinely be able to pay her back.

Instead of dwelling on what had been taken away, I was dedicated to gaining as much as I could from the opportunity I'd been given. Emails flooded in from promotors and bar owners that I'd met from all over the country asking if I was available for gigs and I certainly was. I went and played as many as I could fit in. A student union in Wrexham, a gay bar in Leeds. I got paid £1,500 for one gig, which was insane. That was literally ten times more than the most I'd been paid for a gig before that. I was making money, real money. Soon, the phone rang again.

'You need to stop playing gigs,' the lawyer said. Were they joking? I asked if Syco or Fremantle (another television production company) were going to reimburse me if I was to cancel the shows. After all, they reimbursed people with 'normal' jobs for the time off needed to take part in the show. If I was to turn down work for them, they'd need to cover the cost. The answer was no. It was clear that they weren't used to dealing with gigging musicians; before 2012, most of the contestants had day jobs.

'This is my job,' I said. I agreed that I wouldn't book any more gigs than I already had.

In 2023, after more than a decade of being a professional musician, songwriter and recording artist, I have no doubt at all that agreeing to remove that album from sale was one of the worst decisions of my career and was never, in any way, in my best interests. It is one of my only regrets in life and I still feel that my naivety and lack of industry knowledge was utterly exploited by *The X Factor* and the lawyer involved.

In 2012, the mentor for the girls' category was Tulisa Contostavlos. I don't know how much money she made from N-Dubz but I'm fairly sure it wasn't enough to buy an entire hotel in the Caribbean, so instead of going to her *house*, on 2nd September, the six 'girls' left in the competition were flown – cattle class, with Tulisa and the producers up front – to St Lucia and put up in a five-star hotel for the Judges' Houses episode.

If the producers were hoping to get a shot of me in a bikini by the pool, they must have been disappointed when I turned up in a jumper. A fucking jumper. In the fucking Caribbean. I didn't know what to pack when I left Sheffield and I panicked, putting on a jumper before the flight, with just a bra underneath. As soon as we arrived at the hotel they started filming before I could change my outfit. They interviewed me and this was the first time I learnt that, for television, you have to film everything five times. I was also introduced to 'noddies' here, too. Noddies are where they film you nodding in various ways, so thatthey can use this in the editing suite. The first time they did this I thought, 'Fuck no, I've got no idea what question I'm going to be nodding in agreement to.' It could be 'Do you think Hitler had some interesting ideas on eugenics?' Nod. 'Do you fancy Nicole Scherzinger?' Nod. Anyway, by the end of the interview, I felt like a dog in a hot car. I was overheating.

It's called 'reality TV' but things were so far from my reality at this point. I was in the Caribbean. I was surrounded by famous people and there were producers and runners telling me what to do every minute of every day. It may have looked like a holiday on TV but this was one of the most exhausting weeks of my life. It would be a slight understatement to say that I have never been one who likes being told what to do and with every new request/instruction/demand, the more and more resistance I felt. I started to get this overwhelming conviction that this wasn't for me, that I shouldn't be there.

We'd been there a day and talk of the song they wanted me to perform for Tulisa and her guest judge, Tinie Tempah, was beginning. It was Whitney Houston's 'I Will Always Love You' (actually a Dolly Parton song but I knew which version they wanted me to massacre). It wasn't fair; I'd already done the embarrassing section, the bit where I looked shit. I'd sung 'Moves Like Jagger' without my guitar. Why did they want me to do it again? I argued and argued with the producers and fought for the right to play my own song. They said no. This wasn't what I wanted. I didn't come here to play other people's songs. I went to my room and had a long think about it all.

Later that evening, I asked to speak to one of the producers, Caz, in the hotel's bar on the beach. It was a fancy wooden shack with swinging benches and white draped curtains that billowed in the breeze. A tall, handsome waiter in cream linen made cocktails in the background. It was such a peaceful, dusky evening and the humid air felt so foreign.

'I don't want to do the show anymore,' I told her, once she'd sat down with me on the long bench. She made this face, like I'd accidentally put something in her shopping basket and she was removing it to hand it back to me. A respectful refusal. 'Oh, Lucy. Come on! Why would you want to leave?!'

She started to look a little more serious as my explanation went on.

'Millions of people have seen my audition. In the best possible way, I have already got what I wanted – exposure. I could get a record deal without doing the rest of the series; a few companies have already been in touch. I don't want to sing covers, I never did. I'm so grateful for this opportunity but something just doesn't feel right.'

My instinct was telling me to leave and it seemed like the right decision. I try to avoid feeling regret but, looking back, I can see how different things would have been if I had listened to it.

As soon as she realised how serious I was, it was immediately clear that me leaving was not part of the producer's narrative.

Caz called Cait, another producer, and she came down to the bar too. She was softly spoken and had a kind face. I'd met her a few times before and I genuinely liked her. Caz was the more forceful of the two and I think that, by this stage, they'd started to see that the softer they were with me, the softer I became, whilst the more resistance I encountered, the more I'd push back. They both took it in turns to prompt my reversal.

Don't you realise what an opportunity this is, Lucy? This could be life-changing, Lucy. You'll always wonder what might have been, Lucy. You'll have to live with that regret, Lucy.

It didn't matter. I was adamant that I wanted to leave the show. Through tears, I stuck to my guns. Caz and Cait both knew they needed a more effective game plan. They called in the A-team. The two producers quietly walked away as Tulisa and Caroline Flack just so happened to walk into the beach bar and sit down beside me, ordering a cocktail for each of us. Fucking hell, they were fit. As the alcohol flowed, both women repeated the same narrative as the producers had – how this was my golden opportunity and I shouldn't waste it. That this would be the biggest thing I'd ever do.

The whole setting was so surreal. I knew they'd been asked to come down to the beach and talk some sense into me. The production team had sent beautiful women to convince me because beautiful women were (and are) my absolute kryptonite. They already knew this: it was Layla, Syco's beautiful talent scout, who got me to sign up for the show in the first place. There was probably a file on each contestant kept somewhere, documenting their likes and dislikes, their attributes and flaws. On mine, it probably said 'a sucker for a pretty girl'. It worked. I agreed to stay.

So, there I was, on the terrace of a fabulous hotel overlooking the Caribbean Sea with my bashed-up guitar, sitting in front of Tulisa and Tinie Tempah, two artists who

I grew up a huge fan of and had influenced my own music, unable to show them my potential and my talent because I wasn't playing my own song. I started to play 'I Will Always Love You' as requested. The key was uncomfortable, the lyrics felt foreign and, needless to say, it was shit. Again. Tinie Tempah looked at me through his sunglasses and said, 'I don't get it.'

'Mate, I'm not surprised you don't fucking get it, *I* don't fucking get it!' I thought to myself, 'because this isn't what I do.'

After the conversations at the beach bar, it wasn't such a shock when Tulisa told me I was one of the final twelve to go through to the live shows, despite my uninspiring performance. I can't remember feeling overly happy about it, I was more curious just to see what would happen. All I knew was that I was already fucking exhausted.

I know now that this was all part of my storyline. By giving me such an inappropriate song that they knew I would suck at, the producers were creating jeopardy and baiting the viewers: 'Oh, no! Maybe Lucy won't go through.' That's their job. I get it. They have to create a story to evoke feelings in their audience, just like I do with my songs. But I use words and they use real people. The stress they put the contestants through is real. I *hated* doing that song but someone in the production team told me that this was my big moment. This would either change my life or I'd slink back to a flat share in Sheffield. 'If you don't make it now,' they whispered, 'you'll never make it.' As it turns out, tired, confused and emotional people make great television.

★

After a week away under immense stress, I flew back to the UK for a reunion with my girlfriend at the time. Harriet had just accepted a contract to teach English as a foreign language in Thailand; we would only have a couple of weeks together before she left the country for six months and I moved to London for the live shows. After a mental week in the Caribbean, my body felt heavy with jet lag and emotion, and there was a lot to fit in before Harriet's flight.

The day after I got back, we'd been to get some shopping and I knew I probably shouldn't have been driving because I felt so tired and out of it. We were nearly back when her flatmate asked us to stop by and pick her up too; she was only one block away from us and, oh, there she was, on the corner! I turned the wheel left to pull in, without looking, straight into the bus lane where a bus, doing 30mph, smashed straight into the passenger door. The car spun round and Harriet was covered in glass.

I got out and apologised to the bus driver. I'd never been in an accident before. I sort of knew you were supposed to swap details but were you meant to call the police? As my cottonwool brain tried to figure everything out, a camera flash momentarily startled me. People on the bus had recognised me.

The remaining twelve contestants were moved into the Corinthia, a very swanky – we're talking Saudi princess swanky – hotel in London. *The X Factor* had taken an entire floor and placed security guards by the lifts, ostensibly to keep fans and the press out, but it also had the effect of keeping us in. Top Room at the Corinthia, eh?

Every hour was spoken for. We were woken by one runner and taken to the dance studio for the choreography lessons, or off to some location for filming with Tulisa, and then back into an Addison Lee minicab and handed a lukewarm Tesco sandwich on the way to the Corinthia for a singing lesson. Yes, a fucking singing lesson. All twelve of us together. I literally couldn't bear it.

I don't know if we weren't allowed to see our families and friends or if there just wasn't time. Suddenly, my entire life was about being an *X Factor* contestant and we were not allowed anywhere without a chaperone. We ate together in the hotel dining room and were constantly accompanied by a runner. Have you ever heard of the Stanford Prison Experiment? You know, the one where they told half the participants they were prisoners and the other half they were guards? The runners were only a year or two older than me but, somehow, they seemed so much more authoritative. They had power. Some of them were casual and relaxed with us and others took their role very seriously indeed, almost like prison wardens. At times, I found myself just doing whatever I was told, which was very unlike me. I guess a slightly less extreme Stockholm syndrome had kicked in. They were our keepers and we did what they asked.

Everything was new to me – the month before, I'd been flirting with the boy in Cash Converters in the hope he'd pay me more for my CDs so I could make my rent. I didn't know how to behave in a five-star hotel. I didn't even know that the Addison Lee drivers weren't *X Factor* staff. To me, they were just magic cars that turned up when you needed one. My life was now as far away from my old one as I could possibly imagine.

Even our social life was taken care of and it was a step up from my regular nights out. We were invited to the premiere of the new James Bond film, *Skyfall*. What the hell? We didn't need to find an outfit as one was picked for us. Thankfully, the stylist was queer and understanding and, instead of a frock, I wore a tuxedo with my hair slicked back. I'd never been on a red carpet before. Later, I saw my expression in every paparazzi photo that was taken of me – dumfounded. My mouth is open in some pictures.

Everything was arranged for us. Within weeks, possibly within days, we all became dependent on the production team. With the ability to look back on this time, I can see that there was definitely an element of coercive control to it all. It was there in the dynamic between production staff, too. At the top were the executive producers who made all of the decisions, rarely seen but often heard, then the producers who organised the plan, and then the runners who followed the orders. And then there was us. Everything was drip-fed down the pipe, and I imagine the runners were just as fearful of losing their low-paid, but high potential positions on a show as big as *The X Factor* as we, the contestants, were. The lower down the ladder you were, the greater the leverage was for what you'd do to climb up it.

Thankfully, Rylan Clark, the contestant I'd met in the lift at Bootcamp, had also made it through to the final twelve and we instantly became friends. He is six-foot-four and I am five-foot-three. He is gay and I am a lesbian. I don't remember saying it out loud but we both knew that neither of us really cared too much about winning. To us, it wasn't a competition, it was an opportunity to win in other ways. It was exposure. And we were terribly good at getting that.

From the off, we were the troublemakers and ringleaders. We weren't allowed out unchaperoned so we staged day-time escapes from the hotel, gathering the other contestants and sneaking them out of the staff exit so the security guards wouldn't see us. One time, we all ran away from the hotel and went to Trafalgar Square – it's not far from the Corinthia – but once we'd got there, we realised we didn't really know what to do. Freedom didn't feel like it had before; we were almost conditioned to be scared of being outside alone without a runner. Another time, we snuck off to Nando's. Hardly rock'n'roll but we were so conditioned by this point that we knew we were always going to go back.

When the producers gave me and Rylan a bollocking, it was always with a smile. It's extremely hard not to laugh when Rylan is around. He has this charm which melted even the strictest of runners. Rylan and I were getting a lot of press for our antics, and *The X Factor* wanted all the press they could get. I didn't understand back then but it's a relationship. The red-top tabloids need stories to sell papers and TV shows need stories in those same red tops to get more viewers and make more money from advertisers. It's a business and I was a commodity. We were young and excited, and pretty bloody famous, and we loved going out and being seen.

Unlike me, Rylan was built for showbiz. He'd already been on *Signed By Katie Price,* was friends with some other stars and he just seemed to know how everything worked. I reckon we were offered an hour's worth of media training but I learnt everything from standing next to him.

Wherever we went, an Addison Lee took us there and when we arrived, the drinks were magically free. And after several hours of free drinks, we'd make fools of ourselves

– SNAP – and get poured into another Addison Lee – SNAP – and in the morning the tabloids duly reported our escapades. One night, Rylan and I snuck out of the hotel and a couple of paps spotted us, clearly drunk, and followed us. We stumbled – quite literally – onto a building site. I fell down a gap between two slabs of concrete and Rylan had to try to pull me out. SNAP. We walked past a stationary bus and stood in front of it posing as if halting it in the street, cackling. SNAP. The headline the next day, supported by that picture, said we'd 'stopped traffic' in the middle of London.

Luckily, the production team liked us and the press did too. There was an appetite for more stories about us and it was striking how often a conversation one of the contestants had had in private ended up in the papers. We were always told to tell the publicist anything that worried or concerned us but, as if by magic, once you did, it was those stories that ended up being printed. That show had more leaks than any of the jobs Paul and I attended. Mostly it was harmless.

We were prepped for our first performances by a styling team, hair team and Julia Carter, who was the head make-up artist. As soon as I heard her speak, I didn't like her. She lined us all up against the wall, like a military operation, and went down the line pointing at each of us, describing how she would commandeer our faces. 'I'm gonna make you look like a boy band member,' she'd say to one of the boys. 'You're going to lose the stubble and look a little sweeter, maybe some eyeliner,' to another. I couldn't believe it.

When she got to me, she looked me up and down and

said, 'You're going to be a gothy rock chick.' She'd already moved to the next person when I said, 'Er, no. No, I'm not.' Her head turned so slowly, astonished that someone had dared to speak. It was like she was a baddie from a cartoon, Cruella de Vil maybe. Her eyes bulged.

'What did you just say?'

'No. No gothic rock chick for me, thanks,' I said, plainly.

'This is MY job and I will be doing what I decide,' she barked.

We then had this big barney in front of everyone. I quite enjoyed it. I asked her if she'd actually watched our auditions. She said she hadn't. It boggled my mind that she was employed to emphasise our style when she had no idea what our styles were. It was like our identities and bodies were being pirated and we were being appointed new ones. I noticed that I was one of the only contestants who questioned what was going on. Or maybe I was the only one who was vocal about it.

I loved the styling team, led by a gay man called Frank, and in queer solidarity and an understanding of the importance of identity, we settled on a beanie hat, a plaid shirt and boots for most of my 'looks'. Lesbian chic, I call it. The hair team were just as lovely. Jamie Stevens and his wife Megan, who led this team, didn't want to push me out of my comfort zone. I appreciated that so much. They loved to watch the weekly bust-up that Julia and I had. She'd come into the dressing room and begin to dictate what face paint I'd wear for that week's show and I'd protest. As soon as she stormed off down the corridor we would all burst into laughter. The most painful part of the transformation was having my eyebrows threaded and my teeth whitened.

We all had to have it done and, fuck me, that hurt. I ran to the local shop to smear Sensodyne all over my teeth as they became so sensitive. They had a lady come in and give us a super posh facial too, which brought me out in a massive rash. Another reminder that I didn't really feel like I was supposed to be there.

For the first live show, I was allowed to perform one of my own songs, 'Mountains'. The musical director had to create a backing track so that it wasn't just me and my guitar. They felt it needed to sound 'more Saturday night' but I thought it was way too floral, a bit cheesy. But then again, I was on *The X Factor*.

At this stage of the competition, it's the viewers who get to decide who goes through, not the judges. Not that you'd know it from my 'performance'. I didn't know how to look into a camera, I never once smiled and I was so distracted by the acoustics – terrible – that I looked thoroughly miserable throughout. I was playing but I definitely wasn't performing. Not like I had in my auditions, or at the festivals, or in the pubs. The cold, hard TV studio didn't smile or laugh back. I didn't know how to navigate that kind of performance.

By week two, the institutionalisation had really kicked in and I started to play the game a bit. *The X Factor* was famously a covers show and I accepted that I had to do one in the anticipation they'd let me sing one of my songs the following week. In an attempt, I guess, to show my versatility, I agreed to do a version of Kanye West's 'Gold Digger'. I'd arranged a little acoustic version years ago that I sometimes pulled out when a crowd got a bit rowdy in a bar.

At some point that week, I got a phone call from my

grandad. My grandma had died. Grief and trauma, I've discovered, can have the same impact on your memory as a head injury, so there's a lot about the next few weeks that I either don't remember or I can't put in the right sequence, the memories present themselves in a random order and I struggle to get them lined up. I have a memory of being on the tube, on the Circle Line – I think I was trying to get to my grandad's house in Kent – but I ended up going round and round and getting totally lost because I'd never navigated the tube alone before. Then I was at the funeral. I have a memory of being back in London with the filming team, sitting on a stool, high up on an empty floor of a tall building, light flooding through the windows, a white backdrop behind me and a camera in my face. They were filming VTs. That's the bit they play before you walk on stage, the clip that helps the public make their minds up about you. The director was asking me what I had done that week. 'Oh, nothing much.' I replied. I didn't want to talk about my grandma. That was private. It was personal. But they *did* want to talk about my grandma. They wanted the emotion for the screens.

'What have you been up to, then?' They tried a different tack.

'Oh, just playing my guitar, practising my song for the show.'

That went on for about an hour, them throwing out a line that I was supposed to bite but having to reel it back in empty-handed and cast it out again. I wasn't playing ball.

They started to realise I wasn't going to crack. The production team walked off into a huddle at the back of the room. They came back and assumed their positions:

the producer was in the director's chair in front of me, the sound man had his boom mic above my head, the camera man was behind his lens, and the runners were onlooking either side. I noticed the red light on the camera flick on and the director took a deep breath in.

'Your grandma died this week, didn't she?' The question hit me like a train. I hadn't thought they'd go that far. I couldn't speak because I knew I'd burst out crying. My lip started to shake and a single tear rolled down my cheek. Bravo to the production team. A well-executed extraction.

The first time I saw that VT package was when I was standing backstage, just seconds before those big mechanical doors opened and I went out to perform live on Saturday night. I was watching that VT footage at the same time as millions of other people across the UK, but the difference was, that was actually me. I was watching myself crying about my grandma who had just died. My grandma who I would never see again. On the screen, I saw my chin start to wobble and then, as if cued by Disney, a single tear fell down my face. My heart broke for that girl.

Immediately, I felt like I was going to cry again and a huge lump wedged itself at the front of my throat. I remember thinking, 'I can't physically sing now' because my neck felt so tight, so constricted by the emotion. But regardless of my feelings, the mechanical doors opened up and the hot spotlights spun down the stage revealing me, with only my guitar to protect me, to millions on live TV. I felt ambushed. Thank God they let me keep the guitar. Thankfully, I wasn't on stage alone for long.

That week, the choreography had been organised by Brian Friedman, who was very excited about the fact I was going to do an up-tempo number. I had agreed to have dancers, but only on one condition. As I stood on a podium in my beanie hat and plaid shirt I began to sing 'Gold Digger'. The huge screens across the stage lit up with animated green dollar signs and simulations of gold dropping down the walls behind me. Four of the most beautiful women, dressed in cargo pants and crop tops, danced on up to me and started twerking. At one point, they were on all fours, doing that cat-cow yoga move whilst circling the podium I was on, giving definitely the most lesbian performances I'd ever seen on the show. It was one of the stranger performances of my career but it was unbelievably fun. I was playing the game but on my terms, and the audience loved it. The judges, again, mentioned the fact my grandma had died, said some nice things, and the viewers sent me through into week three.

After every successful show, Rylan and I would paint the town red, and that night was no exception. That Saturday, we ended up in G-A-Y, lapping up the attention. The following week, possibly on the Wednesday, Caz and Cait came to tell Rylan and I that we were being moved out of the Corinthia. Just us two, not anyone else. Apparently, it was because we were so badly behaved. The funny thing was, we weren't being that badly behaved and, to be honest, the way we did behave was being encouraged. We hadn't done any damage and certainly no one from the Corinthia had said anything to us – and Rylan was friends with everyone, from the concierge to the kitchen staff. That's just the kind of guy he is. We'd been reading the inflated stories about our escapades in the red tops and noted that most of the sources for these stories were 'someone close to the show'. Rylan told me he'd had a conversation with a producer to get to the bottom of it all, to know the truth, and came to the conclusion that this was, again, all part of our storyline. Hellraisers being kicked out of one of London's poshest hotels was another convenient bit of publicity.

We were moved to a shitty hotel in Wembley near to where the live shows were filmed. When I say shitty hotel, I mean shitty. Not just because our standards had been raised by the £1,000-a-night Corinthia but because it was fucking dire. Rylan took one look at the place and announced we would not be staying there, and so we were moved again to another hotel on Edgware Road. Again, it was no Corinthia. Not only was it not luxurious at all but there was no security, no infrastructure; it was just the two of us and a single runner to look after us. What was their plan? Were they hoping that we'd be unleashed to create more headlines?

Despite the change of location, the cycle of singing lessons, the dance studios, rehearsing and filming continued. On week four, I agreed to do a cover of David Guetta's 'Titanium', but only if I could change the lyrics. I think I was hoping they'd never get permission and I'd get to sing one of my own songs again, but somehow the producers got Sia and co-writer Guetta to say yes to my request.

The show had its weekly rhythm of rehearsals, arguments with the production team, getting drunk and ending up in the tabloids with Rylan, filming behind-the-scenes stuff for Caroline Flack and Olly Murs on *The Xtra Factor*, and then performing on Saturday night followed by looking at my Twitter feed and seeing what everyone was saying.

Week four was Halloween week and, given the response the previous weeks, and the bookies declaring I was now the favourite to win the whole thing, I agreed to stick with the formula and do another cover. 'Gold Digger' had actually been quite fun. This time it was going to be The Specials' 'Ghost Town' but with Justin Timberlake's 'Cry Me a River' thrown in.

That week was also the week of Rylan's twenty-fifth birthday, providing the show with another event to plan some publicity around. The party was at Mahiki, a.k.a. Wanksville, one of those posh Mayfair clubs that everyone's very pleased to tell you Prince William and Harry used to go to. It's got a Polynesian theme and it's all tiki huts, fake Hawaiian cups and very expensive sugary cocktails.

All the contestants were invited, as were the judges, and we were all given costumes to wear. Rylan got given a sexy quarterback's outfit and Hannah, the runner staying at our hotel, turned up with a pumpkin for me. A big, round, felt pumpkin. Lesbians are always something plump and jolly on television, aren't they? Funny and rotund, but never sexy.

I felt so humiliated about the prospect of going to this glamorous party dressed as a punchline to a joke that I spent several hours on Edgware Road looking for a replacement outfit. Not only did I not find a costume, all that time spent shopping meant I didn't have time to eat before another Addison Lee appeared, as if by magic, to whisk me to the ball.

The place was full of celebrities. Nicole Scherzinger – the mentor to the 'boys' group – got up, wearing a PVC catsuit and seductively sang 'Happy Birthday' to Rylan. Tulisa was there. I think someone mentioned a Spice Girl. The whole place was littered with faces. There were journalists there too. A face I recognised as Dan Wootton, the head of showbiz at *The Sun*, had been invited. Ed Sheeran's producer at the time was there and *that* was who I was most excited about meeting.

Normally, the point of exclusive Mayfair clubs is that they are, I suppose, exclusive, so royalty and movie stars can socialise away from prying eyes. On this occasion, however, there were paparazzi inside the club. That's how much publicity the show was trying to generate. By this stage, I knew my role: get drunk, do something funny, appear in the headlines the next day. Win the hearts and minds of the voting public, and coast through to the next live show. There are photos of me picking up a bottle of beer from the table with my teeth, knocking my head back, drinking the entire contents, then returning the bottle to the table. People were cheering. Classy party trick, eh?

Everyone was drunk, even the runners. It was like everyone had let their hair down and was blowing off a *lot* of steam. We'd all been churned up in this crazy machine and the pressure was so intense. There were just two sober runners, standing in the corner of the bar, watching on as chaos ensued, unable to control it. There were contestants falling down drunk, kissing people they shouldn't kiss, ordering more drinks. 'Someone's going to get hurt,' said one of the sober runners to the other. She was right.

★

When you're used to having very little, you'll take anything that's free. We had endless free drinks that night and I knew I was playing my part to perfection. Adhering to my storyline. The girl who sings about drinking getting drunk. The girl who parties with Rylan. I kept drinking.

On an empty stomach. Much of that evening, unsurprisingly, is a total blackout to me. I remember bits of being in the club, or maybe I remember what I've seen photos of. Because of what happened that night, and the police investigation that followed, I was given a fairly good idea of the sequence of events.

I ended up paralytic. Blackout drunk wasn't new to me, as we know, but it had been an awfully long time since I'd been that drunk. Hannah, the runner who was looking after both me and Rylan, a girl not much older than me, and who had also been drinking all night, was responsible for me putting me in a cab and taking me back to the hotel on Edgware Road.

Obviously, I don't recall any of this part of the night from my own eyes because my eyes were closed. I was unconscious. Instead, I imagine how it all unfolded from above, as if I'm watching haunting footage from a hovering CCTV camera that followed my movements from the Addison Lee to my hotel room. I know how it went based on evidence that was found by the Metropolitan Police and from accounts of people that were there.

Outside the hotel, as an intoxicated Hannah struggled to get me out of the car on her own, a hotel porter saw her and offered to help her take me to my room. They hoisted me up, one arm around her shoulder, my other arm around his, I was carried – still dressed as a fucking pumpkin – into my room and thrown onto the bed. Not under the covers, just dumped in the middle of the double bed. As they left me in my room, Hannah must have walked out first. Behind her, Hannah too tipsy and tired to notice, the hotel porter flipped the metal security latch over, to prevent the door from closing properly. He wanted to make sure my hotel room was not locked. Hannah fell into her room a few doors down and closed the door.

I don't know how long I was in that room, unconscious on the bed with the door unlocked, but I do know that without Rylan – heroic, gorgeous, brilliant Rylan – I would know a lot less than I do now.

Rylan arrived back in the middle of the night and, knowing him, and that it was his birthday party we'd all been at, I imagine he was quite pissed himself. Regardless, for some reason, whether it was his good nature, our solidarity or just a gut instinct, he thought to himself, 'I'm just going to check that Lucy is alright.' I can tell you right now that I wouldn't have done the same thing for him back then. I'd have just gone to bed. He changed everything by checking on me.

He arrived at my door and saw that it was open, that the latch had purposefully been put across. 'What the fuck?' he thought and he walked in. That wonderful man checked that I was breathing, took my stupid pumpkin costume off and tucked me in, pulling the covers over me. When he left my room, he made very sure that my door was shut. It closed behind him and he gave it a push to make sure the lock had engaged.

If Rylan hadn't done that, the hotel porter who had given Hannah a 'hand' to get my deadweight upstairs wouldn't have needed to get a key card, a *traceable* key card, to let himself into my room when his shift ended in the early hours of that morning.

And they would never have found the man who raped me.

When Your Body Is a Crime Scene

At 7.30 a.m., my eyes shot open to the thudding of a fist on my door and the recognisable voice of the runner ordering me to get out of bed. 'There's a car outside, Lucy. We are already late! Get up . . . Now!'

Some of the runners had started to consistently speak to contestants in this way. It had become quite normal to be spoken to by them in that regimented, almost aggressive tone but, as used to the shrill as I was, it catapulted my body into consciousness, clanging into my ears. Immediately, I felt my brain trying to catch up with my physical awareness but it was like turning the key in the ignition of a car with a flat battery. Click, click, click in rapid succession, the awakening thoughts interrupted again with the voice bellowing, 'Get up, NOW!'

My eyes had been open for seconds. My heartbeat felt irregular and my chest felt like it was tremoring. The sound of blood was rushing around my temples and palpitating in my ears. My mouth was dry. I was physically incredibly hungover with all the usual signs but alongside that I was also so, so confused. That's the best word I can find to describe it, even though it felt like so much more than that. How I imagine dementia to feel. It was as if my thoughts were misfiring or I couldn't reach them.

In the 1990s, there was a gameshow where the finale would have the contestant standing in a clear Perspex tank with paper money propelled into the air around them by a giant fan underneath their feet. The contestant's job was to grab at notes flying about their body and past their face, each bill artfully dodging their grip, whichever grabbing method they used. I was reaching out for my thoughts but my brain wasn't letting me hold a single one of them for more than a fraction of a moment: 'There was a man in my room last night' *FLASH* 'I need to get up' *FLASH* 'Something very serious has happened' *FLASH* 'You are late' . . . Then the voice again: 'You've got two minutes! I am going downstairs to wait in the car for you. Hurry up!'

Head soup, I call it. When your brain feels like a can of Alphabetti spaghetti. It's full to the brim of vowels and consonants, but they form no legible words. My eyes focused and I looked around the room. I felt utter dread.

Stone-cold, not-sober dread. As my thoughts started to formulate, my personality zapped itself away. There was an emergency unfolding, a high-pitched alarm ringing out across all of my senses, a message of danger telling me that something was very wrong. Without consciously making the decision to do so, my brain switched into autopilot and I stood up, pulled on the clothes that were on the floor and walked towards the door.

Survival is the deepest instinct that we, as living, breathing, creatures, have. Even creatures that don't breathe, the smallest micro-bacteria or single-cell organisms, have it. We'll all do just about anything to survive. That day, as soon as I woke, the instinctive, subconscious part of my brain that dictates how I survive assumed its responsibility. And I'm glad it did. Had I woken up and immediately considered the reality of what had happened to me just hours before, had the truth that trickled in during the next twenty-four hours and day by day after that (some details didn't arrive until a decade later, whilst writing this book) hit me all at once – I don't think I'd have been able to survive that morning. I'd have just shut down and died.

That is exactly what I wanted to do in many of the years that followed.

Peppered throughout the last decade of my life, I have experienced hours of distraught, guttural pain from knowing what just one action from another human being took away from me that night. If I'd have woken up on that morning and known of the harrowing inspection of my body that was about to happen, or of the illness I was about to endure, the opportunities that were about to fragment and crumble away from me, the dimming of the promised future that had brushed my fingertips or the way I was about to be treated like a corporate problem by the people who had the responsibility and the duty of my care, the loneliness, the shame, the sadness, the anger, I'd have wanted to die. I'd have wanted to close my eyes again and never wake back up.

Instead, the part of my brain that survives stood up my legs and marched them downstairs to the lobby of the hotel, with my hair and teeth unbrushed and my face unwashed. It walked me outside into the street and into an Addison Lee. I opened the door and climbed into the back seat of the car. I registered the runner in the front passenger side, her messy blonde hair tied into a side ponytail and her fingers furiously jabbing at a BlackBerry phone. My head turned itself to the right and my eyes made out a person sitting next to me on the opposite side of the car. I blinked. A face. A familiar one. One that I liked. It was only when I saw Rylan that I remembered I was alive. It was only then that I remembered that I was a person. That I was Lucy. The autopilot switched back off.

My brain started running playbacks of waking up in the night and realising there had been a body on top of me. That it had been a man. That there had been hands around my throat. Chaotic memories of smells and sensations and of a struggle rushed through me and then faded into blackness. I still didn't have a name for it; I couldn't say the R word. As Rylan's eyes connected with mine, his smile dropped. His eyes widened and he grabbed my hand with both of his. 'What's happened?' he asked, in something just louder than a whisper. Aware that the runner's keen ear might be trained on us or that the driver of this car might be listening, I leant in close to him and, very quietly, I told him.

That morning, Rylan saved my life.

Upon hearing the very basics of what had happened, similar to the instinctive way that my brain had buckled and shut out my ability to reason or process, his brain transformed him into a calm, rational leader. No flapping or shrieking. He wasn't Rylan from his famous audition video, sobbing into Nicole Scherzinger's lap, he was Rylan, my friend, my saviour. From the second the mumbled story left my mouth he was a beacon of support and a source of stillness. A steadfast, pragmatic thinker.

'We're going to get you the Pill,' was the first thing he whispered, nodding at me and studying my face. 'We're going to tell the police.'

The car ride was over and Rylan and I were back in the Corinthia hotel. At this point, I'd stopped speaking; autopilot had flicked back on. Rylan took me up to the floor that the contestants had, past the security guard outside the lift, and sat me down on a bed in one of the vacant hotel rooms. When he knew I was safe, he literally ran off to make contact with the show's producer. His job was to find someone who could help us. Rylan was already very aware of the public implications of telling the wrong person, as he himself had been the subject of countless stories in the papers. He knew how fast 'news' travels. Besides, this wasn't a problem that could be fixed by a runner; he needed someone at the top.

When I recall this day, the whole thing happens in the style of a slide show. There are no middle bits – no being in a lift or walking down a hall. No eating anything, no ordinariness. The projector clicks and one photographic slide is replaced with another, and another, each memory independent of the last. One minute, I am in the room I was attacked in; the slide changes and I am in the car with Rylan. The next slide: I am in the Corinthia. The next thing that I remember, despite everything that was unravelling, I am being walked out of the room Rylan left me in and marched down a corridor by the same runner, who clearly has no idea what is going on, her hand around the back of my bicep, pushing me through a tall door, into a light and airy room with tall, white walls and wooden cladding across the back. I realise this room is full of all of the other contestants and our singing teacher. It's a group singing lesson. I can't even talk.

As I walk in, I feel as if I'm floating. I am watched by every single eye in the room but I'm staring straight ahead into nothing. I must look like shit; I am wearing the same clothes that were under my costume last night but I don't care. I don't care about anything. The runner lets go of my arm and leaves. They're mid-lesson. 'Eeeeee's' and 'Ooooooohs' harmonise with the alarm that's still ringing in my mind. Amazingly, I try to participate but within seconds I can no longer stand up. My legs give way and I slip down onto the floor and lie in the foetal position.

'La-la-la-la-la, lala, la-la.' The class is continuing and is communally climbing up a scale whilst the singing teacher, who is loudly singing along, stands above my motionless body, grabbing me by the arm and trying to drag me up onto my feet to join in with the rest of the class. 'Fa-la-la-la-la-la, lala, la-la,' she bellows, as she tries to lever up my deadweight. She clearly suspects I am purely nursing a terrible hangover and being dramatic. She's visibly frustrated by the level of my disrespect. I can't move.

Click, the next slide: I have been rescued by Rylan and I am sitting on the edge of a bed in a large double hotel room in the Corinthia. I used to share this room with Ella Henderson before Rylan and I were kicked out. Despite the room being huge, with floor-to-ceiling curtains and tall, smooth, ultra-modern white walls, dressed with sculpted brushed-brass wall art, it feels tiny, dark and suffocating. I'm in front of a mirror and looking at my own face in it. I realise I'm grimacing a bit. I'm doing that thing I do when I am completely overwhelmed and I can't bear to look at myself any longer. There's a such vivid juxtaposition between the regality of the luxury that surrounds me and the reality of what is happening. The soft, luxurious linen on the beds, the spotless mirrors and marble tops make no difference to this kind of situation. Nothing like that matters when you know you have been raped.

A male producer is in front of me, asking me what has happened. Rylan is standing against the window frame with his arms crossed, his head cocked to the side. He looks frustrated that nothing is happening, that there are no sirens, no policemen. I notice that Ella has appeared in the back of the room and is sheepishly looking around. No one has figured it would be a good idea to keep her away from the situation and it is Rylan who ushers her out.

Another producer arrives. It's Cait. Cait had been so maternal and caring in St Lucia when I had decided I wanted to leave the competition. She was softly spoken and calm. Hers was another face I liked, but a new face all the same. There was no one from my rooted past, not yet. In these early hours, everyone around me was part of The Show, part of the circus.

It gets foggier at this point. The police did come. Not the kind that wear uniforms. The decision was made for me to go back to the hotel where it had happened. I don't know if this is police protocol, perhaps to help a victim recount the way it went? I remember being so scared that they were going to make me go back in that room. Instead, they put me, Cait and someone else from the show (someone who I can't place) in the room opposite. They made us wait in there for quite a long period of time. My brain was spinning. Eventually, a blonde, petite policewoman in plain clothes came in and introduced herself as Micky, my point of contact during this investigation, ascertaining the facts and details to come to a conclusion. Micky interrupted my thought process by saying, 'Our team has already made an arrest and we are very confident we have the right person.'

For the first time that morning, I felt something close to positive. I don't remember what I asked but I had a waterfall of questions for her as I tried to comprehend what was going to happen next. She waited patiently for a moment to tell me just that I would need to give my statement and be as detailed as I could possibly be. She told me how important the early stages of a crime as serious as this are and she asked me if I had showered that morning. 'No,' I said, feeling disgusted with myself. She brought my eyeline up from the floor to meet hers. 'That's really, really good, Lucy. It means that we are in the best possible position for the forensic collection of evidence.'

My blood ran cold. I hadn't considered that my body was going to be the main source of evidence here. It wasn't just the room across the hall, metres away from where I was sitting that was a crime scene – my body was too. The reason I hadn't showered when I got up was because I had no control over what I did then, because of the autopilot, not because I'd thought ahead to the 'collection of evidence'.

★

The Haven is the name of a specialist centre in London for victims of rape or sexual assault. I find the name incredibly ironic because The Haven sounds like a place you'd want to go to. The name makes it sound like wellness retreat in a tropical country, where the linen curtains sway with a sea breeze that drifts through an open window frame, with flaking but charming magnolia paint cracking off it. The Haven sounds like somewhere you go to feel better, to be wrapped up, to be covered and protected and warm. The reality is as far away from those things as you can (or quite possibly can't) imagine, unless you've experienced it.

After Micky had told me that I needed to be examined, she gave us the information for The Haven. Cait and I made our way there. She didn't say it but I knew Cait was aware that we couldn't be seen going there, despite it being designed to be inconspicuous. I didn't have the foresight or energy at this point to consider that the news had already been leaked to the press, but I suspect that she did.

In same way that children describe to you the monster they saw in their bedroom – the sleeve of a jumper hanging from a chair that, to them, was the long, wicked arm of a demon – there are things I remember about The Haven that I know not to be true. At least, I assume them not to be true because, thankfully, I've never been back there. What I can tell you with firm certainty is that being examined at The Haven the day after being attacked in my room whilst I slept was one of the most traumatic things I have ever endured. I've had to use the website to get a more realistic image of the process that's carried out there because for the entirety of what I experienced, I was inconsolably hysterical.

The crisis worker who carried out my examination was a professionally calm and understanding woman who was wearing scrubs and a medical mask. She spoke very softly and slowly and asked for my consent before doing anything. Though I'm sure it wasn't in reality, in my mind's eye, the examination table was a big, steel slab as if in a mortuary. For a part of my time on the table, my legs were in stirrups. My twenty-one-year-old naked, bruised and trembling body was assessed from head to toe, followed by an internal examination. This woman, who had examined hundreds and hundreds of women in the same circumstance, included in her report that I was one of the most hysterical patients she'd ever seen.

Towards the end, she told me that victims of rape were at risk of sexually transmitted diseases and they strongly recommend taking PEP – post-exposure prophylaxis – a drug that, if taken within seventy-two hours of an attack, prevents HIV from taking hold of the body. She said that the side effects of the medication vary from person to person, but can be very, very rough. Even at that point, I was still convinced that I was going to carry on with the show. In my mind, I couldn't risk being ill because that would mean I had to leave the competition. I told her I needed to think about it.

When we left The Haven, Cait and I sat in a café a few doors down. I told her what they'd said about the medicine. I don't know if my clothes had already been taken for evidence back at the hotel or if they were taken at The Haven but I was wearing clothes that didn't belong to me, being mothered by a mother who wasn't my own and trying to understand how the reality TV show I was a part of had become so distorted from my own reality. Running underneath the lights and the TV cameras and the runners and the storyline the producers had written was the storyline of my life, which had just changed forever.

I don't remember much from the days that followed. I was moved to another hotel, the London Hilton on Park Lane, and put in a room on the eleventh floor, with big sliding double doors that led to a balcony. My favourite runner, Clara, had been moved into the room next door. She was northern too. She was small and quiet with mousey brown hair and this gentle, kind energy. She was like a lifeline for me. The police had taken my phone for evidence, so I communicated with everyone through her. I needed Harriet back from Thailand; I needed her to be here with me. Clara had called her and told her what had happened, and she was already on her way. She hadn't enough money to afford a flight back, so she had borrowed it from her mum. When Clara told me this, I asked if *The X Factor* would cover her costs to get back. They said no.

At some point, a female security guard was appointed to stand outside my door. Cait would come in and visit me, just to see how I was doing, but I was mostly silent. Clara would come and sit in a chair by my bed and we wouldn't say anything to each other, we were just there, together. Comforting each other.

Late that night when I was on my own, the security guard knocked on my door. She had her blonde hair tied up in a ponytail and was wearing all black. 'What's going on with you? I'm not being funny but I'm a close protection security guard, I'm normally looking after Saudi princesses or F1 drivers and I'm sitting here outside the door of some

tearaway *X Factor* contestant. You must have been bad.'
I closed the door without saying anything. They clearly
hadn't told her what was happening.

I didn't know this then but that hotel is famous for
suicides, specifically people leaping to their deaths. That
evening, I had to relentlessly shake away the constant pull
to go towards the balcony doors. 'All of this could go away
so quickly,' I thought.

★

In the morning, Cait turned up at my room again. She was
my point of contact for the police because I really didn't
want to speak to anyone I didn't know. I knew they'd
arrested the suspect at this point and Cait had an update.
Lucy, the police have let us know that the . . . man who
did this . . . He is from India. It means that the likelihood
that you have been exposed to HIV is much greater.' She
looked at me with tears in her eyes. 'You have to take that
medicine, Luce. You're going to run out of time.'

I knew that if I took those pills it was all over. Don't take
the drugs and be well enough to continue but risk getting
HIV. Or take the drugs and the show is over, but your body
is protected. Throughout the last four months, I'd been
conditioned over and over to think that this TV show was
the biggest opportunity I was ever going to get. Just like
in St Lucia, if I walked away, I was throwing it all away.
I had done everything I didn't want to do just to stay in this
competition and now it was over. I took the PEP.

Two nights after what happened, Dermot O'Leary
announced live on the show that I was ill for Halloween
Week and that I would be permitted a pass to the next week.

The side effects were horrendous. I was very, very unwell almost straight away. At some point, Cait told me that my mum was on her way to the hotel and I just stared at her. I couldn't think of anything worse than seeing my mum. I don't know why. Maybe because I'd done all of this alone, so much of my life alone. I'd always proved everyone wrong and been the strongest, most independent person in the room. I needed someone but I didn't think I had the kind of relationship with my mum for it to be her. A few hours later, Cait left the room as my mum walked in and grabbed me. We sat on the edge of the bed, she cradled me on her knee like I was a baby again and we neither of us said a word; we both just cried. And then she left.

I couldn't stay in a hotel any longer and I told Cait that. Clara had been absolutely golden to me and I hadn't been away from her for more than ten or fifteen minutes at a time. I didn't want to be without her. She didn't want to leave me either. Cait told me that they were going to move me to an apartment in Westminster and that Rylan was going to come and stay with me. He had told them he needed to be by my side.

On the way to the new apartment, I travelled with the security guard and, without discussing it with either of us, they separated me and Clara, replacing her with two other runners, Saz and Nick. I walked into the apartment. It looked like cheap student accommodation. As soon as I saw Saz in there, I wanted to scream. I had never liked her. She was one of the runners who had always been scolding and dictating. Where was Clara? I did not want to be around Saz, Nick, or anyone else I didn't know. Or in this shitty little bedsit-style apartment, with white walls and sticky IKEA furniture.

I didn't want any of it. The drugs were making me feel so fucking sick. I needed to lie down.

That medicine and probably the trauma made me sleep, and sleep, and sleep. I didn't know what day it was. I would wake up to one of the runners knocking at the bedroom door and announcing the arrival of someone who needed to talk to me. At some point, it was Harriet. Beautiful, tanned Harriet. Someone from my old life. She climbed into the bed and stayed there with her arms around me.

I don't know when it was but the next knock was Rylan. My hero, my best friend of that time. I can't imagine the pain he was feeling inside but he brought his energy, his light and his jokes into that room. He picked up some of the medicine on the side, read the label and laughed. 'These anti-sickness tablets are Domperidone? Fuck off!' He found great irony that the name was so close to the champagne Dom Pérignon. He made me laugh.

In that apartment, I got sicker and sicker. The next Saturday, I watched Rylan's performance on the show. He pranced around, bright and bubbly and brave and strong, and, mid-performance, in front of millions of viewers, he shouted, 'This one's for you, Spraggan!'

Faces that I hadn't met before started to arrive. People in suits. High-ranking people from Fremantle, the company that produced the show, and ITV. They were here to talk business. They wanted to know what I *wanted* to do. I wasn't in any fit state to make decisions, plus, I don't think I had many options. A woman, with short hair and a pantsuit on, asked me if I wanted to talk about what had happened to the press or whether I wanted to keep my right to anonymity. I didn't have the capacity to think about this stuff and I didn't know what the implications of any of it were. I was so unwell and the room was spinning. I sat there, with a blanket over my head, whilst the people in suits stood around, talking at me.

At first, I told them to just tell the truth, to put it out there: the real reason why I couldn't continue. I hadn't really had any time to think it through. As soon as I said that, it was clear, once again, that my decision did not align with the narrative that the production company saw fit. They told me all of the reasons why speaking out might harm my position and they left to let me keep considering my 'options'.

Much like in St Lucia, when I had told the producers I wanted to leave, it was time to help me change my mind again. Once again, it felt like my storyline had already been written. The next knock that woke me was a runner telling me that Tulisa was at the apartment. We sat on the cheap black leather sofa in the living room and she said how sorry she was. She asked me what I was going to do and I told her what I thought. It reminded me of sitting in that little shack on the beach with her and Caroline when they told me exactly what the producers wanted to tell me: 'This will stay with you for the rest of your life.' I was grateful that she'd come to see me but I felt like I had no independent advice, like I was fully out of my depth. I mean, I *was* out of my depth. Nothing could have prepared me for what happened to me and no one else had been through it.

My mum wasn't being kept updated and she was panicking about what was happening to me. She knew I was in London but didn't know exactly where. Despite our complicated relationship throughout my life, she was my mum and she stepped in just at the right time to save the day, exactly when I needed her to. Like me, she had no idea how to deal with the legalities of this situation but she had a friend who she knew could help. Behind the scenes, my mum was trying to rally independent support for me, so that I could be advised properly on what to do next. Her friend had recommended that she speak to a privacy lawyer, Dominic Crossley, and she did everything she could to get in touch with him.

Back at the apartment, I was still on the sofa with a blanket draped around me, pale as a sheet, surrounded by the people in suits who had returned to do more talking, this time with a heap of paperwork that was on the coffee table. I heard a loud knock at the front door then this bellowing voice, posh, like Hugh Grant. 'Where is she?' the voice asked the runner. In walked a tall man with dark brown curly hair, wearing an overcoat over a suit and shiny shoes. 'Lucy.' He put out his hand as he stood in front of me. 'My name is Dominic Crossley and your mum asked me to come here.' He turned around and looked at the people in suits, at the pile of contracts and paperwork on the table. 'I need you all to leave, right now,' he said to them. They all froze like animals in a snare, exchanged looks and did as he said. 'Let's get you to your mum's,' he said to me.

All the time I'd been in that apartment, and to be honest, for the months leading up to it, nothing had felt real. When I'd been on the show, it felt hazy, like it could have been a dream, and now, it felt like a nightmare. All of the decisions that had been made for me had led me to this place; I'd put my life in someone else's hands and here I was. I'd been trapped in a personality-less apartment and was still being told what to do by runners who were not much older than university students whilst my body responded badly to HIV medication. The production company's representatives came into that space and kept asking me what *I* wanted to do. But it didn't feel like I had many choices at all. What did I want to do? I wanted to curl into a little ball and/or throw myself in front of a train. *Do you want to talk in the press about what happened?* I don't fucking know. *Do you want to carry on with the show?* My body is being ravaged by this medication. *Are you willing to sign this?* I don't know what *that* is. There was clearly no protocol for what had happened to me, no guidelines for what to do when a reality TV contestant under the show's duty of care is raped.

I had a lot of things on my mind, things that any victim of sexual assault may well have racing through their heads: what the fuck just happened? Why did that happen? Have I been exposed to HIV? Will he be convicted? Is this *my* fault? I was dealing with the police and I'd provided the evidence, done the interviews. Now, in this apartment, I was asked a new question every few hours. I was asked to make decisions about the rest of my life and about my career.

I was told that the security guard had been appointed to be by my side until the final of *The X Factor*, so she and I and Harriet travelled down to my mum's house from London. In 2012, my mum and Colin had left Buxton and moved to Deal, Kent, so Harriet and I stayed in their spare room and the security guard stayed in a B&B. I was so grateful to be away from the un-reality of it all. The day after we arrived, I wanted some fresh air, to be outside and to feel normal. I thought I was safe there, away from London. Harriet and I, and the security guard, visited Canterbury Cathedral. That place was a familiar landmark from my childhood, calm and quiet, a sanctuary. As I walked down the stretch of tarmac after the gates, I noticed a man taking pictures in my direction with a professional-looking camera. The cathedral was behind me, so I scolded myself for being paranoid and walked away from the direction his camera was pointed. As I did, he started walking towards me at a pace. At the same time, I saw the security guard, yards away, trying to get to me first.

It all went in slow motion as he lifted his camera to his eye. 'Feeling better, Lucy?' he smirked from behind the lens as the flash went off in my face. The next day, that picture was published in print and online newspapers, alongside a bounty of others – images from outside my mum's house, of us getting out of the car in Dover on the way to Canterbury – pictures that showed the paparazzi had tailed us for the entire day, miles and miles, hours and hours, without us knowing.

Dear Lucy,

I'm pretty sure I speak for all the researchers on the show when I say we all felt very responsible for what happened and I think we always will.

We were told not to say anything to anyone – not our families or friends or anyone else on the production about any of the details – but that meant we didn't even talk to each other. We were all so young, just a few years older than you, and I don't think any of us were equipped to really help you.

A couple of days after it happened, there was a meeting with the entire team run by Richard Holloway, who was the head of Thames TV at the time. You weren't even mentioned; we were just told the importance of not drinking when working and, of course, a lot of the team had been drinking that night. I remember thinking how weird it was that we'd all been summoned for this really important meeting but then nothing was said about you.

I felt very uncomfortable about how the situation was talked about, or maybe that should be how it wasn't talked about. I sensed a lot of fear among the people at the top, like they were scared of information getting out.

I knew you needed things like clothes and toiletries, and I was sent out to buy those things for you, but I only really had practical conversations with my bosses. I never heard anyone talking about you negatively but I don't remember people doing very much to offer you emotional support. I know they put you up in the Park Lane Hilton, and maybe they thought that by putting you somewhere swanky they were taking care of you. Mostly it was just you and me in that room – I had my own but I didn't want to leave you alone – and it felt a little bit like we'd been hidden away so decisions could be made without you. We saw very few people from the production team that week, though Rylan did come to visit a couple of times.

Your mum came to the hotel and I sat with her in reception because you didn't want to see her. You couldn't face seeing anyone, not even your mum. Or maybe it was that you didn't want to be seen? I know you did let her in eventually, but I think that was one of the hardest moments that week.

PROCESS

I was so upset that one night, whilst you were having a bath, I went to my own room and called my parents. I just broke down on the phone to them. They drove to London the next day and checked into the hotel next door. I've never told anyone they did that because I was so scared that I'd told someone. I saw them for half an hour before they drove back up north. That's what it did to me, so I can't imagine how you coped.

It was reiterated at another meeting how important it was we didn't tell anyone anything. It was sold as 'Lucy wouldn't want anyone knowing about this, so you could potentially do some real damage if you tell anyone.' Most of us just started crying after that meeting and the abiding feeling among the researchers was just of sadness and guilt.

We were all made to go to a one-off counselling session with the show's psychologist a good few weeks down the line. It was just one session and it felt very much like a box ticking exercise. I know now that's more than you were offered.

I don't think you were in a space to make any reasonable decisions. I remember you wanting to go and get a tattoo only a few days later, but a woman from Syco talked you out of it, thinking you might regret it. I know that's not an important detail but it's interesting that it's what I remember. I think a lot of decisions were probably taken out of your hands, but because I was with you so much in those days, I didn't see what was going on outside your hotel room. I do remember that you didn't want to drop out of the show to begin with. I never knew if that was your decision in the end or if that was made for you.

I hope I helped you that week but I'll always wish that I could have done more.

It's been amazing to see you build your career in the years since. I've watched with such admiration and I've often wondered how different your career might have been if you'd stayed in the show. For many, many reasons, I wish that was the case.

Take care,

Clara

Dear Lucy,

I don't really know what to say.

I don't want to tell you I'm sorry because you spent so long feeling guilty and responsible and I don't want to give the impression that you were ever right to feel that way in the first place. I don't want to apologise just in case you feel like you did something wrong.

There are so many things that change irreversibly once you have been violated in that way. Once someone breaks into your room in the middle of the night, you never quite sleep the same again.

Once you are shown a certain kind of wickedness, you will never forget that it exists and can never trust humans quite the same way you did before.

I wish I had, like so many other times in these letters, been able to swoop in and scoop you up that morning. To take you away from the show, the people, the suits, the storyline.

PROCESS

I wish I had been able to sit by your side and give you what you needed, as opposed to those people asking you what you 'wanted' to do, how you wanted to 'move forward'. The only person who did comfort you was Clara, and she was snatched away from you without either of your consent. The next time you saw her was in 2023, when you reached out and said you were writing this book. It was so good to see her. We went for lunch, and when we parted ways she gave me a pyrite crystal, she said she'd read that it offers protection. Then she said that she wished she could have protected me back then and I told her she really did.

Yeah, it was just a game show but it was also the biggest opportunity you'd ever had and that was snatched away from you – it's only in the last couple of years that I've given us time to mourn that.

I'm sorry for how it followed you around for so long and for all of the ways we tried to hide from the trauma. I know I said I didn't want to apologise but I am just really sorry. For everything.

I wish I could tell you that, one day, it won't be as bad, but I know you wouldn't have believed me.

I love you very, very much.

You deserved so much better.

Love,

Lucy x

An Unhappy Experience

By writing this, I have relinquished my legal right to anonymity more than a decade after the rape. For those of you who don't know, victims of sexual offences have a legal right to anonymity, for as long as they choose to do so. The only way to give up that anonymity is with written consent. By giving up that right, I am intensely aware that I open up the opportunity for people all over the world to discuss what happened to me and that it will probably become a 'story' that is passed from person to person, that the most vulnerable part of my life will become a shocking headline and a link that is sent from friend to friend over WhatsApp.

Over the last decade, many people have told me they are aware of what really happened to me in 2012, some very directly. A journalist from Sheffield sat me down in front of a camera in my dressing room before my show for a 'relaxed interview' and in the middle of nonchalant questions about what it's like on the road, and what bands I'm into at the moment, said, 'I heard you were raped when you were on *The X Factor* and that is the reason you left the show.' A man in a London bar once shook my hand and blurted out the exact same sentence, waiting for my response as if he'd just asked me if I was having a good night. In those moments, the *story* was more important than the fact that I was a human being.

What I want you to remember whilst reading this is that this isn't just a story. This is my life. This all happened to me. When you finish this book – or if you just came here for the previous chapter – please remember that I am real, that it has taken great strength and years of rebuilding to be able to share this with you, and that, when this all happened, I was a twenty-one-year-old girl.

Dominic Crossley, the lawyer who had burst into that horrible little apartment – in my mind's eye, wearing a superhero costume – unshackled me from the runners that had been appointed to me and shooed the legal representatives from the show out the door, then very calmly, and very unbiasedly, explained my legal options and rights to me in a way that no one else had. In the UK, an individual with the right to anonymity must not be named or identified in or by the press, either expressly or by implication. Nothing can be published which is likely to lead to any member of the public being able to identify the victim. There are many reasons why a victim's right to anonymity is in place. Over the previous two weeks, I'd been repeatedly informed what everyone else *thought* I should do and was told plenty about the repercussions of telling the truth right then and there. It's something you can't retract: once the right to anonymity is relinquished there is no rewind button. I considered that then and I've considered it every single day whilst writing this book.

The announcement of why I was leaving the show was time sensitive and the public would need an answer. I couldn't just disappear. From the viewer's point of view, the show had given me a pass to the next week of the competition. This was the production team buying time to work out what the fuck to do.

It was decided that I would not tell the truth about why I had left the show and it was announced in the press, and live on television, that I would not be continuing due to 'illness'.

I don't remember being hugely involved in the excuse decision making process but what else could they have said, really? It needed to be vague enough for there not to be too many questions but believable enough for the public to accept it.

I don't know how much the story of what had happened to me was worth in financial terms but it was sold, or leaked, to the papers – allegedly by someone within the Metropolitan Police – within hours of it happening. Reddit, Digital Spy, Twitter and all of the other gossip websites started to flood with rumours of what had happened to me, of which hotel it had been in – details that should never have been public. I don't know if it was *The X Factor* or Dominic Crossley that instructed specialists to enforce my right to anonymity but when they did, it was quite something to witness. As the speculation on discussion forum webpages went up, they were pulled down. Tweets containing my name and allegations of what happened to me disappeared. It was quite amazing, really; I had no idea that this kind of thing could be done.

Not everything was caught in time, though. In the weeks that followed, my dad, who I hadn't had much contact with over the years, had been trying to call me. He wanted to know what had happened and where I had gone, but I wasn't in the right frame of mind to pick up. Searching for answers, he took to the web forums, where painfully descriptive stories of what happened to 'X *Factor*'s Lucy Spraggan' were being posted.

One day, I did pick up one of his calls. I had never heard my father cry until then.

'I just want you to tell me one thing.' A breath caught in his throat and his pitch went up, 'Is it true?'

'Yeah,' I said, and I heard a crash of something being thrown across the room on the other end of the phone. Then I heard a noise that sounded like a scene from a wildlife documentary: a primal, guttural cry, the kind that a buffalo makes when it watches helplessly from a distance as a lion kills its young. The line went dead.

The police arrested and charged the hotel porter almost immediately due to the evidence that was available. Thank God. Privilege sounds like an odd word to use when talking about sexual assault, but an arrest and charge *are* a privilege that not many victims are afforded. The court case began quickly.

In this country's courts, we have public galleries to ensure a 'transparent justice system'. It means that any member of the public can be present for a court case. During the trial of the man who attacked me, the entire gallery was full of press. All the transparent legal system did for me was ensure that very, very private information about exactly what happened to me was dictated directly to the people who wanted to hear it.

Because the defendant pleaded guilty, I did not have to be present for the trial, which I am incredibly grateful for. I couldn't have sat in the same room as that disgusting human and listened to his defence lawyer. I don't think I could have been in court whilst all of those journalists ferociously scribbled down notes for their 'stories'. It harrows me that some victims do have to be there. His defence in court was that he was 'a man floundering in a culture which he hadn't quite come to terms with'.

At the sentencing hearing in April 2013, after the judge had announced the defendant's ten-year sentence and deportation to India upon release, he directed his attention to the gallery and said, 'If any of you allude to or speculate the identity of the victim of this crime, you will face being charged with contempt of court. Let this be known.' It turns out that they didn't care very much about that warning.

Straight after the verdict, my closest friends and my family didn't know what had happened, but if you were reading the right online newspapers, you did.

At least, you knew it happened to someone that sounded very closely, but not explicitly, like it could be me. The press shared sensitive information and evidence from the trial for everyone to read, as if it was light fiction. They had found pictures of the man casually posing outside Buckingham Palace. The only way I can describe how that felt, and still feels now, is soul-destroying. It's like the feeling when someone reads your diary or goes through your phone but times 10 million. A feeling of infiltration of privacy and exploitation of vulnerability. I would never have shared that information and no one else should have been able to.

When I use my name to book a table at a restaurant, or it flashes up on the screen at the doctor's, lots of people study it, look at me, then back at my name, and then say, 'Lucy Spraggan – are you the girl off *X Factor*?' That has happened ever since 2012. It's pretty mad to think that something as personal as the name I was given when I was born, the one I had for twenty-one years before the show, ended up being synonymous with a TV show. And, by default, synonymous with what happened to me. I thought about changing it for a while because every time someone asked if that was me, it triggered that chain reaction.

I've had to lie, almost every single day since. When I'm introduced on a podcast or written about in the paper, it's always, 'Lucy Spraggan, who quit the *TXF* due to illness.' People still ask me why I left the show. And with each lie came a flood of extremely painful memories. It's not good to lie, to hide, to harbour. But that is why we're here. I have spent ten years in my very own prison, a small box, nodding my head in agreement to a narrative that I didn't even choose. My storyline: I want to set the story straight.

It happens less now but when members of the public asked me, 'Why did you leave the show?', it was usually very genuine. Some people would joke or scold me: 'Must have been a pretty fucking bad hangover to miss out on that opportunity. What a waste!' That always stung. But when a journalist asked me that question, I knew they had an ulterior motive. They would quiz me about my 'mystery illness' and I would know that they knew just as much as I did about why I left.

Do you know what? My experience was fucking awful. It has been a terrible thing to live with and was a hideous thing to endure. But being in the public eye has meant that every time I spoke to a journalist and they repeatedly asked me vague-but-not-vague questions, which I quickly learnt to sidestep, just in time for the next re-phrased one, I knew that what they really wanted was for me to relinquish my right to anonymity. Every time they have asked me their version of the same questions, they have inflicted more pain.

In 2013, on the day the judge sentenced her daughter's rapist to ten years in prison, a journalist offered my mum £35,000 for an exclusive. She put the phone down on them.

In 2014, in response to a press release for my upcoming album *We Are*, my manager received an email from a popular newspaper that breached a low I didn't even think was possible: 'Unless Lucy is willing to talk about what happened in 2012, we wouldn't be willing to interview her in relation to this album.' They never gave a shit about me being ready.

To them, the fact that a twenty-one-year-old woman had been raped was a 'story', an 'exclusive', a chance to get one over on their rivals and win bragging points with their editor. A chance to expose *The X Factor* or, in the actual words of a journalist trying to get the story out of me, to 'take down Cowell'. Even when they were nice to me, it was an attempt to coerce the truth from me, and some of the methods they used to extract the headline they were after were pretty despicable. Like turning up at mine and Ben's house, handing over a business card and offering to 'beat any price *The X Factor* has paid for their silence'. No one paid me for my silence; as a matter of fact, I paid a price to stay silent.

In 2014, I'd been out drinking all day in Brighton and a woman befriended me. She joined onto the group I was out with and appeared to be getting more and more drunk as the day went on. She waited until the group had disbanded and just she and I were left. Both of us were sat slumped against a wall in the smoking area on a roof terrace of a club. She started to divulge her deepest, darkest (almost certainly made up) traumatic secrets to me, and then asked me, 'What's the worst thing that's ever happened to you?' The security guard who had been quietly chaperoning me noticed a red light in her breast pocket and approached her. She was using recording equipment. When asked what it was, she got up, sober as a judge, clearly not drunk at all, and left very quickly.

Honestly, it was masterful how some journalists could phrase a question without actually using the language that would get them in trouble. And occasionally they were completely brazen and asked me outright, but off the record so no one could prove they'd asked. In the summer of 2013, just before performing at V Festival, a very well-known journalist approached my dressing-room cabin, which was home to not only me but my band and crew too. She spotted me and walked right up to the door, almost like she was going to walk right in.

'How are you doing then, Lucy?' she asked. There was a woman I didn't know standing beside her.

'I'm doing great, thank you,' I said, at this point unaware of the intention. I considered this to be too out in the open even for a journalist of this calibre. There was an awkward pause and I instantly knew what was coming next.

'No. I mean, how are you . . . *really*?' she said, with a gaze fixed on me.

My crew in the room behind me sensed the shot of ice that whipped up my back and I felt them stop what they were doing and turn to see what was wrong. Time slowed down as she waited for me to answer. Tears pricking at the backs of my eyelids. Why was she doing this? Why here? Why now? I had a huge show in a couple of hours.

I could see Ben walking up the path towards the cabin. He would have absolutely no issue with telling these people to 'fuck off' on my behalf. But he was just a little too far away to see what was happening.

'I don't know what you're talking about,' I replied, taking a deep breath and pushing off the door frame, turning my body away from her.

She snorted a nasty little laugh. 'Of course you don't.' She smiled sarcastically. 'Never mind then!' She looked at everyone in the team, shot one last look at me, and turned away to walk down the path.

And it wasn't just journalists. A greatly disliked former winner of another reality show sent me a DM on Twitter, out of the blue, saying he had 'found out what happened in 2012' and was about to 'announce' it. He wanted to know if I would like to 'make a statement' before he did. Clearly not only a cunt but a stupid one. I sent proof of his threats to Dominic Crossley, who responded with our own threat of legal enforcement: contempt of court carries a ten-year sentence. Dominic had become accustomed to doing this by then. Lots of newspapers had flown so close to the sun whilst reporting on me, but not using my name. Remember, it was illegal to even imply it was me. And yet under the headlines it would read: 'a twenty-one-year-old, female, reality TV contestant, made famous by a song'. The full truth was kept out of the papers and the mainstream media. It was still out there and whilst most people didn't know, plenty of people did, and lots of them made that very clear.

Wherever I went for work, whether I was in London at my management offices, or in the Sony building, I would walk into a room and have to deal with the fact that – possibly, probably – the people I was meeting knew what had happened, yet we had to spend the entire interaction pretending that it hadn't. That fucked with my head a bit. *Do they know?* It definitely impacted the choices I made and the way I conducted myself. I always had my guard up. And that sort of thing can shape an entire career.

I sometimes wonder what those journalists, or the trolls on social media, are doing now. I hope they've had daughters since. I hope they put them to bed and looked at their sleeping little bodies and know that I looked like that once.

None of the Twitter trolls or journalists have ever faced any consequences for their behaviour, even though they *must* have known that every threat, every blatant attempt to extract my truth, or oh-so-innocent suggestion transported me backwards.

★

I always knew that one day I'd talk about it but for years, I didn't want to. I wasn't ready. I watched the rise of the Me Too movement in 2017, when it became even more clear how many women had a story to tell. But I just couldn't bring myself to tell mine yet. Like many – most? – rape victims, I was scared of what people would think. I was *petrified* of what people would say. I was so fearful of being 'That Girl' so early in my career and for that to be what I was known as for the rest of my life. I stayed quiet and I got to work to show people who I really was. In 2021, six albums into my career, and after years of touring around many parts of the world, I told myself: 'If my next album makes it to the top ten in the UK, I will get serious about writing this book.' *Choices* charted at number five and in the video I put up that day, thanking everyone for their support, I was incredibly emotional. When I watch it now and see the tears roll down my face, the shortening and staggering of my breath, I can see how scared I was to know I'd finally be doing this.

Truthfully, I've been terrified of being seen as an attention seeker. Or finding out that it was actually all my fault. Or that new information would appear and his conviction would be overturned. I know now that these feelings, along with guilt and shame, and the belief that you deserve what happened, are very common amongst survivors. After nearly a decade, those feelings have started to loosen their grip but they haven't gone entirely. The difference is, these days, I have the tools to manage them.

If I hadn't gotten sober, if I hadn't started therapy, I would not be in a position to tell this story. It took years of pain for me to know that when a man lets himself into a paralytic twenty-one-year-old woman's hotel room in the middle of the night, using a master key, to carry out a prolonged sexual assault, it is only the fault of the man who made the decision to do that. I should harbour no guilt for what happened. And yet, sometimes, I still do.

My friends hate it when I say this but I consider myself to be a 'lucky' victim. I am luckier than so many other women when it comes to the evidence presented in my trial. The fact that my rapist had used a traceable key card to enter my hotel room. The DNA. The bruising. Lots of things that other rapists fail to leave behind. I consider myself lucky because there were so many catalysts to the evidence of that man's guilt that he was convicted and sent to prison.

But that's not why I call myself a lucky victim: I am a lucky victim because my door was locked.

I call myself a lucky victim because if the door hadn't been locked, there may have been no conviction. There may have been a level of disbelief. A level of blame. They might have even asked what I was wearing.

I am a lucky victim because if I'd have been just another unconscious drunk girl on a sofa at a house party, or in the back room at a nightclub and not behind the locked door of a hotel room, a lot of people would have a different view on what happened to me.

I have listened to people's opinions on drunk women who are sexually assaulted and I've had to remove myself from those conversations. I've had to talk myself down from becoming a screaming, shaking oblivion of fury in response to the way that people talk about victims of rape. Through listening to people, reading articles and paying attention to societal narratives, I've learnt that their perception of rape is different dependent on the setting in which it took place.

Often, when I have told my story to a friend, the outrage

of a man letting himself into my locked hotel room has superseded the fact that he did so to rape me. I am a lucky victim because there is proof my door was locked. I am lucky because my friend locked it.

When I walked into my hotel room on holiday in Malta in 2022, I realised my first-floor balcony door's lock was broken. I told the man on reception. He came to the room and told me: 'Malta is very safe, you do not need to lock this door.' I nearly went fucking ballistic. He argued with me for nearly an hour about the fact I did not need to lock that door. When I got back to the UK, I was livid. I told a male acquaintance about the argument in passing. 'Fucking hell!' he said. 'Of course you need to be able to lock the door in a hotel – you have passports and stuff in there!' I told him that the passports would probably be the last thing a woman thought about. Lots of my male friends don't like to acknowledge their male privilege but this is a great example of that. The passports, the money, the gadgets – if someone breaks into my room, they are welcome to those things. I can get most of that stuff back. A lot of men have never considered the sinister risk that comes with being a woman.

Whilst it was offered to me like it was my choice not to talk about it at the time, my silence was extremely convenient for a lot of people, most notably the producers and broad-casters of *The X Factor*. It's my belief that *The X Factor* (and that includes Syco, ITV and Fremantle) handled it all very badly.

I also believe that they are all, in part, responsible for

the deterioration of my mental health afterwards. I was not offered support. As a matter of fact, until I started writing this book, I had never heard from anyone behind the scenes of the show ever again. I was let down so badly.

No one ever contacted me to ask if I was OK. No one ever followed up after three agonising months – the time it takes for HIV results to come back. No one called or emailed when the trial was over and he was convicted. No one offered me rehabilitation or ongoing mental health treatment. No one contacted me years later when I spoke openly in the press about my suicide attempt. There was no corporate shift within ITV when Caroline Flack died to repair the historic trauma that happened to people on their shows.

No one came to save me: I was on my own from 2013 onwards.

The night my *X Factor* audition aired, my life completely shifted. I was given an opportunity. I saw that fame as a little jetty I could push my rowboat off from and out into the big, wide world of showbiz. But on another evening, a few weeks later, it was all ripped away. All those opportunities dissolved. The jetty crumbled. The rowboat sank. No one threw me a life jacket.

I have not been able to say the word 'rape' for ten years. I have not been able to see rapeseed oil in a supermarket, drive past a field of rape, watch a film with a rape scene in it, hear a jibe about a 'Facebook rape' or read about any kind of sexual violence in the news without being 'triggered'.

We all have different words that trigger us. You now know mine.

Some people who have lost family members to illness can't hear or say the word 'cancer'. Some families that have suffered miscarriages or lost a child cannot bear to look at, or acknowledge, other people's living children. You might read this and think of your very own example and you might not.

Some people use the word 'triggered' as an insult. It's used in memes about people who hear something they don't like or agree with, and react in an explosive way. They were 'triggered', someone might say, mockingly. Some people even set out to find out what 'triggers' someone else and use that information to cause harm. Some people even find that funny.

I'm going to explain why I do not.

I understand why we call it a trigger because hearing certain words is a bit like a gun going off. With a gun, you squeeze the trigger, and a series of events happen. The trigger releases the hammer. The hammer hits the primer at the base of a bullet, which explodes and ignites the propellant, which drives the bullet down the barrel of a gun. There is a loud bang as the bullet is sent towards its target.

A few years ago, I was fishing at a very peaceful lake in Cheshire with my best friend, Josh. We sat about six metres apart, deliberately too far apart to talk as tranquillity is part of the experience of fishing. Being able to concentrate on something with no other distractions or interruptions around you is a bit like meditation.

I was watching my float bob calmly on the rippling water when my entire existence was shaken by what I can only describe as a huge flash that I felt with every single sense in my body. I *saw* the flash, I *heard* the flash, I *felt* the flash. I smelt it and tasted it at the back of my throat. But I still had no idea what had happened.

Milliseconds later, the barrel of a long, sleek, double-barrelled shotgun appeared in my peripheral vision, the butt of the gun still positioned high up on a farmer's shoulder, his eye looking down the aim.

'Fucking herons,' he growled, then fired off another round, right next to my ear, before I could even put a hand up to cover it.

I was completely stunned. Not stunned by what had happened, stunned like I'd been actually stunned. Tasered. I couldn't register it. I could see the event unfold but it didn't make any sense. Both of my ears were ringing so loudly that the only thing I could hear was my own breath. The birdsong had stopped. My heartbeat pulsed behind my eyes and I could see tiny shapes flickering with each beat. My ears were hot and there was a small delay in what I could see. Like when my eyes moved, my brain took a while longer to swing my vision around.

The farmer grunted, lowered his gun, turned on his heel, started up his quad bike and rode away into the woodland. I turned to Josh; his face was a pale, wide-eyed mirror of my own.

'What the fuck just happened?'

This is what being triggered feels like. It is the perfect metaphor because when that shotgun went off, it sparked something freezing cold and terrifying in my very core, and I feel that same rush of panic, and the same physical sensations, just by hearing the word 'rape'. This is the legacy of sexual assault that most people don't realise and even if they do, they belittle it.

It doesn't even have to be the word 'rape'. I recently got a DM from a stranger saying she'd worked in a hotel in Shetland where I'd requested to have the bed put next to the door 'so that you could fall into it pissed when you got in'. It chilled me to the bone. That wasn't why I'd requested the furniture to be moved.

I always asked Ben to ask for right-facing rooms so that when I walked in, the TV was on the right, and the bed was on the left. But it was never because I wanted to fall into the bed drunk. It was because I was raped in a left-facing room. In a locked, left-facing hotel room. A locked, left-facing hotel room at the end of a narrow, long corridor. The last room on the left. At one point, I couldn't get myself past the threshold of left-facing rooms.

To this day, hotels which have familiar décor to *that* hotel – similarity to its carpets or doors or panelling – can stop me in my tracks completely. A long corridor can cause me to physically fold. It feels like I've been punched as soon as I walk out of the lift. A left-facing room can set off a mental reaction that I can't control. The times that I've been allocated the last room on the left of a long hallway, which coincidentally happens so often, it feels like all of the blood in my body drains out of my feet. Patterned carpets and walls merge as my vision blurs and my legs drag underneath me, like I'm staggering through quicksand. My heart beats so fast and so loud that it feels like it might implode. My entire being gets filled with a panic I can only describe as primal. A panic that insists I escape, that I remove myself from the immediate danger. A deafening yet inaudible alarm fills not only my ears but all my other senses. A frenzy replaces every rational thought in my head.

When this happens, I have to acknowledge the feeling of the bag in my hand, I have to let my eyes focus on something recognisable and control my breathing. I have to bring myself back to where I actually am.

I am in a different hotel, not *that* hotel.

This is what PTSD is. And when you're not prepared for it – when it just slams into your day without warning – it's unbearable and unfair and it's exhausting.

My job is to tour, so I stay in a lot of budget hotels. Ask any touring artist if they could do what they do without budget hotels and they'll tell you they can't. If I can, I stay in serviced apartments or an Airbnb and when I can afford to, I stay in boutique hotels which are far less likely to have the traditional layout. But my first choice, on the bigger band tours, is to stay on the bus. I might be in coffin-sized cot but I am surrounded by my team. My safe, trustworthy team. In 2015 I bought a campervan and have had one ever since, almost always feeling safer sleeping in that, whether in a car park or campsite, than in a hotel.

I had a lot of issues, like most of us do growing up, before *The X Factor*, but what happened prevented me from fixing those problems; it delayed me for years and years. I had no space to heal because I was constantly trying to claw back what I had lost.

And I lost a lot.

★

You might have noticed that I haven't talked very much about the man who committed this crime. I find it hard to. Like you, I have never been able to relate to his actions or to be empathetic towards his choices. He did what so many men have done to people all over the world. It was calculated and it was reprehensible.

I don't want to think about whether or not he is sorry. I don't want to know either.

When another human has destroyed a part of you, a part that will never return or be fixed, sorry is not enough. Maybe some victims would cope by hoping that their rapist has been changed by what happened, too. They might hope that either the act they carried out, the punishment they received or the shame they experienced changes them so that they will never inflict that kind of evil on anyone ever again. They might hope that their crime makes them feel as sick as it does them. That's not how I feel. I have forgiven many people in my life but not him. In many religions, forgiveness is paramount, but not mine. Truthfully, I hope that the repercussions for his disgusting actions have and will be karmically delivered, and will continue to plight him for the rest of his life. I hope he experiences trauma as deep as the kind he inflicted on me and I have faith that the stars have already aligned in that way.

He will soon walk free. The judge ordered him to be deported upon release but I don't know if that will happen. The reality is that, due to my job, it would be very easy for him to find me if he so chose to. Anyone can see my social media and anyone at all can find out when and where I am playing a show. If he felt that his punishment was not deserved and he has spent the time in prison plotting against me, then I could be an open target. There are so many things I've considered.

Writing this has not been easy. I have put every ounce of strength I can muster into telling my story and at times it has pulled me back into a darker place. No matter how many times I have written the word rape, I am not immune to its power to wound me. It's still hard for me to say out loud. However, I hope that by sharing this, I might make it easier for other victims to find the right words to tell someone else what has happened to them. And I hope that, like me, it leads to them shedding their guilt.

In my opinion, the worst moment of my life didn't happen to me because I was drunk and alone in a hotel room. It didn't happen to me because I wasn't looked after properly on the show. It didn't happen to me because of Simon Cowell, or anyone else, bar that one man. Ultimately, it was all down to choice.

It happened because some people in this world choose to be fucking horrible creatures.

Everything we do is a choice. Regardless of pressure, or culture, or education. Our actions are all preceded by our choices.

Through my horrendous experience, learning this also exposed me to a contrasting fact that gives me faith every single day: some people in this world choose to be kind. They choose to care, to change, to nurture and to heal. Look for them, and be one of them, regardless of what happens to you.

Dear Lucy,

It took you more than a decade to talk about this.

You were ten when you moved to Buxton; ten years later you went on the show and all of this happened, and ten years after that – here we are. Seems like no time at all when you put it like that, but it is. It happened one third of our life ago.

I wonder how many times you had to lie about what happened. I know it's got to be hundreds of times, if not thousands. 'I was ill' even started to seem real to you.

People would ask 'But what kind of illness?' and I remember wondering whether they'd ask a work colleague, a stranger that they'd never met, why they weren't at work last week.

It's always been strange to have people think they deserve an answer to that.

You were punished for not telling your story earlier and I am so, so proud of you for enduring and waiting until YOU were ready. For not giving in to the bullying. You didn't deserve that punishment, the backs that were turned on you or the ultimatums that were given to you by the press.

I wish you could see what that did for you. Instead of giving in, you built this incredible fan base, you talked openly about your struggles with mental health and, more importantly, you persevered. I don't know how. You created everything you have now on your own.

If they give you nothing, they can't take anything away from you.

Incredible work, you.

Love,

Lucy x

All or Nothing

'£74,000 all on red!' I was leaning over a roulette table in London's Hippodrome Casino as every single person in the room whipped their heads towards me to make sure they'd heard me right.

'£74,000 all on red.' I was using a stool as a crutch to stay upright.

Standing next to me by the green felt table, his mouth open and pure bewilderment across his face, was my tour manager, Ben, and my newly acquired band (who I had literally met that day) – my bass player, Matthew, and my drummer, Alex, both of whom were wearing confused smiles, as if someone had just told a joke that they didn't quite understand.

Up until then, from what I recall, I had been on a relatively standard night out in terms of the amount of chaos I had left in my wake. Although, we were in a casino, and I've told you what that means: I must have been kicked out of a bar or club nearby and was so pissed I couldn't get in anywhere else. Or it's so late that a casino is the only place that's still open and serving alcohol. And that means I'm late-night wasted. Either way, me being in a casino is bad news.

Between 2013 and 2015, I experienced some of my most intense battles with depression. Perhaps during this particular bout, when I wasn't truly experiencing highs *or* lows anymore, just a muted mash of indifference, I was looking for something to make me feel more alive. Or, at the very least, just make me feel *something*.

The croupier, with his hand on the edge of the roulette wheel, about to spin it, said, 'For high stakes bets we need to notify the floor manager.'

I always admire how nonchalant croupiers are. They must watch people lose their life savings on a pretty regular basis. I always wonder if they think all people who gamble are fucking idiots because the croupiers know – more than anyone – that the house always wins. But whatever it is they are thinking, you'd never know, because they have this wonderful talent of keeping their faces in a neutral, ventriloquist dummy-esque expression and their body language gives away nothing as they float their hands about like a close-up magician.

'She is *not* betting £74,000.' Ben instantly looked sober.

The croupier looked back at me. How did a twenty-one-year-old idiot have the very precise figure of £74,000 to gamble away at a roulette table?

I was the last of a rare breed in my industry and in 2013, when I signed to Columbia Records, I was given an advance. A pretty decent advance of £75,000. Nowadays, it's rare to see an advance like that in music, especially as a new artist, but I'd been in the great position of being seen as hot shit after my stint on *The X Factor*. At that time, I had absolutely no concept of the value of money. When I auditioned for the show I was broke. Something strange happens when you go from being skint to being, well, rich. As I mentioned earlier, when my audition aired on the television, I had an album online. In the 24-hour period that album was on sale (before I was told I had to remove it to continue in the show), I made £56,000.

I went from genuinely scraping together 50p coins to make my rent at the end of the month to having enough to probably buy a one-bed flat in the area in which I lived overnight.

I remember meeting Louis Tomlinson of One Direction not very long after that £56,000 had landed. I can't remember who introduced me to him but we were in a dimly lit Mayfair bar. Before whoever it was could say 'Louis, this is Lucy', he told me he was a big fan of my audition, which blew my fucking mind. One D were huge at this point and every time someone famous acknowledged my existence it tied my mind in knots (though none were as mind-blowing as when Lily Allen tweeted that I was like a younger version of her).

Louis asked me what I wanted to drink and I proudly told him to keep his wallet in his pocket because this round was on me. He tried to insist but I, looking a bit like an emoji with stars for eyes, told him: 'I have just made £56,000.' He laughed, patted my shoulder and let me pay for the drinks.

I now know what that laugh meant. From a man probably deep into his millions by then, it meant 'you have no idea'. And I didn't have any idea. To me, I was a millionaire now.

To me, £56,000 was like winning the lottery. Like I was made. £56,000 was, and is, a LOT of money. But then it was an inconceivable amount. Like the feeling of being given a twenty-pound note when you're six years old, times by hundreds. Or thousands.

I'd love to know how many lottery winners invest their winnings and end up with a successful stream of passive income, enough to supply them with a healthy salary for life. I'd bet on it being very few. The thing is, a regular working-class person only comes across tens of thousands of pounds in one of a very few ways: winning the lottery, inheriting money from the death of a family member you knew nothing about or claiming compensation for an accident at work. Or, if you're lucky, being mis-sold PPI. Oh, yeah, or going on reality TV.

I know people who have inherited large sums of money or property from their parents or grandparents. As well as the money itself, the privilege that is passed down with generational wealth is decades of financial knowledge. It's how the rich stay rich. Buying and selling property is in their blood, medium- to high-risk share ownership is commonplace, managing business and tax implications are all part of their lives already. I'm from a household that was visited by bailiffs; I was raised by a single parent that cast FINAL NOTICE letters aside and who told us to tell the companies that phoned the landline that she wasn't in.

When I was handed £56,000 it seemed to me that all of my problems had been solved . . . I was rich now. It didn't cross my mind that not every transaction from here on out would be this substantial, but why would I question that? In a few short weeks I went from struggling to pay my

£75-a-week rent to buying a member of One Direction a drink in a dimly lit bar in Mayfair. Fast forward to 2013, less than one financial year on from that first cash injection, and I was being signed to Columbia Records for £75,000.

So, alongside the big-headedness that comes with a successful *X Factor* audition – one that many reality TV contestants have suffered – my head had ballooned three extra sizes because I now perceived myself to be unfathomably rich. The Hippodrome casino in central London is not a good place to learn you are wrong.

The croupier ignored Ben. I was quite clearly the one in control here. In control of the purse strings, I mean. I was obviously not very in control of anything else. With his hand still on the roulette wheel, he beckoned a man in a shiny grey managerial-looking suit over to our table, which had now amassed quite the audience, to give me the green light for a high-stakes bet. Ben turned to me, my eyes swimming about in my head, barely able to meet his, and pleaded with me to think about what I was doing. What the fuck *was* I doing?! I still can't tell you to this day. I don't know where the thought came from; I don't know what I was trying to prove, or whether the point to be proven was to myself or to other people.

I don't remember everything from that night but I do remember the sharp seriousness in Ben's face. It made me want to do it even more. The man in the suit asked me how much I'd like to bet. The croupier had not spun the wheel since I had made my intentions known; I was adamant that his next spin would land on red. I knew it from the very deepest part of my soul. But it had to be *that* spin. He had to hold the table until I put my bet down. And here I was with the manager, the only man who could press the 'yes' button and let me put my money where my mouth was.

The croupier, who had begun our interaction with non-judgemental eyes, definitely developed a bit of a menacing smirk at this point, clearly on the side of the little white ball settling on black and not red. He looked at the manager, who was side by side with Ben, willing to let him spin the wheel. The manager looked directly at me and spoke to me in a soft voice with an empathetic look which he must have refined over the years. Both he and Ben talked to me as if I was a terrorist, my thumb hovering over a little red button that could only lead to catastrophe. This tag team of sensibility somehow managed to talk me down.

'Maybe you could bet £1,000,' one of them said, which I clearly liked the sound of as we shook hands in agreement.

There was an audible, collective groan, a bit like air being gently let out of a set of bagpipes, as the crowd realised the show was going to be a bit more like fireworks at a local cricket club in Peckham rather than outside the Bellagio on Las Vegas Strip. They still watched anyway. A thousand pounds on the line. All on red.

'No more bets, please.' The croupier effortlessly drew back the wheel and let go.

No joke, that was the longest I have ever seen a roulette wheel spin. After what seemed like about twenty years, it started to slow and the little white ball began to duck and bob three, four spaces at a time. It took on a life of its own, reversing backwards and then jolting forwards, each time it fell onto a number falsely implying that would be its final resting place. It settled on black. And then red. And then black. And then, dink, dink, dink.

The ball sat in red thirty-six. Staring at me.

The table erupted with cheers. Even the croupier gave me a nod of support. Ben, Matt, Alex and I rejoiced with glee, the manager seemingly disappearing into thin air. I was paid out £2,000 in fresh fifty-pound notes, each thousand in its own little clear blue bag. I tipped the croupier £50. I tipped our taxi driver home £50. Up until then, I'd probably only ever seen two *real* fifties in my life. It just felt like Monopoly money.

What's worse? Losing £74,000 on a roulette table or knowing you had £148,000 in the bag all along? I still don't know.

Moderation is a skill I have struggled so hard to grasp since, well, since I can remember, really. I have always found it hard to moderate, whether that's with alcohol, food, work or other humans. I've partied, eaten, worked and loved very hard throughout my life, but not always by choice. And moderation really is a skill. Up until a year or so ago, I didn't know what it even felt like. I didn't know that there was an option between ALL or NOTHING. When I quit drinking, I didn't moderate. I quit. That's why it worked for me. Because the option I chose there was 'nothing'. I'd done the 'all' – I drank to oblivion and one day I woke up and said, 'No more of that now' and my inability to moderate thrived. For the first time, I consciously used my 'all or nothing' as a superpower. I put my 'all' into cutting out alcohol. I couldn't cut *down*, so I cut it out. What I didn't know at the time, though, was that my issue wasn't with alcohol. It was with moderation.

PROCESS

I think it's important to document how I've learnt some moderate habits and, by discovering and harnessing my extreme side, I've also used my 'go hard or go home' attitude to my advantage. It's also important to be honest with you and tell you that, if you also have this affliction, I'm not sure it's completely possible to go from being an integrally extreme person to a moderate person. I think you can learn to moderate parts of life. You can adopt a savvy, moderate angel to sit on your shoulder and whisper pieces of sage advice to you in impulsive moments, but there'll always be an extremist devil inside you whose first instinct is to go balls deep on everything, every time.

Join the Club

As 2012 was ending, I was already in a very dangerous mental space. *The X Factor* final had been and gone, which meant ITV's contractual duty of care was up, so the twenty-four-seven close-protection security guard that had been appointed to me in the immediate aftermath of being attacked was relieved of her duties. Just like that, I was left alone for the first time since it happened.

When you leave a reality TV show, there is a process waiting for you. There is work to be done, money to be earned. And in those specific post-show months, you are a glowing, honking, golden goose. A cash cow whose moo can be heard for a thousand miles. Everyone around me in a professional capacity knew what I had been through weeks earlier. Quest, the management company I had been appointed by *TXF*, Columbia (the record label), my agent (the company that books shows) and the production team all knew, but no one said: 'Hey, Lucy, do you think we should look at doing this differently to other people who have come off the show? You've been through a lot.' By December 2012, not even two months after the attack, I was doing up to four public appearances every weekend.

The final show was due to air on 9th December, 2012 and I was contacted to be given the option to join all of the other contestants for the finale. I didn't want to, of course I didn't, but the narrative that had already caught alight and spread was that I'd left because I thought I was 'too good' for the show. If I didn't turn up for the last week, I'd be the only one who wasn't present. Eight weeks after the biggest trauma of my life and I was defending my public image. I had been since the morning after it happened.

I opted not to join in with the group singing of the 'I Wish It Could Be Christmas Every Day' medley because I didn't wish it could be Christmas every day; I wished that time would reverse itself and I could go back to how it was before. I wasn't the only contestant who didn't want to be a part of the performance, so I didn't stand out. It was a strange experience, being there in Manchester's Central Arena back with all those familiar faces. Contestants, producers, runners, judges: they had been cogs in this abnormal juggernaut that, for me, had malfunctioned and derailed so badly, spilling its oil and corrosive contents all over my future. I still wasn't well, either. I had reacted badly to the PEP and my mental health was at an absolute low. I was drinking and eating excessive amounts, piling on weight.

I was also invited to join *The X Factor* tour in the coming February, which would visit arenas all over the country, but as they were offering a mere £500 per show, along with the fact I couldn't think of anything worse than doing it, I said no. *The X Factor* reminded me that I was actually contractually obliged to do the tour, but that they would kindly afford me the right to say no. How lovely of them. Again, in what looked like a desperate bid to feed the narrative that the problem was all me, when it was announced that I wouldn't be there, ITV's website ran the headline: 'Lucy Spraggan: "I am not doing *The X Factor* Tour." The singer-songwriter pulled out of the show four weeks into the live episodes after being ill for two weeks.' To the public, another typical, obnoxious move from Lucy Spraggan. Who does she think she is?

As soon as the show was officially over, I booked flights for me and Harriet to get out of the country with no return date. I needed to leave reality behind, or whatever reality had become for me. I had to leave the UK at the very least. We flew to Thailand, where she had been teaching, then on to Malaysia, Japan, LA and California. When we arrived in Thailand, we booked something similar to an Airbnb, a tiny little IKEA-esque apartment. I always thought the symptoms I experienced in that apartment were the side effects of the anti-HIV medication, but now I don't know how much of it was just sheer physical exhaustion and stress. I spent most of the time lying on the laminate floor, wrapped in a blanket, in 40-degree heat. It wasn't an enjoyable experience, running away from my problems, but I do think it helped. It reminded me of what it felt like to be anonymous. That, actually, what was happening back home wasn't everywhere and that it was escapable; it didn't have to be my reality.

Until, that is, I was in a tiny village in Thailand, in a bustling traditional food market, when out of nowhere, someone tapped me on the shoulder. When I turned around, a British family of four with their camera pointed at me said, 'Are you Lucy Spraggan?!' I looked into the lens as the flash went off.

I couldn't tell you where I was that Christmas or New Year's Eve because, honestly, I don't remember much of that trip at all. I ended up in Vegas, briefly, expecting to be relatively unknown there, but due to the number of British tourists, that wasn't the case. I was crossing the road on the Strip when a young man, covered head to toe with tattoos, pointed a finger at me and said, 'Are you Lucy Spraggan?' in a strong Irish accent. I told him I was and he asked me if I wanted to party with him. His name was Buttsy and he was a drift car racer for Monster Energy and a stuntman for the *Fast & Furious* films. It's funny how sliding-doors moments like that carve out parts of the future: not only did I end up partying with Buttsy at the rapper Coolio's house, Buttsy was also the reason I met my future ex-wife.

Early 2013, I was travelling the world and it should have felt good, like a once-in-a-lifetime opportunity, but I was numb. I yearned for a place that I'd feel comfortable in, moving from country to country to find that. But the misery followed me wherever I went. So did the drinking. And so did the drugs. Misery loves the company of those two things.

I knew I had to come back at some point. I had to go home and make a record and start touring or I'd have nothing. Where was home? 'Do I go back to Sheffield? Buxton? The Corinthia?' I asked my management. They organised for me to move into an apartment in Commercial Street in east London.

I've been feeling under the weather, there's a big, black cloud and it's hiding me from me. I'd never trade in my guitar for an umbrella, but I let it go, let it go, let it go.

So, I leave 10,000 miles between me and the place I know, I ride a moped through small alleys, so I can come back home. I will accept the wind and rain – I'll be back in a hurricane. Wait for me, wait for me, it's not too late for me. I'll be back in a hurricane.

('Wait for Me' from Join the Club, 2013)

When it came to playing live, this wasn't going to be my first rodeo. Using the contractually appointed agent and a grassroots promoter, we organised my first ever headline tour for 2013. Albeit a run of only 150–300 capacity nationwide venues, but there were more than twenty-five of them, and they all sold out immediately. There were people who wanted to come and watch me play, even though I had been gone.

It seems a bit naïve that I hadn't considered how hard I would find staying in hotels after what had happened to me. I skirted right over the intensity of that issue. As did the rest of the team. And, Jesus, touring was expensive. Even whilst travelling in the back of a van there were so many overheads, and there was definitely no tour bus at this point. Tickets had been cheap, so it meant that the tour just about covered its own costs. Payment for Ben as tour manager, Alex the drummer, and Matt the bassist, hotels, catering, fuel, van hire . . . It meant that there was no element of luxury. It was budget hotels and tiny, damp dressing rooms. This is where the signs of PTSD started: I'd be given my key card at check-in and walk along the corridor, chasing the numbers down the wall, odd, even, odd, even, trying to anticipate which kind of room I'd get and how far down the hallway it would be.

If I'd checked in before sound check and knew that I was going back to a left-facing room, I would drink myself into oblivion after the show and be carried back to it by Ben. Back into the vulnerable position I'd been in before: drunk and unconscious, alone in a hotel room. I didn't know that I could ask to change it.

Whilst recording my latest album, *Balance*, at the back end of 2022, I stayed in a few Airbnbs in Swords, Dublin, and went through my ritual at each one: checking the doors and windows, ensuring I knew where the light switches were in case I needed to jump out of bed and turn them on, getting a kitchen knife from the kitchenette and leaving it close to my bed so that it was easily reachable if needed. Oh yeah, I still haven't been able to leave behind the issues I have. No matter how many good people I meet, when I am alone and in the dark, I think about the bad ones.

From a business perspective, the first 2013 tour was a roaring success. All the tickets had sold out, merch was flying and the fans were engaged and eager for more. They were an intense bunch, in the best possible way. An army, right from the get-go. On a personal level, I was nose-diving. I'd gotten into the idea that being rock and roll would act as an appropriate barrier from the truth – that I was in a very dangerous frame of mind. My drinking was becoming more and more out of control. But, personal problems aside, it was time to record my album. The show must go on.

A few months before starting the album recording,

Columbia thought there were a few songs missing so they coaxed me into my first ever co-writing session. I didn't think I needed to write with anyone else; I liked the songs I'd written myself and writing with other people was new and outside of my comfort zone, which was probably my biggest turn-off. But when I heard that this session was going to be with Preston, the frontman of the band The Ordinary Boys, I lost my shit. I was a huge fan of The Ordinary Boys' music but mostly of their British, punk, I-don't-give-a-fuck attitude.

Living right up to my expectations, Preston was the coolest person I'd ever met. As well as being the most talented musician and songwriter I'd ever encountered, he was unashamedly, self-assuredly out of control. He was covered from head to toe in scribbled tattoos, little random doodles and colourful, messy writing. He was fashionable in a way that I hadn't seen anyone be fashionable before: he made everything he wore look cool. He could pull off grandad slippers and a fez if he'd wanted to. I idolised him. A decade my senior, Preston saw a lot of himself in me, I think, and I wanted to be him. We shared the way we expressed our pain. He knew about fame. He knew about drugs. He knew about rock and roll. You can imagine my excitement when I was told that Preston was also going to co-produce my debut major album, *Join the Club*. We were to spend more than a month, together with James Flannigan – the shit-hot producer-of-the-moment – in the iconic Wendy House studio in Shepherd's Bush. THIS was more like it! We could get whatever we wanted delivered to Wendy House; you could just press a button and someone would come and see what you wanted. My lord, we pushed that button a lot. Bags and bags of takeaways, unlimited crates of wine and beer and blizzards of cocaine.

After its release, I read a review of *Join the Club* which mentioned that the vocals in the song 'You're Too Young' sounded rushed and messy. I'm not surprised. I recorded that vocal at 1.30 a.m., completely off my tits on coke. Every time I hear that song, I can see my twenty-two-year-old self in that booth, teeth stained from red wine, frustrated at not being able to keep the pace of my mouth in time with the lyrics in my brain. It was undeniably one of the most rock and roll (in its most traditional sense) times of my life. A few years after recording the album, Preston fell from the balcony of a hotel whilst intoxicated, shattering his pelvis and breaking most of the bones in his body. He survived, just about, and worked on his relationship with intoxicants. One more reason why I still think he's the coolest person I know.

The album was released and charted at number seven in the UK. It was a crazy experience. Music videos being filmed, going on TV shows, photoshoots, styling, live streams with fans at Sony HQ, red carpets. It's all kind of exactly how you'd imagine it. I was a bona fide popstar. Every day, a car showed up with one of the management team already in it and I just got in and did whatever was on the agenda that day. Everyone said 'yes' all the time. I was distracted and delighted in the frenzy of it. And yet, out of nowhere, I would often break down. Sometimes I'd burst into tears, sometimes into rage, sometimes into silence. I started getting these headaches behind my eyeballs. But drinking made all that go away.

With every album comes a tour. After the success of *Join the Club*, the agent and promotors decided to step up a gear and ramp up the size of the venues. This wasn't anything like the tour before – everything was being done for me. A bigger band had been put together; there was a lighting engineer, a set designer, sound engineers, a tour rep and a tour bus. I couldn't believe it. I kept having these life-affirming highs – the bigger venues selling out, the tour bus, the team – but they were countered by these life-shattering lows. I didn't know how to navigate any of it.

After the first night of that tour, I got so drunk I didn't remember anything I did once I got back on the bus. The morning-after anxiety was crippling. Proper beer fear. Ben told me I'd been 'a bit of a dick' (which I guarantee was an underestimation) and that I needed to apologise to a couple of the new band members. I felt so shameful but I kept doing it. Night after night, I got so fucked after the shows. Blackout fucked. The rider had a different bottle of spirits on it every night: tequila one day, whiskey the next. I decided to ban myself from drinking spirits, thinking that must be the problem, I told myself I got so drunk because of *what* I drank, not *how* I drank. I'd chug bottles and bottles of red wine to myself. One morning, I woke up in a bunk on the tour bus and realised I'd pissed myself. I needed help. I couldn't carry on doing this.

I called my manager at Quest and she told me to visit her in the west London office on my day off. As I walked in, a man with floppy brown hair and half-asleep eyes was walking out, wearing a big green parka. He recognised me and put his hands out, palms facing upwards, 'When you gonna have a number one then, our kid?!' he said, in a nasal,

Mancunian accent. I knew that Quest managed Beady Eye but had no idea that Liam Gallagher knew who I was. More surrealism. More rock and roll.

The good news was my manager, a middle-aged, upper-class white woman, who drove a Lexus and collected art, had a remedy for my predicament: 'It's a little clinic on Portobello Road; you're going to see a private GP. I've booked you an appointment with a lady who has looked after me.'

I told the private GP everything. That I was desperate and needed to stop the drink, the drugs, the chaos. It was all too much. I was scared of what I was capable of. Instead of observing that I was in crisis, or recommending going to rehab or cancelling the tour, that private doctor prescribed me a plethora of drugs to plaster over the deep wounds I had presented to her. Fluoxetine (Prozac) for the depression. Beta blockers for the anxiety. Xanax for the edge. And Antabuse for the drinking. Antabuse, if you don't know, is what they use to treat alcoholism. If you take Antabuse, drinking alcohol will make you violently sick. I started the Prozac straight away, as if something magic and dramatic would happen as the tablet slid down my throat. This day stands out to me as a catalyst for the next few years of disaster.

They say I need this, they say I am not OK. I said,
'I can't read this,' they said, 'take it anyway'.
('Prozac', from We Are, *2015)*

I carried on touring. The thing with Antabuse is that you have to take it for it to work. I think I lasted a day. The doctor didn't think to mention that drinking on the Prozac would increase the blackouts and, of course, she didn't need to tell me Xanax could be abused. I was already very aware of that when she prescribed it to me. It wasn't that I didn't want to get better, I just couldn't do it. The pressure I was under was so immense.

I cheated on Harriet on that tour. The girl who had come back from Thailand and put everything on hold to come and rescue me. Any opportunity to find a high, I'd take it. Playing to thousands of people, drinking straight after the show, taking drugs and sleeping with the support act. The tour rep who had travelled on the bus with us quit, telling Ben that he'd been on tour with Marilyn Manson and I was worse.

When I returned from tour, I decided that I didn't like living in London. Preston and I had stayed great friends after the record and he told me he'd quite like to move back to London. One day, we both packed our apartments up into vans and swapped dwellings. I moved into his flat in Brighton and he moved into mine in London.

Whilst living in Brighton, just before my twenty-second birthday, I bought myself a dog. A brindle, black and white Boston terrier. I'd wanted a Boston terrier since I was little and I'd always wanted to call him Steven, after Stone Cold Steve Austin, the wrestler. So, I did. Steven was both amazing and awful in the way that puppies are. Challenging, sharp-toothed, flip-flop-destroying bundles of absolute joy and despair. I adored him with my entire heart from the moment I saw him and from then on, we were inseparable.

I started getting tattoos, quite a lot of them. To begin with, getting tattoos was an attempt to cover up the parts of me that I didn't like. The parts that were vulnerable. Lots of my body is covered in dark, black artwork, and it's not how I'd physically present myself now, had I the chance to make the choice again. My tattoos were a way for me to look meaner and harder because I felt like I needed to be those things to feel protected. To keep people away. I'd lost so much of my identity, my trust and my softness that I started to present myself as tough, or what I thought tough should look like.

The first significant purchase I made when the money from *Top Room at the Zoo* landed was a tent. I went to Decathlon and spent hours picking out a big, multi-room, family-and-friend-sized tent because that is who I am. I would do that now. Now, I drive a van and I camp a lot. But during 2013, and for the next few years after, I lost myself whilst trying to reclaim who I was. I started buying things to project an image of myself because the parts of me I used to value had gotten so small. I bought Rolexes (I know), a white Mercedes and branded clothing, all in an effort to try to pass as successful and happy and complete.

I don't do that now. I know that the version of myself that is projected out to others comes from the way I conduct myself and the words I use. My tattoos serve as a reminder of who I have been, or who I have tried to be. I still get the odd tattoo now and again – small things, reminders, like the word 'yes' on my forearm and the word 'run' on my ankle.

I got dropped by Columbia once the album and tour were done. It hurt at the time but I've come to learn that's what happens in my industry. It is a rarity for a major label to stick with an artist. My album had gone silver after selling 60,000 records but it was nowhere near matching the amount of money Columbia had spent on recording, marketing, promotion, videos – and probably the cost of all of that food, wine and cocaine that Preston, James and I ordered via the landline at Wendy House. What no one told me, and it seems incredibly irresponsible of me not to have asked where the bill for everything went, was that all of the shit we ordered went on my account at Sony. Every day a car would take me from east London to west London, taking an hour each way. I didn't know any different. I still didn't know how to get the tube. I recently got access to an online Sony portal where artists can see how much money is still recoupable by their label: ten years on, after years and years of sales and streams, I still technically owe Columbia £150,000.

Spotify, as of right now, says that 'Last Night' has had nearly 50 million streams and 'Tea and Toast' is at 10.5 million. They're just two of the songs from that album. It says an awful lot about the music industry to know that it's unlikely that Columbia, or I, will ever make money on those recordings.

I stayed on the Prozac for three months and during that time, for the first time in my life, I was completely unable to write songs. I wasn't told this when I was prescribed them, but antidepressants are renowned for dulling creativity and causing writer's block. It made me even more miserable. I came off it, cold turkey style, in the summer of 2013. Again, I didn't know that doing that could make you ill. I vividly remember the side effects of coming off it so quickly, but not being able to understand why they were happening.

PROCESS

Just before my set at V Festival in August 2013, St John's Ambulance was called to my dressing room because I was experiencing what I described as 'brain tremors' and 'electric currents zapping my head'. After that set, I got so drunk that I refused to leave the festival with the band and the driver, despite Ben pleading with me to do as I was told. Instead, he and I got stuck into the festival as punters. I blacked out and woke up in the tent of a journalist I knew, thankfully with Ben. We had to ride a public bus back from the festival with all of the other punters.

> *Label you then leave you,*
> *No they won't stay for the fight,*
> *It's the closest thing to empty,*
> *And the furthest from alive,*
> *I got what I asked for,*
> *Now I'm lonely and I'm tired,*
> *I am hurt,*
> *And even worse,*
> *I'm uninspired.*
> *('Uninspired', We Are, 2015)*

Operation Self-Destruct

It was early 2014 and Lloyd and I had been on a big one (Lloyd is the blond-haired friend that you met in the Earl of Doncaster at the beginning of this book). We'd had very little sleep, if any at all. At this point, I could not bear to be alone. The silence that came with being by myself scared me so much that I knew it just wasn't an option. If I didn't have someone with me, my thoughts could overwhelm me so quickly, like a flash flood. Steven made life so much better but when I was intoxicated, my need for other humans was overwhelming. For me, the worst time to experience the silence was right before I went to sleep, so my options were to get so fucked that I'd black out and fall unconscious or, if I'd been on drugs and was going to lie in bed awake, writhing and thinking about how to kill myself, I'd need to find somebody else to lie next to, to prevent action.

That manifested at the time as a bit of a Tinder addiction. I'd scour the app for a girl who was around and who wanted to party so that I could at least be around the comfort of another body, even if it was one I didn't know. This particular Saturday night we ended up in Oxford. Lloyd had to work in the city on the Sunday morning, so I knew I'd be alone the next day. My Tinder date for that night didn't pan out as planned. We'd been banking on her knowing a local dealer and as the coke started to run out, I knew the panic would rise with the sun in the early hours. The baggies were empty, ripped open and scoured for every last microgram. It was time to concede to bed. I writhed around sleeplessly, trying to bat away the demons that started to creep in from the dark corners of my mind. I used to spend hours and hours doing that.

Despite having done my fair share of it, I've never really understood coke. It's the go-to of the drug world for most casual drugs-users. I've always felt like coke is the drug without an actual high – like, as soon as you do a line, you're chasing the next one. With most other drugs, like MDMA or even mushrooms, you're up until you come down. With coke, it's like you're coming down as soon as you're up, but, God, is it moreish. If you haven't done coke and can't relate, I would best describe it as eating an entire family bag of Haribo, waiting twenty minutes, and then craving to eat another family bag of Haribo. Then another. There's no real point of satisfaction, or if there is, it's fleeting, which I guess is what makes it so addictive. I would get so drunk I needed to sober up, and coke makes you feel more sober, and then I'd drink more so that I would be able to sleep. I do have a friend who told me that proper cocaine, like the stuff he tried in Columbia, is nothing like the drugs we have here. He said he had one line and was up for three days, had the best time of his life. I guess I'll never know.

At about 6 a.m., I said goodbye to Lloyd. As soon as I heard the door of the Airbnb slam, it's as if a timer started to count down towards something very sinister that was somewhere deep inside my mind. Immediately, I knew I had to leave right then. I remember having the 'I need to leave' feeling for the first time when I was primary school age. If I was at a sleepover and I woke up first in the morning, I'd see and hear my friends around me sleeping, and everything would be quiet and calm, but I would get this overwhelming sense that I needed to escape with immediate effect. To leave right then and there.

Have you ever walked into the road without looking, accidentally stepping right in front of a car, then, at the very last minute, you were able to pull yourself back from the road and out the way? You know that instant feeling when you realise the danger you have put yourself in and the ice cold of adrenaline is shooting up your body, the most primal part of your brain setting off a siren, a scream, to warn you of the emergency? When the door clicked shut and I knew Lloyd was gone, all of my senses were overwhelmed by that feeling but on a magnitude I had never known was possible. This feeling I had was worse than anything I'd ever experienced before and the force of it was getting greater with every second that passed, like it had fallen on top of me and I was pinned beneath it.

I grabbed my bag from the Airbnb and put Steven in the car, on the passenger seat. My emotions became fire ants and were crawling all over my body, biting and injecting their venom into my bloodstream. It was spreading. I was running out of time. I needed to get home, now. By getting in that car, I, in no uncertain terms, put not only myself but other people at risk. But, that morning, I had lost the ability to make considered decisions for me or for anyone else. My wheels spun as I pulled off; my head was sweating. I used the buttons on the steering wheel to try to call Ben, over and over. But it was 6.15 a.m. on a Sunday morning; he wasn't going to be awake. I frantically, desperately, called other people, some I didn't even know well, but no one picked up. Tick, tock, tick, tock. The timer was counting down to something.

By the time I reached the M40, I knew I was going to kill myself. Knowing you are going to kill yourself is different to wanting to kill yourself. I didn't *want* to kill myself; I didn't consider killing myself. I just needed to die. It's a very strange feeling to explain but it's quite as simple as that. There were no other thoughts. It was like everything I had been through had been growing silently, like a tumour inside my body. That morning, that tumour erupted into a pure desperation and panic. The only understandable message I could discern from my brain was that to die was the only way to stop it. I could hear a high-pitched white noise. It felt like screaming for my life but being unable to make a single sound. Like the rational part of my brain had been obliterated and I was paralyzed from the neck up. A computer that has too many applications open at once, crashing, and failing, and spiralling. Oblivion. The fire ants were chewing and the toxins were rushing towards my heart.

I was just a rubber band that had stretched itself as far as it could possibly go, and I had snapped.

My brain, much like it did when approaching those left-facing hotel rooms, had turned into liquid. Alphabetti spaghetti. There were no words, just sobs, as I gripped the steering wheel and put the accelerator all the way to the floor. The engine roared and the speedometer shot up. I felt the car lunge forwards, like I was goading it and it knew exactly what I wanted. Sobbing in a way that I have never sobbed again since, my breaths between the sobs shallow and barbed, I looked at the central reservation. I closed my eyes, I took off my seatbelt and went to turn the wheel.

Dogs do this thing when they're playing, when they want you to know that they aren't being serious. It's like a little fake sneeze. They push air out of their nose and throw their heads forward in an effort to say, 'It's OK, I'm yours, I would never hurt you.' Sometimes they do it mid-play fight with another dog, with their front legs outstretched and their head close to the ground in a play-bow. It's their way of demonstrating that there's nothing to fear.

As the timer counted down the final ten seconds to what I had realised was to be the end of my life, everything slowed right down. The seconds were heavy. I felt suspended in nothingness and numbness as I waited for the car to connect with the metal railing. Until I heard this noise. This sobering, familiar noise that cut through the static and the panic and the relentless oblivion.

A fake sneeze. My eyes shot open. Sitting in the passenger seat, his eyes fixed on my face, was Steven telling me the only thing I needed to hear in that moment: 'It's OK.' At the very last moment I could have, I yanked the steering wheel in the opposite direction, almost losing control of the back of the car, and cut across three lanes onto the hard shoulder. I sat there and cried. I cried, and cried, and cried, until I couldn't cry any more.

I can't tell you what it's like to die. But I can tell you what it feels like to need to die. Sadly, this wasn't the last time I'd be suicidal.

★

When I finally got back to Brighton, I went straight to see a therapist. I broke down, hysterical, and I told him everything. He let me talk and, once I was finished, he very calmly and very kindly told me that he specialised in CBT and that, right then, I was in crisis and he did not have the resources to be able to help me. My face burnt. I was so embarrassed. He began to rummage in his drawer for some leaflets about where I could go but before he could hand them to me, I was already out the door.

That year, 2014, was probably the toughest year of my life. What happened on the motorway that morning just outside of Oxford was the only conventional attempt I've ever made on my own life, but it's clear to me now that I made so many attempts at dying since that, they just looked different. The flagrant disregard that I had developed for my own life and safety should have terrified me, but I was still numb. I was like a balloon that someone had let go of, floating off into the sky.

★

A couple of months later, still in early 2014, and Ben and I wanted a weekend of carnage. Carnage we got. Way beyond the realms of the carnage I anticipated. Our flight to Amsterdam was delayed, so we sampled one of every beer Manchester Airport had to offer. We were having so much fun we nearly missed the flight. Oh, how I wish we had.

It surprised me how much I was recognised in Amsterdam. Apparently, the Dutch watch a lot of British TV and *The X Factor* was popular there. We were supposed to watch HAIM play at Paradiso that night, but the flight delay had meant we arrived just as they were about to do their encore. We were gutted. What's the next best thing to do in Amsterdam? Drugs.

Within the hour, we got hold of a few grams of MDMA. Before my life got swept up into hurricane-like chaos, I'd always been quite sensible with drugs. It was rare for me to take too much; even as a teenager, I'd take a pill and then I'd wait until I'd come up before I took more. I always stayed hydrated and had been prudent about who I bought drugs from. By 2014, this had changed. I'd started doing lines of coke that were extraordinarily large, like the whole bag at once. I'd buy drugs from people I'd never met before; I'd swallow little rolled-up Rizlas of far too much powder. I had formed a habit that was indicative of my blatant disregard for survival and, in effect, was not dissimilar to actively trying to kill myself. I was kind of making a passive attempt at my own life every time I took drugs. Like a bully, I was provoking my body to have a reaction, an overdose, all in the name of fun. The numbness was so present in my life at this point that I had to be extreme to feel just a little. Unflinchingly taking lethal amounts of drugs just to see how it would play out didn't feel like an attempt, but it was. 'Go big or go home,' I'd say.

PROCESS

That night, doing my knife-edge dance, I took an entire gram of MDMA in one go. That's about five times more than a normal dose. Ben had his own baggy and hadn't seen me take mine, so I imagine he took a safer dose. He and I sat on stools at a high table in The Bulldog, a pint of beer each in front of us, waiting to come up. About an hour later, I was mid-conversation with Ben when he interjected and said, 'Lucy, you aren't making sense.'

I didn't know what he meant. I tried to ask him but noticed I was struggling to string words together. 'You are slurring so badly,' he said and I looked at him, because the way he was talking had changed now. I saw his eyes roll back a little bit, then focus back on me. He was coming up, hard. I felt my eyes start to drag back into the top of my own skull. Fucking hell, this shit was strong. Both of us were trying to tell the other one something but our jaws were starting to clamp shut. MDMA makes you gurn. Uppers in general set off a compulsive desire to grind your teeth and, as we know for me at least, make you develop a bit of a claw hand. We had to get out of the bar. We were rushing. Not like 'in a hurry' rushing, physically rushing. That's what you call it when you come up hard. You lose control of your eye movement and endorphins start to envelop your body like a warm hug made of gold leaves, as wildly intense as panic but as full of love as your first relationship; worries and pain evaporate, euphoria rains down in their place and you float. You just . . . float. We were floating.

Ben had taken a relatively normal dose and I could see that he was fucked. We had both become clouds, existing suspended in the sky, best friends with the sun that was shining on our smiling faces, not a care in the world, not a thought in our minds. I imagine the people of Amsterdam are used to seeing tourists that look like they've just left a lobotomy unit. Space cadets. We were in orbit.

I don't actually know how or when we got separated because my memory becomes partial after The Bulldog. I wish I had more information for you – well, I wish I had more information for me, to be honest – because the repercussions of that night were fucking stressful. I don't know in what order things went down that evening. In the memories I do have, I don't know if it was dark or light and I don't recall looking at a clock. I cannot tell you which of these things happened first or last, or if what I remember is legitimate, so forgive me if I'm vague. I don't remember any of this in the normal way I recollect memories. I don't see any of it from my own eyes; I see it as if watching it back on TV, almost as if it was filmed by one of those body cameras that bouncers wear.

I joined a cult that night. The memory is of me in a room, potentially an apartment, with perhaps ten or fifteen people wearing baggy, robe-like tops. I was sitting on a wooden chair with my bare feet in a washing up bowl of soapy water, and someone was rubbing/washing my feet. I might possibly hold the record for the shortest ever cult membership, given that I wasn't aware that I'd joined a cult until I saw a £600-ish payment on my bank statement months later. I managed to trace it back to a bizarre, half-arsed spiritual organisation but by then I had much bigger worries. I wish I could I tell you that was the biggest expense of that evening. It was not.

I remember being in the foyer of a very grand hotel.

Chandeliers and gold architrave, an ornate glass reception desk and concierge pushing those metal-framed luggage transporters around, wearing all the fancy get up.

I remember being on the back of a moped, shoeless but wearing a helmet.

I remember walking down the street with a man. A slightly overweight, tanned guy, maybe in his thirties. I remember a blip of a conversation. His name was Luciano – I remembered because it was so close to Lucy. I remember kissing that man.

You're probably shocked to read this. Imagine how I feel! They call MDMA the love drug because of its ability to make you experience (what feels like) overwhelming love; your brain floods itself with nearly all of the serotonin you have, all at once. On MDMA, you don't have to have had any previous interaction with a person in order to feel like you are legitimately in love with them. I don't recall any emotions from that evening, so I can't tell you for definite that I was experiencing that, but judging by the fact I'd necked a whole gram, and this man, I'm going to assume I was.

I remember being in a quite fancy hotel room with that man and he was wearing a white dressing gown.

My last memory, the only one that I know the order of, is of being reunited with Ben, in a park, in the dark. I distinctly remember his eyes – his pupils were like dinner dishes, black and round and huge. Somehow, I had shoes on.

We had plans for the next day but I was completely unmovable. If you've never had a comedown from MDMA, then, take my word for it, you've done the right thing. That serotonin that your brain used to make you feel on top of the world? That's all gone now and you have none left. Your brain feels dry and dehydrated, your body aches from the tension in your muscles, your jaw hurts and, in my case, there is a whole lot of doom about the parts of the night that are just large, black voids.

Fast forward to October 2014, six months on from the Amsterdam mess. I received a WhatsApp message from a Dutch number, from a man claiming to be Luciano. He said that he had taken a video of the two of us having sex in a hotel and that someone (a journalist) had offered him 3,000 euros for the tape. I have no way of knowing if this was ever true or not, but after the intervention of my lawyer, Dominic, (and Interpol, the international police), he retracted those threats and said he would not make the video public. And that's as much as I ever knew about that. The work Dominic did across this was far more expensive than what the man was allegedly being offered for his alleged tape.

I still can't find the words to describe how any of this felt. I felt very sick. I felt full of shame and guilt. I felt powerless. Panicked. Traumatised.

★

In 2014, I was suicidal. Everyone has a different understanding of the word suicidal. I realised a while ago that there isn't just one kind of suicidal, and that being suicidal feels different to every person. The one defining thing that binds all suicidal people together is that they all actively know or have known that they want or wanted to die. I have nothing but deep sadness and deep under-standing for anyone who has been suicidal and even more so for those who succumbed to suicide. I hope this chapter helps you realise that some of the things you are ashamed of in your life were just parts of your process. Just things you did to survive.

Dear Lucy

I don't know if maybe a little part of you had always considered suicide as an option.

The first song you ever wrote was about suicide, remember? Your uncle and your maternal grandmother died by suicide. Maybe it's in our blood?

> *'My eyes are fixed to the ceiling as you stare at my face,*
> *your heart's in your throat,*
> *you wish you weren't in this place,*
> *because my expression is angry and my lips are blue,*
> *please remember it was never you.'*

I've got theory about being suicidal: once you've been there, if you were lucky enough to make it out alive, there is a part of you that will always consider suicide as an option. Like an outfit that you once wore that now sits at the back of the closet, waiting to be worn again. I know that sounds very dark, that's because it is. Everyone has a friend who at primary school got a little bit of pencil lead stuck in their skin and it's still there, decades later, a little black mark just underneath the skin, a reminder of times past.

Since being sober and having therapy, it got a lot easier to stay alive, but sometimes, even now, out of the dark, our brain sends me a little reminder: you could always kill yourself.

The trick to staying alive is to override that voice. My motto in life? Don't fucking kill yourself. If we can adhere to that simple rule, we're going to be OK. The motto makes it sound a lot easier than it is, of course.

As for Amsterdam, I want to tell you something that you didn't know for a really long time: it's OK.

You and I both know why you were taking the sheer volume of drugs that you were and the irony of that coming full circle, making yourself vulnerable to another man, wasn't lost on you. I know how broken you were during those years and, that night, if you did have sex with that guy, it's OK. Simple as. You felt the most intense shame about all of that for years, and I mean years. Shame of not knowing, shame that you were in that kind of mess after what had happened to you.

You wondered that, if it did happen, maybe there was a part of your subconscious that wanted to reclaim control or make you feel like you had control? I'm not sure it really matters. If that is how it went, you weren't in a position to make consensual decisions anyway, and I'm really sorry I put you in that situation again. The shame had me consider whether or not I'd include this episode in this book, but I want to be clear, it's here for a reason – shame breeds in the dark. It suffocates in wide open spaces.

The involvement of the press wasn't surprising. You figured, if there was a video, it would be used against you if you ever told your full story, or perhaps even used as leverage to prise your story out of you. Well, who knows the truth? I certainly don't, and I have made peace with that.

I want you to know that I'm not ashamed of you at all. I am unbelievably proud of you and of everything you have ever overcome. You did not have the resources to process any of the trauma that you experienced, but you tried. The drugs, the blackouts, the behaviours – they were all part of your process.

You did the best you could.

There are some bad people out there, I'm sorry they let you down.

Love,

Lucy x

Lesbian Warp Speed

I got married when I was twenty-four years old. I don't have enough fingers to count the reasons why that was not a very good idea.

As with most decisions I've made in life, I look back and think, 'Well, what did you expect?!' The older I get, the more I realise that in a few years, I'll revisit some of the decisions I'm making right now and think, 'Well, what did you expect?!' What you expect to happen and what *is* going to happen will never, ever be the same thing. Despite making countless guesses, I have never once correctly read the future.

To me, life in general feels a bit like throwing darts in the dark. When the lights are on, you have a good look at the target and decide where you intend your arrow to land. The lights go off and you think you still know the general position of the dart board on the wall, and you might have relatively good aim, so you throw with your best intention and hope that one of the tips lands in or around the bullseye. In the dark, you might even be confident that you scored a triple twenty, only to turn on the light and see a dart hanging out of the skirting board. I've always moved forward with the best intentions, aiming for the right things, only to end up absolutely fuck all near where I thought I'd be. When I got married, I threw a dart in the dark, hoping it would land in the bullseye of happily ever after. I missed, smashed a window and dropped the rest of the darts I was holding.

I am in no way going to make any excuse for the fact that, in the end, the way I behaved resulted in the ending of my marriage. I played a massive part in the breakdown of it, too. I promised myself that I'd be incredibly open with you about everything in this book, so that is going to include the fact that I had an affair. Your opinion of me probably just plummeted reading that one line. Especially if you have been cheated on in the past. There is absolutely no excuse for the damage that I caused and for the decisions that I made at that time in my life. I didn't just hurt my ex-wife; I damaged the very infrastructure of our lives and the plans we had, and it had a wider impact on our family and friendship circles. I don't have any excuses for it. I don't have lies that I tell myself (or others) to make it seem like I had no other choice but to be unfaithful. The only thing I have is an explanation of my thought processes at the time, a retrospective analysis of the reasons behind those choices, and genuine remorse for all of the pain I caused to everyone around me.

Had I known what I know now, if I'd had the coping mechanisms and ability to set boundaries, I would not have acted the same way. I've heard a lot of people speak about being cheated on; I've listened to the impact it had on them and it's only ever emphasised the guilt that I still feel about cheating. I've tried to speak in depth to other people who have cheated and, mostly, they are reluctant to talk about it. I think most people who cheat don't want to accept that their actions were wrong. Once you accept that what you have done is wrong, that leaves space for shame to rear its head, and most people will do anything to steer clear of shame.

I know that I will never be unfaithful again. That is not a preface, just in case the next woman I marry is reading this chapter. That is something I know deep in my soul. I now know how to say what I feel, and I didn't then. I know how to walk away from relationships without throwing a grenade into the situation and turning my back on it as it explodes. I know that relationships don't have to be in tatters and ruins before you call it a day, but I do understand why I thought that was the case. I want to explain what happened from the perspective of the person in the wrong because it's rare to hear it that way round. I guess I should start from the beginning.

When I met my ex-wife, Georgina, who we all called 'G', it was clear that things were going to move extremely quickly. We were the definition of a stereotypical lesbian relationship. For those of you who don't know, a lesbian relationship moves at superspeed. Approximately three months of hetero time = one year of lesbian time. When most heteros are considering meeting each other's parents, us lesbians have already moved in together, have adopted multiple pets and have matching tattoos. Things are almost always very intense, very quickly.

On 12th April, 2014, Ben and I got out of a taxi at a bar in Kensington just in time to see Buttsy, the drift-car racing friend I had met whilst crossing the road in Vegas, whose thirtieth birthday it was, standing atop a table, shaking a bottle of champagne and spraying it across the room. I had a hangover so bad that I had missed two trains and had to keep my head tilted slightly to the left to prevent my headache from making me puke, so I slipped around the edge of the champagne spray and headed to the bar for a hair of the dog.

This bar was an island in the centre of the room, oval shaped so that the bar staff could serve 360 degrees around it. Frosty beer taps with rubber mats at their feet stood atop the bar between the servers and the thirsty people. Cocktail glasses hung above and light filtering through them set up a kaleidoscopic lightshow at the moment I locked eyes with a very beautiful blonde girl standing opposite me on the other side of the oval bar. It was intense and direct, as though everything else in the room had been muted.

As if it was a film, our gaze was interrupted by the barman, asking what I'd like. I quickly ordered, trying to look past his head to make sure she didn't leave my eyeline, but as he turned away from me to pour my drink I looked back for her and she'd gone. I spent the next hour looking around for the blonde girl with the round eyes and the white smile who I'd shared more than just a glance with over the bar.

Despite the hair of the dog, the hangover was developing, and I was struggling to get into the party mood. I told Ben that I was going to get going. I reached for my coat from the back of a chair and, as I turned back around, the blonde girl appeared right in front of me. I lowered my coat back onto the chair and adrenaline surged through my body as I took my opportunity to start a conversation with her. My hangover floated off as we flirted but I felt completely out of my depth. She was beautiful. The eyes that had captured me across the bar were brown and wide and stayed on mine as I spoke. She was petite and had a small frame with well-placed curves around it. She wore a dress that had a deep V-neck front, the point sitting just below her sternum, where she had a large tattoo of a mandala. It was intricate and I love tattoos, so my eyes stayed on it.

'Are you looking at my tits?!' She looked quite seriously at me.

'No! Oh God, I'm so sorry, I was looking at your tattoo!' I tried to explain through my embarrassment.

She gave me the tiniest essence of a smile and we both laughed. We stood in the same spot and carried on our conversation, lost in it. A little while later, whilst I was trying to get another look at her tattoo, she raised her eyebrow and said, 'Are you looking at my tattoo again?' I looked right into her eyes and grinned. 'Nah,' I said. 'I'm looking at your tits.'

We openly embraced the lesbian stereotype. Just three weeks after first meeting each other, G quit her job in Liverpool and moved into my house in Brighton. Steven took to a stepmum with glee. From then, we were joined at the hip. Wherever I was, she was. We were obsessed with each other.

When she moved in with me so quickly, a few friends flinched. She had quit her job and was moving out of a spare room in her mum's house and into my house with no income. From the outside, I can see how it looked. To make matters worse, G was absolutely gorgeous. Strangers would regularly comment on her beauty. Despite the concern about motives, however, most of my friends were just relieved that I wasn't going to be on my own anymore. I do have to say that I have no doubt that G's intentions were completely pure, I never did doubt that.

Very quickly, it was us against the world. Without her, I felt unguarded and weak. I'd been through an incredibly difficult few years and all I wanted was to feel safe. She made me feel safe and she cared about how I felt. She was exactly who I needed, and I really mean *needed*. It's such a healthy thing to want someone but to need them can be dangerous. Instead of learning to regulate my own emotions and to take steps to look after myself, I reached for her to look after me.

Up until I met G, I had to keep the party alive to stay alive. I convinced acquaintances to stay up late with me and have *just one more drink*. I paid for the drugs and invited strangers into my house because I was so scared of what might happen if I was left alone. She was there and she didn't want to leave me, even when the party was over. She wanted to be a stay-at-home wife and I wanted to feel in charge. We depended on each other. The perfect storm.

I have no doubt that without G and her ability to support and care for me, things would be very different now. I was not a well person when we met. She was a natural caregiver and, at that point, I needed to be cared for. G would prop me up when my brain was letting me down in periods of depression. She would offer me support in the form of food, wine and emotional reliability. She rarely questioned my way of doing things, which, as unhealthy as that is, worked just perfectly for me. Instead of a two-way relationship, at the very beginning at least, I leant on her like a crutch. In return, I felt like I needed to give her the world.

We spent the majority of our relationship being the life and soul of every party, as well as the hosts. We held raucous house parties and took charge of the planning of group outings to festivals. We loved to drink. Along with every other aspect of my life, alcohol played a very significant part in my marriage too. I've struggled to find a picture of us in which we are not holding a drink. The night we met, we spent the evening romantically trying to find a drug dealer as we'd both independently run out of drugs. On our wedding day, she was so drunk I had to carry her to bed. I pissed the bed (with her in it) on multiple occasions (but not on our wedding night). We were what the professionals would say 'enablers' when it came to alcohol and drugs.

I didn't know it at the time but I was relying heavily on those two things to get through life. This makes it sound like we had a terrible relationship but, without those things, I don't think we'd have made it past the first date. We didn't have a terrible relationship, by the way, we actually really got on. G was funny, fierce, caring and knew how to have a good time. And we did have a good time. I told her everything about me, everything that had happened, all that I was ashamed of, and she never even flinched.

In 2015, exactly one year after the day we met, I proposed to G. We went for anniversary drinks in the Kensington bar we met in, then for a walk across a beautifully lit Chelsea Bridge, with each bulb sparkling in the pink, sunset sky.

Halfway across the bridge, I pointed down to the water at a huge, beautiful, wooden yacht that was moored up. I turned to her and said, 'Wouldn't it be amazing to ride down the Thames on that?' Before she had time to agree or take part in the fantasising, I put my hands either side of my mouth and shouted down to the man who was on the deck of the boat, adjusting its resting sails. 'Hey! Excuse me! Can we come and ride up the Thames on your boat?!' G was mortified and turned towards me with the most shocked expression. She pulled at my arm and told me to stop being embarrassing. Then, to her surprise, and as if we were the main characters in a blockbusting rom-com, the man on the boat shouted back up: 'Go on, then!'

There was a brief moment of still where we exchanged a look of complete disbelief and then hurried down towards him before he changed his mind. As we speed-walked down Cadogan Pier and stepped onto the boat, the man appeared with two glasses of champagne and a pair of flat shoes for G. She couldn't make sense of the fact that her shoes, from our house, were already on this boat. She looked at me and twisted her head, somewhere between confusion and realisation that perhaps there had been some planning involved in this after all. The man walked us to the back of the boat, where we sat alone in a little nest of bedding and fairy lights as we sailed down the river. On the way back up, just before we got back to the quite spectacular Chelsea Bridge, I walked her to the front of the boat and told her to look up at the lights on the bridge. 'The traffic lights?' she said. 'No, you eejit, look closer!'

As we got closer, we could hear whooping and cheering. Lined up along Chelsea Bridge were her family and friends, holding sparklers and the lights on their phones. I dropped to one knee and asked her to marry me. Our friends on the bridge came down to Cadogan Pier and climbed aboard for an evening on the boat.

★

In 2015, just after I'd released my first independent album, *We Are*, we moved from London to Stockport, to a large, detached farmhouse, dating back to the eighteenth century. On the face of it, it looked like we were a blissfully happy couple, with a beautiful house in the countryside, even though things inside the house were not healthy.

It was a 'fixer upper' and needed a lot of work doing to it. I reached out to my dad, who has always worked in the building trade, to see if he would help me renovate it. He came to stay periodically and we worked on the house together; it was the most time I'd spent with him since I was a child. He drank a lot, often starting in the daytime. We drank together at night. One Thursday night, we went out for drinks in a nearby pub and my dad got into a fist fight. We all got barred. By the time the house was finished, it looked beautiful – but the neighbourhood never fully felt like home and something wasn't quite right.

Our pace continued. In 2016, we got married. Our wedding was cracking. It was at the picturesque Fountains Abbey in North Yorkshire and then on to a farm in the middle of nowhere – a barn with bunting and candles and hand-tied table gifts. We had a rodeo bull and a tattoo artist; they ate steak and chips and got absolutely wasted, which, to me back then, was a sure-fire sign that everyone had a great time. It was the kind of wedding you saw in the magazines and we did see it in magazines. From the outside, things looked just as they should be.

It wasn't until after I got married that I heard the phrase 'some people are ready for a wedding but not ready for marriage'. That was me. It would have been better for me to have just thrown a party to tell everyone how much love there was between us. I was trying to do what you're *supposed* to do: buy a house, get married, have children. At that point, I'm not even sure I was aware that there were other options.

In 2017, my fourth album, *I Hope You Don't Mind Me Writing*, hit number twelve in the UK. What a result. I released it independently again and production costs had been high but it was selling so well. Things were looking great but it meant that I had to keep the momentum up. I toured it twice in the UK and I jumped straight into writing and recording my fifth album, *Today Was a Good Day*. Just as my home life began to feel askew, things started to pick up in my music career. At that time, although imperfect as ever, life did feel happy and markedly more grown up than before:

> To *live fast and die old, what a perfect work of art*
> To *live with someone you love and both get in bed*
>   *before it's dark.*
> *Life gets better, the hangovers get worse.*
> *When did I get so old?*
> *I even pay train fares now and most days do what*
>   *I'm told.*
> *I wake up every morning with someone I truly love,*
>   *and every day I act more like my mum.*

I watch what I eat, I stay in and watch films.
Man I have to pay my bills, I guess I must be
   grown up.
I'm working on my house, I'm building a career.
How on earth did I get here?
I must be grown up.
('Grown Up' from I Hope You Don't Mind Me
Writing, *2017)*

For the first couple of years, G not having a full-time job wasn't an issue but, eventually, I think we both started to struggle with it. Music and writing is my life, it always has been, and I can't imagine not feeling the way I do about it. It drives me forward. Storytelling is my purpose. It felt, at times, that G didn't know what hers was. She'd mentioned that she thought her purpose was to become a parent. After several conversations about passion and purpose, she told me that she wanted to become a foster carer. I wanted to support her in that endeavour because, more than anything, I wanted her to be happy. Fostering looked promising – she was great with children. That would be her thing, music was mine. I naively saw fostering as something she would be doing, though, of course, I would help where I could. I didn't see that as another profession I wanted to take on. That was not how it worked out.

We applied to become short-term and respite foster carers for Stockport City Council. We went through the long and detailed process of background checks: character references from ex-partners, addresses, school and police history. Even Steve was poked and prodded and deemed to be (and I quote) 'the most gentle-natured dog' the assessor had ever come across. A few months later, we were approved and ready to foster.

We were assigned a twelve-year-old boy, who I took to straight away. I realised that having a child living in our house wasn't something I could just work around and not be involved in. This little person needed nurturing, parenting and care. I was told to baton down the hatches and fix my TVs to the wall because there would be outbursts and showdowns. But I never saw a single one from him. I understood him. He was a frightened little child. I saw a lot of myself in him and I liked him a lot. He came along to a couple of shows – his identity protected, of course. It showed me how near impossible it would be to ever tour with my own children. In another life, I'd have adopted that kid. We fostered twelve children in total and, as lovely as they were, I found it absolutely overwhelming.

One sentence kept repeating itself over and over in my mind: 'I can't do this.' I was exhausted. It wasn't the children and it wasn't G. It was me. I was being all or nothing. I'd opted for 'all' and, once again, I couldn't handle it. That's when I decided I couldn't continue to foster anymore. The balancing act was too much for me. My mental health was deteriorating again and I knew I had to call it a day.

I didn't want to be responsible for dashing her dreams, so instead of telling G that I couldn't carry on, I'd make excuses as to why a placement wouldn't work. I couldn't just say, 'This is too much for me, I'm sorry.' I was on the verge of mental collapse but more scared of letting people down than letting myself get ill. One of the placements we were given was two toddler-age boys; it was then I knew I wasn't ready to have children at that time in my life.

And I knew that my wife had only ever wanted to be a mother. I knew in my heart that I was nowhere near being ready to have a child, but I was married to someone who was. That was a big problem.

None of my close friends were away from home for long periods of time. They weren't waking up in a different city every day. They were buying houses, having children and getting family-sized cars. Not only did I have a different job to those people around me, I'm also a lesbian. By default, my life was not the same as theirs, but I tried to buy into it all the same. I guess it's a testament to the progressiveness of this country that I never really noticed the fact that I wasn't in a heterosexual relationship. However, because it was illegal to be openly gay in the UK until 1967, it means that there isn't really a blueprint for LGBTQ+ people yet. G and I had a weirdly gendered relationship, like two women trying to adhere to the stereotypical lives of all of the other men and women in our lives. I work, you stay home. You wear a wedding dress, I wear a suit. I'll be a rockstar, you do the washing up.

Although the ground underneath me at home was beginning to feel shaky, in my career, I began to feel a growing sense of self-assurance. I played Glastonbury on the Acoustic Stage in 2017. As an independent artist, to help with costs I had been flip-flopping between playing full band shows, which is five-piece (including me) with drums, keys, bass and violin when I could afford to, and 'acoustic' shows, which is just me and my keys player, Josh. As it was Glastonbury's Acoustic Stage, and there wasn't much wiggle room in the low fee, we opted for the latter. For me, the fewer people on stage with me, the more nerve-wracking the show has the potential to be.

My band and I have played plenty of low-quality, first-year festivals and dodgy Christmas festivities. When there's a few of you on stage, it's easy to shake off the fact that the actual event you are playing is a bit soul-destroying or naff, and you can just enjoy making music and exchanging sarcastic looks with each other. However, when, for example, you're alone up there in the middle of a 'corporate' show performing songs for a company that, quite frankly, massively over-budgeted for their mid-dinner entertainment, to the point where you cannot help but sell your soul and accept the offer, it's pretty challenging. All musicians at one point in their career have to contend with a gaggle of middle-aged men in suits and women in sparkly dresses finishing off their desserts (and their ninth glass of wine), talking very loudly over the very inconsiderate noise you are creating, whilst only one or two of the approximately 200 people in the room give you all of their sympathetic attention and clap with all their might when you finish a song. It's just a rite of passage for performers.

Obviously, Glasto isn't anything like playing a charity dinner in middle England. It was actually unlike any show I'd ever played in my life. I had never been so nervous about a show in my whole career. From the second we woke up, both me and Josh thought we were going to puke. I don't suffer with performance nerves in general, unless my mum is in the audience (I have no idea why) or someone I fancy.

I learnt as we arrived at the festival that a) the Acoustic Stage tent was absolutely massive and b) it was about a mile from basically anything else at Glastonbury. It sits atop a lonely hill which is a mission from the middle of the action, and this combined with the fact it was a very early afternoon slot on Saturday meant I convinced myself that no one was going to show up for the set.

At 1.20 p.m., with fifteen minutes to go, I poked my head around the curtain . . . I was right. There were about forty-five people dotted around this huge circus tent; four instantly recognisable super-fans were leaning on the front barrier smiling away and the rest of the people just looked a bit lost.

My mouth got watery, like I was going to be sick. I went and sat in the shared green room with my head in my hands and wondered how I'd even blagged a spot at this festival. I was completely unworthy of it and the lack of audience proved that. I felt miserable. A short while later, Ben craned his neck around the door and told me it was time. Josh was waiting in the wings. We nodded to each other and headed out onto the stage . . .

The tent was absolutely jammed to the rafters. I looked to stage right and Josh was beaming at me. I couldn't believe it.

The whole show was a total blur that felt like it lasted all of five minutes. There were thousands of people, all kinds of people, singing along at the tops of their lungs, waving flags and dancing around. I'd heard people talk about the magic of a Glastonbury audience and I never really got it. Until you're there I don't suppose you can. With the final word of the last song came uncontrollable tears, and they didn't stop for a good fifteen minutes after the show. It felt like a true milestone. It was, really. I was the first ever *X Factor* contestant to play at Glastonbury. I believe I still am. Again,

I was also a touring artist who, at the time, had released four albums and put in all the graft that so many artists with the same beginnings do, but no one else had made that cut.

I was so full of pride that five years after my audition I was slowly shedding being 'that girl'. Something was changing.

A hectic work schedule, an epically busy festival season and my first multi-continent tour meant that 2018 sped by. The plan was to start 2019 with a bang. In March, I was to support rock legend and lesbian icon Melissa Etheridge on her UK and European tour, and then I was going on my own headline tours in the US, then Europe and then the UK again.

Although in my career I was going from strength to strength, I noticed myself pulling away from my life at home, slowly creating distance between me and G. At the beginning of 2019 I'd been away from home for nearly a year, spending most of my time without her. I started to learn about who I was when I was freestanding, when I was independent. I started to discover a whole other person underneath the skin I was shedding. I know G felt me pulling away but we both pretended like nothing was happening. We buried our heads in the sand and said that I was just struggling with being away and that when I got back everything would be fine.

My therapist once told me that couples are supposed to grow together, like trees standing side by side. We are supposed to grow in the same direction and at a similar rate, so that the tips our branches are always touching, whether one tree is leaning downwards to touch leaves with the tree slightly below it or has to bend slightly to connect with the other tree that has unsteadied in a storm. The key is to grow independently but in a way that compliments and connects to your partner. G and I had two parallel lives but we weren't like trees. We were like brambles, intwined and merged. We shielded and protected each other in many positive ways, but we also stunted each other. We were so co-dependent that neither of us knew what it was to be independent. It was as if were one of us to die, the other one would just stop living.

During the months and months I'd been away from home, the brambles had started to unravel. I'd started to deviate, like a rogue shoot untangling its way out of the thorny scribble, seeing how much room there was to grow outside of it. I didn't know what to do with that. I'd been so broken before G that I'd never felt independence as an adult and tasting it for the first time made my relationship, and our plans for the future, feel like a shackle. I genuinely thought that love was making each other happy and I had done everything I could to feed her, but I forgot to look at my own plate. I was starving. I didn't know what I wanted because I didn't know who I was. I'd grown into being two people and I didn't know if the goals we had were mine or hers. I also didn't know how on earth to say that out loud.

When I think back, I sensed that things wouldn't work out from early on.

It was the night before my wedding and I was sitting opposite Ben at a table in an Italian restaurant in Harrogate.

Ben launched into his projection of the trajectory our lives, mapping out the constellation of the future with his hands in front of him, grand and bold gestures outlining the life-long commitment I was making to not only my as-of-tomorrow wife but to him too. The permanency of the relationship I was about to commit to for eternity, and the permanency of our friendship. I waited for space to interject.

'It's going to end in divorce,' I said, plainly.

Ben, who was simultaneously chewing and rolling more pasta around his fork, immediately stopped doing both and shot his eyes from his plate to my eyes. His face was shadowed with an expression of misunderstanding, like I'd just spoken to him in Cantonese. Then, the deep, confused crease between his dark bushy eyebrows softened and his face straightened out.

'You dickhead, don't make jokes like that!'

There was a pause whilst he searched my face again, waiting for a wry smile or a roll of the eyes to let him know I was joking. Neither came. I sat there, looking straight back at him, my face still neutral. Not sad, not happy, just matter of fact. His eyebrows met in the middle of his face again and he leant forwards over his plate. He looked like he was about to choke. 'What the fuck are you on about?!'

People gasp when I tell them this story. They look just like Ben did, but without the carbonara sauce on their chins. Truthfully, I didn't understand what commitment was at that stage in my life. I'd never been committed to anything or anyone, apart from music. The people I had grown up around – my school friends, my father, my aunties and uncles – even the house I grew up in, it had all dissipated. I always ended up on my own. I had no roots anywhere, no allegiance to a place, not even to a football team. I had grown up thinking that everything always ends. People leave.

That human relationships, whether biological or not, have an expiry. Getting married, to me, meant getting divorced. I didn't know how to make and keep a promise because no one had ever kept a promise they made to me.

★

It was 2019 and I refused to acknowledge that the life I had created was falling apart. I upped the self-medication with drugs and alcohol because they took the edge off all of the feelings, and I convinced myself that by looking the other way and throwing myself into work, all of my problems would disappear. They didn't.

After accepting the fact that Stockport wasn't right for us, we put the house on the market and looked for somewhere more rural to live, somewhere with fewer people. G had seen this huge countryside barn conversion with a honeycomb, red brick exterior that was surrounded by fields and nature, twenty-five minutes from Chester, right on the border of Wales. It had a large indoor/outdoor space, like a sheltered courtyard inside the entrance of the barn just off the driveway, perfect for parties. It was gorgeous and it was expensive. Though I'd been working so much, it was mostly promotional, so rather making money, it was costing a lot and all of the travel made the overheads insane. Despite that, we secured a buyer for the Stockport house and I put an offer on Barnhill Grange. For everybody else on the outside looking in, life was perfect.

This year was geared to be even more intense than the last year. When the first single from the album *Today Was a Good Day*, 'Lucky Stars', was released, I had my first ever UK national radio playlisting on BBC Radio 2. Work started to pour in in a way that it hadn't before. It felt incredible, like all of the effort I had been pumping into this was starting to show signs of life.

It was March and I was in Leipzig, in my first few weeks as support act for Melissa Etheridge, though I had been on the road for months. By this point, I had started to notice that I was feeling very differently about my relationship. Before the previous twelve months of touring, G and I had been magnets, with an invisible force that glued us together. I could feel my magnet was losing its polarity. I had flown her out to visit me in Germany for a few days and the atmosphere between us was off. We didn't talk about it; I just carried on ignoring my feelings and making sure everything looked OK from the outside. I thought that was what was important – how it looked to everyone else. I knew she had an instinct that I was feeling off, plus I had a huge tell: I couldn't look directly at her face. She would smile at me with sad eyes that I could see were trying to figure out what was going on behind mine. It felt awful, even at that point. It felt like something had pulled out the plug and the happiness had already started to drain away.

Once G had boarded a flight back to the UK, Melissa and her wife, Linda, pulled me to the side of the catering room and asked me if everything was OK. They said they could sense something was up and I said they were right, but I didn't go into much detail. I said that my life was changing. That I was changing. A lot. They both gave me a hug that I really needed. I really got on with Melissa and Linda, they were like parents on tour. Once, after hearing I was suffering with a sore throat, Melissa stopped me in the catering room and told me, 'I'll tell you what I told Adele

and P!nk: Don't eat dairy! It's so bad for the vocal cords.'
How fucking surreal. She was so fucking cool.

Later that day, when I passed her backstage, Linda said,
'You should really meet Bailey. You and she will get on like
a house on fire.' I had heard that Melissa had a daughter; in
fact, I'd seen the *Rolling Stone* cover that she'd featured on
as a baby. She was the first ever celebrity lesbian couple's
child. The sperm doner Melissa and Bailey's other mum had
used was the late David Crosby, of Crosby, Stills and Nash.
I didn't know that Bailey was a lesbian too.

It wasn't unusual for me to visit Melissa's dressing
room before the show but when I wandered backstage
in Stockholm, I was surprised to see this young, tall, slim
brunette leaning against the back wall, wearing a pair of
slightly flared blue jeans and a long-sleeved black top. Bailey,
aged twenty-three, was talking passionately about the work
she had done on Hillary Clinton's presidential campaign
during her time at Columbia University.

I listened as the conversation flowed from what she had
been doing and into her plans for the future. She wanted to
apply for a master's at Harvard because she needed to get
away from her job at Goldman Sachs; she hated working
on the Stock Exchange. She sounded like she knew exactly
what she wanted, and she wanted to do it by herself. Just
from listening to her speak for a few minutes, it was clear
she knew far more about herself than I knew about me,
and I was twenty-seven. I was floored by her. Her drive,
her motivation and her passion were like nothing I had seen
before. At home, I felt pressure to help find motivation and
drive for someone else but Bailey was bursting with it, and
she was dazzling. This girl felt like an escape.

PROCESS

Linda introduced us. 'Bailey, this is the lovely Lucy we told you about!' she beamed. 'Hey, Lucy,' Bailey smiled at me, and they carried on their conversation. Bailey and I connected almost immediately, initially with no idea that we were going to be anything more than friends. We swapped numbers because Melissa's tour was coming to an end but over the next few days, we found ourselves texting and opening up about things we were both struggling with. We related to each other a lot and, not only that, I'd found someone I could fully confide in. I told her about my concerns at home. She didn't know anything about my home life, she didn't know G. She heard my perspective and only my perspective so, of course, her judgement was in favour of my view. With Bailey, I had discovered a separate world and it took me further away from the one I had at home. It made it easier for me to live in this separate world if I had someone else on my team, someone to enable it.

Soon, Bailey and I were exchanging messages that had gone past the boundaries of friendship. It had developed and I felt excited for the first time in a long time. I couldn't believe someone like that could be interested in me. Alongside all the new feelings, I felt so full of shame. Even at this point, when it had gone as far as some inappropriate texts, I was drinking and smoking weed to help me negate the guilt. We hadn't even kissed. What the fuck was I doing?

I didn't have the ability to look past the *right now* and into the future, when the tour would finish and I would have to go home. I was experiencing complete denial. When I tried to think about the future, my attention turned straight to something else. I could not face thinking about the implications of my actions. It's not that I didn't want to, it's that I couldn't. That's what denial does to you if you aren't aware of it: it stops you from being able to access the truth and the severity. I was completely out of my depth.

Bailey offered to fly down and meet in Texas, where I would be playing SXSW Festival, and I said yes. I knew that would be it then. Deep down, I knew I wouldn't be able to return to my other life if she came to meet me. When she arrived, we went straight to a bar. I felt so many emotions. I felt like a teenager again, nervous but brimming with excitement. The fact I was in Texas to perform at a huge festival, and nothing looked like it did at home, encouraged my denial. I could pretend that this was my only life. Out of nowhere, shame would knock at my ribcage so hard that it physically hurt my stomach and when it did, I'd order another drink.

After a few, we awkwardly walked back to my hotel room in Barton Springs, just over the river in Austin. It was such a clear, sunny day. Even the birdsong sounded different here. I knew that if we slept together, I was ending the life I had at home. I wasn't just unplugging myself from it, I was destroying it. Smashing it into tiny pieces.

I cried afterwards. I'd done the unspeakable. I'd done what I never imagined I'd do. I did what I solemnly promised not to and knew that I would never be able to look G in the eye again. There it was in black and white: all or nothing. Once I slept with Bailey, there was no turning back for me. I'd committed to the destruction.

It got worse from there onwards. The more guilty I felt, the more I drank. The more I drank, the more I didn't care. The denial was the fuel and the alcohol was the accelerator. I didn't know what the fuck I was doing, but I do now.

I was running away because I didn't know how to do anything else. All I've ever known is cutting ties and moving away, leaving people behind. Slowly, I stopped speaking to G, until phone calls and texts from me were nearly non-existent. I ignored her calls but stayed in constant contact with Bailey.

When SXSW finished, I had a show in LA and then a week off, so I flew to Vegas to spend time with Phil and Kevin. I couldn't bear a single moment of silence, so when they were working, I hired a Harley-Davidson and rode for miles and miles across the desert and pretended to be someone else. When I'd return, the intermittent shame would flare up as violently as a chip pan fire. I would douse the flames with alcohol, getting blackout drunk.

Pretty quickly, my relationship with Bailey developed into a full-blown affair. I believed that I was in love with another woman. It turns out that lesbian superspeed applies to affairs too.

G sensed that something was wrong but for months I denied it, refusing to face the real consequences of the decisions I'd made. The year continued in a blur of touring, festivals, album promo and career successes, and whenever I was in America, I'd be with Bailey, staying at her apartment in Manhattan. I was living a double life.

I was full of dread but so was my wife. At least I knew what was happening. She was experiencing the dread but didn't have any answers. What a terrible thing to do to a person. I knew it couldn't go on. I was beginning to acknowledge that I needed to take accountability. I needed to tell the truth.

In late July, just after my twenty-eighth birthday, I told G that I didn't want to be with her anymore. I made excuses, some that were true, but only I partially uncovered the reasoning behind them. I was finally able to tell her that I'd been overwhelmed by my responsibilities, the expectations and the pressure, but I didn't tell her that I'd met someone else. I moved into the spare room and we lived in a kind of limbo for a few weeks. She openly told me she suspected there was someone else and I denied it. She told me she wanted to fix things; I told her I was quite sure I didn't want to. It was bizarre. We were living in the same house, avoiding each other and dancing around the huge cracks in the building. Even though part of the truth was out there, both of us were still in denial.

On Saturday 27th July, 2019, I arrived back from a run of shows, the last one being on the Isle of Bute, in Scotland. It took around seven hours for the tour manager to drive me back home. The end of summer was coming. The whole thing had been like a strange dream. Despite the fact that G and I were in confused, unchartered relationship territory, she had suggested that we throw a party at the house that night. I think it was an effort to remind me of our normal life that used to be. It was the same day that the country estate behind Barnhill Grange hosted a large festival in the fields, which they did every year, so the plan was to drink at the house and then attend the festival with four of her close friends, one of mine and a couple of close mutual ones.

I anticipated chaos and started drinking beer on the way back down the motorway. When I got to the house in the early afternoon, as expected, the tension was suffocating. I started on the Jameson whiskey, almost a whole bottle. We attended the festival and, before I knew it, I was absolutely fucking obliterated. We all were. Me, G, my friends, her friends. We had no choice but to drink to appease the fog of unease in our atmosphere.

We went back to the house to drink in the courtyard. Unsurprisingly, it all exploded that night. The more drunk we all got, the weaker the denial became. Opinions started to be hurled around. One of G's friends couldn't hold hers in anymore and let loose at me across the table, with a pointed finger. Voices erupted from every angle. A blur of angry sounds, emotion pouring out of these people whose inhibitions had been left in a field behind the house. Everyone was desperate to keep life as it was. It had been so fun for the last few years. The end of me and G meant the end of an era for us all. Everything has an expiry date.

The next day, I woke up with a hangover, but not like a normal hangover. Yeah, my head was pounding, and my mouth felt like merino wool, but the scale of the emotional explosion the night before had triggered a strange clarity in me. We had all said exactly how we felt. We screamed, blamed, warned and cried at each other. G told me that I tried to throw the table across the courtyard. I didn't remember that. I didn't remember much after it all kicked off, but I knew that everyone had said their piece and the anger had melted a little. That argument had kicked down the door to reality and I knew I couldn't hide anymore. For the first time, the hangover of everything else I had done came home to roost.

I felt strangely calm, like something had fallen into place. I had to stop this. That morning, the first words that came out of my mouth were 'I'm not doing this anymore.' I was right, too. That was the last time I ever drank alcohol.

G and I separated after that. We agreed that she'd live at Barnhill Grange until she was able to find a job and a place of her own. She didn't want to return to the room in her mum's house that she'd left five years ago. I was still paying the mortgage, for her Mercedes, and all of the bills as I had before, but I spent most nights sleeping in my van on campsites or visiting friends to avoid going back to my house and seeing her. I was still full of guilt.

In the September, after a lot of thought, I walked into the kitchen and I told her about Bailey. I told her when it had started and anything else that I thought was relevant. She threw wine glasses at me. I deserved that, and far more. I told her I was sorry, and I still am. I left her to live in the house until February and we began the arduous process that is divorce.

Dear Lucy,

Throughout life, you were given the impression that being in love is all about intensity, pace and high stress.

Think about love songs: every lyric is about how the singer can't breathe, or eat, or sleep without the person they love, how they'd die without them.

Every romantic film's plot is about a stifling whirlwind of a relationship, the desperate quest of unrequited love or giving up everything for one person and the future you might have one day.

'All you need is love,' apparently.

The messaging was clear: love is need, love is desperation, love is hard and romantic love is everything. I don't blame you for believing it.

I realise that your perception of love was skewed –

there were a lot of things you associated with love that I know now are different traits altogether.

You needed your ex-wife; she was part of your survival from the very start of your relationship. You depended on her and she depended on you. But that's not the same as being in love. As difficult and confusing as this whole period of time was, it showed you 'love' in a different light. It taught you that The Beatles were wrong – you need far more than love.

You should have been listening to 'I Want to Know What Love Is' by Foreigner.

This time of our life taught me that want and need are very different things. Nowadays, I want to want my partner but I don't want to need them. I want to be able to satisfy my own needs so that the rest is all the fun bit. The want. The desire.

I don't think love is supposed to feel like anxiety. Of course, butterflies and excitement are a good indication but now, if there is an element of anxiousness or panic that comes with falling for someone, I know something is off and it's usually coming from me.

You used to panic that you weren't good enough or you'd get anxiety that they might want someone else, someone better. You believed conventionally pretty girls were 'out of your league', which is all about self-worth, and I'm sorry you didn't have that back then.

If you had, you'd have wanted to be on a level playing field with G. You'd have known we both deserved the best in life and that we both needed to be happy independently in order for it to work.

You never needed to sacrifice parts of yourself for somebody else. I wish I could have told you that focusing on making other people happy would never make you happy. In your case, doing that for so long is what caused such a backfire. I know you had good intentions but there's only so far you can stretch a rubber band until it snaps.

You were worthy of happiness. You were worthy of it all along. You just didn't know it. You didn't find yourself attractive or special, so when someone else found you attractive it made you feel validated. You couldn't tell the difference between being flattered and being validated.

You are valid regardless of who fancies you, I promise.

The worst part of it was feeling like you dragged someone else down with you and you did do that, but it's not that you didn't have the balls to end it, it's that you didn't know how. All you knew was how to throw a grenade into your life and walk away. That's how it has always been. There was always a path of destruction lying in your wake.

I'm glad you taught me I needed to change that. I did, in the end. I can say no whenever I want to. We had our first amicable breakup in 2021. Woo!

Back then, I'd have told you that:

Love isn't about need, it's about want. It's about choice.

Love isn't desperation, it's calm.

And romantic love isn't everything.

And, by the way, sometimes, love isn't enough.

PROCESS

Relationships are hard but the best way to start is with the relationship with yourself.

You live and learn.

Oh, and no more divorces, OK? That was very expensive.

Onwards and upwards,

Love,

Lucy x

'I Do Not Drink Anymore'

If you look up #sobriety on Instagram you'll see life through the rose-tinted lens of those living the alcohol-free life. I hate to admit it but most sober people (including me) tend to fit into a plethora of terribly accurate stereotypes. The list is quite extensive: the recovering addict, the fitness enthusiast, the hippy, the outdoorsy mountain climber, the solo-traveller, the alcohol-free drink connoisseur . . . there are loads.

Sober people can often sniff each other out in social situations and there's usually an unspoken bond between us. It's based on a degree of shared understanding of what a life without drinking can offer, of the hardships of sobriety, of the assumptions that people who do drink make about you – again, the list goes on. But despite the fact that sober people can adopt predictable stereotypes, I have come to realise that everyone's physical and mental experience in early sobriety and beyond is unbelievably different, as are their reasons for getting sober in the first place. My last hangover wasn't even that bad, physically. I think you'd agree that my rock bottom was long before my decision to stop drinking, though a lot of other people's initial face-first contact with the concrete is enough for them to make an instant decision to quit. Like I said, it's a very individual process.

Let's be real, I'd sunk pretty low. I'd nearly killed myself. I'd got into a few unfavourable (understatement) situations – I'd got into fights and I'd had an affair. I really hurt a lot of people around me and alcohol helped me stay in my cycle of misery: feel overwhelmed > have a drink > feel more overwhelmed > get more drunk > do things I wouldn't have done sober > feel guilty > get drunk > do more things I wouldn't have done sober > feel overwhelmed. And on it went. In order to break the cycle, I had to remove the thing that enabled all of it: alcohol and drugs. But then what would that look like? I didn't know what the new cycle would be. I had woven and woven my problems around the maypole until it was too late to undo any of it. I felt like there was no other option but to walk away from everything I knew and get sober.

I wasn't as motivated by my circumstances as I was cornered by them, but that's not the same for everyone. Some of my friends ascended softly into sobriety, hardly noticing the difference, whilst others kicked the door down and howled in pain. I know which I was.

★

My first few weeks of sobriety were some of the hardest I've experienced. In some ways, they were also the most motivating. When I peeled back the boozy façade of my life, I realised, very quickly, that without alcohol I had no fucking clue who I was. That sounds like an exaggeration, but I'd first got pissed in the garage with Billy when I was seven and I'd been doing it ever since. When I took away alcohol at twenty-eight, I didn't know how to socialise; I didn't know how to talk about my feelings, how to go to sleep in hotels, how to date, how to have sober sex, how to dance, how to talk to my friends. One morning, I looked into the mirror, right into my own eyes, and asked myself out loud: 'Who the fuck are you?'

I felt like I was learning to walk all over again. I was going to have to drag myself along the floor, then crawl, then stand and then practise, practise, practise until I started to get somewhere. I didn't know how or where to start, but I knew I only had one rule from now on: whatever happens, I do not drink anymore.

I'm not sure how long from my last drink it took for my skin to start hurting, but when it began, I initially thought I must have been coming down with an ill-timed bad cold. I had never experienced anything like it before. After approximately a couple of weeks, it felt like every single hair follicle on my body had accrued its own nerve ending and that nerve ending would heat up like a tiny hot little pinprick. Like each hair was a strand of one of those fibreoptic, colour-changing lamps from the 1990s and every time the colour changed the sensation did too. My arms were especially bad; it went from feeling pinpricks of red hotness to acidic, icy burns. When someone touched me, it felt awful. I would wince if a hand brushed my forearm. It was like their skin was made of sandpaper and mine was that of a newborn. I had no idea it was linked to quitting drinking. I've heard other people talk about their experience of discomfort in those first few months, with many different symptoms. I can only tell you about the ones I had.

For some people, the discomfort is a physical symptom of withdrawal from alcohol. Some say the discomfort is mental, that it's all in your head. Who knows what mine was from. Physical discomfort wasn't my only symptom; I was also fucking starving. Alcohol gives you a pretty good bump of dopamine and when you take it away your brain starts to wonder where else it could get a hit. Once I'd abided by my own rule of 'I do not drink anymore' for long enough, my brain realised that sugar was going to be the next best thing. When I say I was hungry, I mean I could literally think of nothing other than guzzling knickerbocker glories and being the first in line for an almond croissant, or two, as soon as I woke up. My cravings were like that of pregnant woman, unignorable and desperate. I'd wake up in the middle of the night feeling like I needed a bag of Haribo Tangfastics. That's actually quite bleak.

Speaking of sleep, for the first month, my sleep was awful. Here's me, quitting alcohol and being a super healthy person for once, and *this* is how it feels? Insomnia?! This is a symptom that most of the sober people I know struggled with in the first few weeks and months of sobriety. I would drift off and wake up an hour later or wake up in the morning feeling like I hadn't slept at all. There's research to say that the effect that alcohol has on your sleep cycles, even if you don't actually drink that much, can make your brain a bit confused when you take it away. My sleep sorted itself out but it was notable at the beginning.

If the existential crisis of not knowing who I was, the

skin-pain, the cravings for an Easter egg at 3 a.m. on an August night and lack of sleep were not bad enough, I started to experience the most evident, and my most challenging, symptom of sobriety: feelings.

It's hard to explain what a feeling *feels* like, isn't it? It's a mixture of emotions and physical sensation. Like, if you had to explain what anger *feels* like, you might say it's hot and volcanic, or that happiness is like floating or calmness. When I look back on those first few weeks without alcohol or drugs, I think that my feelings and emotions contributed to my very real sensory discomfort. Up until the point of sobriety, I had smothered the essence of sadness with alcohol. At the first sniff of shame, I drank. When I was happy, I celebrated by cracking open a bottle. When I was stressed, or when I was overwhelmed, whiskey gave me a diversion to another place, a place where feelings didn't have to be experienced in real time. I could put them off indefinitely. I'd been doing this for fuck knows how long, for my whole life. As soon as I removed the ability to divert my feelings, they crashed in. The dam had broken and those feelings were the flash flood I hadn't prepared for. Feelings started to seep under my front door and the water level was rising around the space I used to live so comfortably in. The instinct was to grab the sandbags to absorb the incoming devastation, to pick up a bottle of something and nullify those emotions, but now I had my one rule, 'I do not drink anymore', so I had to learn on my feet. I was so emotional but I had no idea how to experience feeling like that. I had to meet myself head-on and learn how to feel.

A couple of weeks into my sobriety, whilst sitting in a hotel room to avoid being at home, where my soon-to-be-ex-wife was, I was watching a romantic film and noticed this unfamiliar sensation wash over me. It was the same feeling I used to get when I was a child playing on the swings at the park when the person behind me stopped pushing me. When the swing slowly lost momentum I wanted them to carry on, but it was time to go home. Having to resign myself to the fact it was over. That feeling. I noticed I was crying at the TV and wiped my face. When I stopped running away, moving my attention elsewhere, quit overworking and drinking, I was . . . sad. For the first time, I was mourning my relationship and the life I had before; I was truly experiencing the pain of letting that go. It was excruciating. I sobbed.

'I do not drink anymore,' I said, as the hotel bar called up the lift shaft to me.

> I stayed at the Holiday Inn, I watched a film about a
>   couple in love,
> Kinda makes me sad when I think, like I wanna
>   drink but enough is enough.
> I spent all my time in the heartbreak suites,
> I spend all my time avoiding me.
> ('Heartbreak Suites' from Choices, 2021)

'My name's Lucy and I'm an alcoholic. I am four weeks sober.'

I was sitting on a plastic chair in the basement of a church in New York. I had been in New York for a radio tour to promote my latest album, and to see Bailey. I was at an Alcoholics Anonymous meeting. Around me were a circle of people, each on their own plastic chair, looking at me in a strangely apologetic way.

'Hi, Lucy,' the people in the plastic chairs said, all in unison.

The circle erupted into a short applause. They stopped, as if waiting for me to say something else, but, after a pause, they thankfully turned their gaze to the older man on my right, who began to introduce himself, say how long he'd been sober and tell us a little bit about why he was also sitting in an AA meeting in the basement of a church in New York.

I felt like a fraud. I just told a room full of alcoholics that I was an alcoholic. I was not an alcoholic. Wait, was I? I hadn't even thought about what I was or what I was not. I was just sober. Four weeks sober. Had I just lied or was I in denial? Jesus. I should have just opted not to speak. I spoke because that was what you were *supposed* to do. But I didn't want to do what I was supposed to do anymore. I said I was an alcoholic because I was at an AA meeting. When all of the eyes were on me, I just repeated what everyone else had said.

I was invited to this AA meeting, the first of only four I ever went to, by a man called Garrett Swann. I had met Garrett in New York during part of my album promotion in early 2019. He was an influencer who did a fun little series called 'Undercovers' where he interviewed people under the covers of his actual bed, in his actual apartment on the Upper East Side. When my American PR man had told me the details of that potential interview, sat across the table from me in a café, I'd narrowed my eyes and made a face like I was chewing lemon rinds, 'In a man's bed?' I stuck my neck forward as if I hadn't heard him properly.

'Don't worry, he's gay!' he remedied.

'Oooh, OK. Sounds so fun!' I said, revoking my disgust. And that was that.

We hit it off straight away. Garrett was older, in his early fifties, a silver fox, with a muscly physique and a casual Californian charm. He was flamboyant and a naturally open person, so after the interview we swapped numbers. The next time I was in NYC, in late August, Garrett asked me if I fancied brunch with him and his boyfriend. I did fancy brunch. Matter of fact, at that point, at four weeks sober, I fancied brunch on the hour, every hour. Quite honestly, I'd have done just about anything for French toast at that point.

At brunch I confessed to Garrett and his partner that I was in my first month of sobriety. I wasn't feeling my best because my sleep had gotten so bad and I was struggling to concentrate, so I thought I may as well be honest. I figured that by explaining myself neither of them would think I was like a hungry, irritable zombie all the time and that it might explain the bags under my eyes. I told them I was struggling a bit.

I'm such an over-sharer. I'd only met them once, for God's sake. I didn't know what to expect in return from my overshare but, within seconds, Garrett was looking up to the sky with his hands either side of his face and a huge, white smile. Why was he so happy?

Life has this weird way of throwing you a line sometimes. A care package that falls from the sky right at the exact moment you need it. A reminder that you are on the right path. Of course, they are rare. We know that life can be cruel and tyrannical with its gestures and, most of the time, it feels like life just kicked you in the shin for no reason, but you cannot deny the steadfast, beautiful message that lands like a butterfly right on the end of your nose just at the right time.

'I have thirteen years,' Garrett said, his hands still on his cheeks.

That's sobriety lingo, if you didn't know. It meant that Garrett, the man sitting opposite me, who texted me out of the blue, the guy I'd met by chance in New York City – one of the easiest places to feel completely alone in the whole world – was thirteen years sober. I was sitting there, at brunch, my skin hurting, my brain slow and tired, feeling ravenous, with someone who had been through exactly what I was going through right then. Divine intervention. A butterfly right on the end of my nose.

It turned out that Garrett had achieved his phenomenal thirteen years of sobriety through the Alcoholics Anonymous programme. I knew what I imagine most people know about AA: they have meetings where they sit in a circle, they have a twelve-step programme and they have little coins to be collected at each calendar milestone. Apart from that, I had no idea what went on. The conversation at brunch flourished from there onwards; I had so many questions and I felt so lucky to be getting some answers. As we finished our meal and waved the waiter over to pay the bill, Garrett leant in close and asked me if I wanted to come along to a meeting that evening. I pondered it for a second.

Before I knew Garrett was in the Fellowship, which is what they call people who are a part of AA (I know, it's very *Lord of the Rings*), I had assumed that AA was for the down-and-outs and the rock-bottomers. I don't know why I had thought that. I guess that as a society, we assume those who have issues with alcohol *are* going to be down and outs. But Garrett wasn't one of those people and I wasn't one of those people, so fuck it, why not? Plus, at that point, I had absolutely nothing to lose and a wealth of knowledge to gain.

There I was, in New York City, at an AA meeting in a church basement, four weeks sober with my skin on actual fire and almost everything made me want to cry. The person on my right had just been talking about his lifelong battle with alcoholism, how he no longer had contact with his adult children, how everyone he used to hold close had distanced themselves from him and how it had been a year since his last relapse. When he finished, the group applauded and the Hispanic lady next to him began to tell her story: a series of tragic events that led to her child being put into care, plunging her into a deep depression that she medicated with drugs and alcohol. The applause started again and the young man to her right introduced himself.

I listened intently to each person in that quiet room. It was so, so sad. There was so much pain in that circle. Every story had these cliff drops, things got so much worse and, when you thought they couldn't get any sadder, you found out that something else terrible happened next. Every person in that room told their story as if they'd told it a million times. Most looked at the floor with their hands on their laps, or picking at their nails, unable to tell the story of their life whilst looking anyone else in the eye. Within thirty minutes, I noticed that every story I heard had two things running through it, like a shared vein between each of the people in the room: shame and trauma. Bucketloads of it.

There was such a contrast between the celebration of the

'Hi I'm *blank* and I am thirty days sober' and the sheer sadness of the journeys that transported these people into the eventuality of being in this room. It all felt so dark. It felt like the mission was to be so haunted by your past that you spend most of your time reminding yourself why you can never, ever return there. It felt to me like you were supposed to dwell on the decisions that contributed to the situation you found yourself drowning in.

I didn't want to do that.

I didn't know much about my sobriety yet but I knew I wanted to be able to revisit my past with compassion and understanding. I wanted to look at the struggling, younger version of myself with kindness, to acknowledge her faults and flaws and embrace the idea that my journey has been one of healing and building, and that those dark moments are not to be looked back on with shame, but with an understanding that they needed to happen in order for me to arrive at the place I am at now. I've done a lot of things that filled me with shame. I've done a lot of things that I used to regret. But spending time being full of regret and shame taught me that feeling that way will keep you exactly where you are.

Turning shame into acceptance and telling yourself that it's OK to make mistakes if you learn and grow from them feels a lot better for me personally. Realising that you can't change the past and that replaying events, wishing you'd done them differently, will not change your present and, regardless of how much you regret, there are no other outcomes than the one you are in right now. Accepting that the only decisions you can alter are the ones you make moving forward – that's how I wanted to do it. The only time I've found shame and guilt helpful is knowing that those feelings indicate that I need to get to work on my relationship with whatever period in my life is bringing those feelings around. Unless they are being worked on, they are the most useless and damaging emotions a person can harbour. They will make you hate yourself.

It turned out that AA was not for me. Like anything in this life, we all have different methods of survival. Different strokes for different folks. That said, something from AA that I did continue to do was collect the little coins that AA give out as an act of small celebration when you hit a milestone: one week, one month, two months, three months, eventually a year. I didn't go to meetings to get the coins; I ordered them from eBay or, when I was on the road or couldn't get hold of one, I'd go into the local key cutter's or pet shop and have them engrave a keyring or a dog tag with the milestone I'd achieved and add it to my collection. I stopped collecting them at one year sober but I still have them. Those tiny little medals I awarded myself with.

The part of the ideology I struggled with the most was that those in the Fellowship are, and will always be, alcoholics. The narrative that my relationship with alcohol will never be changed didn't resonate with me. I didn't subscribe to the idea that there was something wrong with me or that my ailment was terminal. In my opinion, I used alcohol as a really terrible coping mechanism as a response to trauma, and I just needed to learn new ways to cope with that trauma. The trauma isn't ever going to go away but I can learn to control my reaction to it. I needed to learn not only how to feel but what to do with those feelings. It wasn't that I was struggling and that I always would be, it was that the struggle I was enduring was an important part of becoming who I was going to be. To shed my old skin and proudly wear my new one.

There's a commonly recited phrase within the AA community, 'If you spend too much time in the barber's, you'll end up with a haircut' – implying that if you go to bars, drink alcohol-free beer, etc., or spend time around people that drink, you'll inevitably end up going back to the booze. I don't agree. I spend time in bars, I drink 0 per cent beers, I attend lairy British weddings and I can do *all* of the things I used to do, apart from drink. I can do that because I exposed myself to those things and learnt how to thrive in any situation as a sober person. There isn't a circumstance that can be sprung on me that I am not prepared for. My method of 'recovery' is head-on and I don't hide from things that challenge me. It's very simple for me now: if I don't like where I am, I leave. I taught myself to choose.

Everyone has the capacity to change and our past is an integral part of our learning process to accommodate that change. To dwell on the past or to look back too much can draw a person away from the present. The same thing happens when you try to look too far into the future. Alcoholics Anonymous agree on that one, as per their famous saying 'One day at a time', which I always repeat back to anyone who says it to me, or comments 'ODAAT' on social media. I see that saying as a nod of respect to anyone who is working on their relationship with themselves and with alcohol. Truly, to be present and to make your way through life, you only need to put one foot in front of the other one and keep going. One day at a time.

After a show, I used to have a beer straight away.

After the high of hundreds or thousands of people screaming my name, my brain would search for a way to keep that feeling alive. For the good shows, it was a celebration, and for the bad shows, a commiseration. Alcohol and drugs offer a pretty strong dopamine reward, just like adoring fans do. Overcoming that was one of the hardest hurdles of sobriety and made me realise why so many performers have substance abuse issues.

My routine now is to come off stage and let my body come down from the high. I sit in the dressing room and take some deep breaths, maybe even have a bit of chocolate. I retrained the part of my brain that needed more and more and more to just embrace the feelings I had and then, to let them go.

When I was three months sober, in the middle of my first ever sober tour, I announced it across my social media platforms by posting a picture of me with a cake with a number three candle on top of it, as well as my three-month AA coin. I guess that is my second 'coming out' story. My mum told me a friend of hers had seen the post and said, 'I had no idea that Lucy was an alcoholic!'

Every single news outlet or interviewer had one question for me: 'Are you an alcoholic?' Some people tried to decide what I was for me. Some assumed, as soon as I said I don't drink or take drugs anymore, that I was an addict. Some friends said, 'But you didn't drink every day, you didn't wake up and drink, did you? You're not an alcoholic!' To be honest with you, I don't care what people think I am. If you want to see me as whatever your idea of an alcoholic is, do that. If you see me as a person who just doesn't drink, do that. The reality is, I'm just trying to be the best person I can be. Not for anyone else but me. I don't drink because I want to be fulfilled and alcohol doesn't help me achieve that. I don't drink because I want to make choices that benefit me and I want to be fully present for my decision making. I can honestly say that becoming sober changed every aspect of my life for the better. Being sober turned out to be my superpower.

Ironically, I wish I could bottle this feeling and serve it to anyone who needs it.

Dear Lucy,

For all those years you drank, do you remember how bewildered you were by sober people?

If you were ever at a party and came across a teetotaller who was smiling and having a great time, chatting and looking comfortable, even bloody DANCING, you would be intrigued beyond belief by them. There were so many times when you swayed up to that person and interrogated them on their ability to be sober AND have fun at the same time. 'HOW?!' you'd say, sceptical as ever.

I know that then, you would never, ever, believe that just last week, at a party, someone swayed up to me and quizzed me with the very same questions you used to ask.

As I write this, it's been nearly four years. I can tell you, and again, you might not believe it, but I have never once looked back. The kind of person who can have fun sober, who can confidently meet strangers and entertain friends, who can dance (badly) at weddings without so much as a drop – that's you. And I am so bloody proud of you.

PROCESS

Those first few months were hellish. The emotions were so all-consuming. But you powered through that, using your all-or-nothing nature for good, for once. Feeling things so intensely is different, but enlightening. Everything feels so real.

You started to find a respect for your body that you didn't have before. Not only were you not putting yourself in dangerous situations, you started feeling so much healthier.

If I woke up tomorrow with the symptoms of a hangover – the headache, the sickness, the anxiety, the lethargy – I would take myself to the doctor's. I wouldn't ever put myself through that now because I know I don't deserve to feel like shit.

All I want to say here is thank you for sticking with it.

I do not drink anymore.

Love,

Lucy x

You Need to Run

In January of 2019, at six months sober, I opted for what some would say is the ultimate test of sobriety – I went on holiday to Vegas. I know. Quite literally a huge gamble. I don't think I really gave it as much thought as I should have, but you see these things in retrospect, don't you?

I flew out with my best friend, Josh. We were going to stay with our wonderful party animal friends, Phil and Kevin, in their house in the Vegas suburbs. Almost every year for the last decade, I had been out to visit them in the States. Together, we had spent many a night absolutely wasted. Puking in car parks, doing shots until we couldn't see, pissing in alleys – you know, *that* vibe. When you get sober, it's hard to know which friends will stay and which will fall by the wayside. But I was wholly confident that this friendship, despite having a foundation built on a decade's worth of beer bottles, would stand the test of sobriety.

Though even with that belief, I knew as soon as I landed that being in Vegas was going to be a challenge.

You know things are bad when you have a drug dealer in each city. I always used to save drug dealers' numbers with the name of the city they operated in, followed by 'up ya nose'. In Vegas, the drug dealer we knew was called Jonny Limo (I'm going to take a wild guess that is an alias) and I hadn't anticipated that my friends might want to have a visit from him. I don't blame them; after all, I was the one who had chosen to be sober. It was my first up close and personal exposure to cocaine since I'd quit and I hadn't prepared for it. It was right there, in little, pearlescent lines on the marble worktop. Though it shook me a little, I knew I didn't want it. My friends picked up on my frustration and it actually resulted in a really healthy conversation about boundaries between us all. We agreed that they wouldn't do drugs in front of me and Phil asked me what he should do if I ever approached him and said, 'Fuck it, give me a drink!' I thought about it for a bit and said, 'Tell me to fuck off.'

I'd been in Vegas for three nights and everything had been the same as it normally was apart from I was doing everything very un-drunk. I was watching live shows, visiting the casinos, eating in the all-you-can-eat buffets and staying in clubs until 6 a.m. A common affliction and renowned short straw that is drawn by the sober people all over the world is automatically becoming the designated driver in a group of friends who are drinking. On this trip, Phil's car keys had been flung at me as soon as I landed on US soil. I'm not sure if they were supportive of my sobriety because of the benefits to me or so that they could drink at breakfast if they so chose. They did indeed choose to.

A strange thing happens to a person who begins their night with a highly caffeinated energy shot called '5-hour Energy' and then goes on to consume more than five Red Bulls in the following six-hour period. I don't know what this says about me but I had always been the kind of person who considers drinking that amount of caffeine to be dangerous; the type of person who would always read and religiously abide by the dosage of paracetamol, who would never take ibuprofen on an empty stomach. Even though I would meet a man I had never met before, climb into the passenger seat of his Vauxhall Corsa and purchase four grams of a white powder that is only verified by him as something along the lines of 'will blow your head off' and then snort it with a rolled-up tenner.

It was 2 a.m. After my fourth Red Bull of the evening, my heart began palpitating and my eyeballs felt like they'd been flattened with a rolling pin, but I was having a great time. I did have a momentary panic about the feeling in my chest but reassured myself that if my heart could deal with Vauxhall Corsa Man's 'blow your head off' coke, it was likely strong enough for this.

As the night continued, we ended up in a gay nightclub called Piranha. Phil and Josh had crossed the threshold of being able to have conversations with, and I hadn't learnt how to dance sober yet, so I just kind of wandered around the club observing all there was to be observed. Then I felt it.

I remember the first time I ever took ecstasy and how quickly, when I started to come down, the feeling of ultimate euphoria dropped away from me and started being replaced by a feeling of sheer, impending doom tinged with guilt and a feeling that I needed to leave where I was immediately, get into my own bed, cover my eyes and remain in the foetal position forever. Somehow, I was experiencing a fucking comedown from caffeine. The audacity. This was not what I signed up for when I decided to be sober.

The doom grew stronger. It was 4 a.m. I found Phil and Josh still swaying on the dance floor, strobe lights flickering them into slow motion, and told them if they wanted a lift home I was going now. They protested that their night was not over yet and that they'd Uber back. Thank fuck. I got out of there, drove back to Phil's and lay in his guest room, eyes as wide and dry as ashtrays, heart close to imploding, wondering why the fuck I had drunk so many Red Bulls. When I got sober and stopped taking drugs, I was excited about the fact that I would never again lie in bed at 6 o'clock in the morning, willing myself to sleep, trying to ignore the spinning anxiety behind my eyes. And yet, here I was.

I tossed and turned for a couple of hours, somewhere between conscious and lobotomised. I couldn't stay lying there. I had this bizarre feeling that I couldn't put my finger on. All I knew was that I couldn't stay in that bed. The feeling told me I needed to go outside and get some fresh air, so I found myself putting on a pair of shorts, a t-shirt and a pair of trainers. I realised that this feeling had developed into a kind of voice in my head and, unlike my constant internal monologue, this voice wasn't my own. By the time I got outside, it was saying one thing:

'You need to run.'

If that doesn't sound wild or abstract to you, you are

probably one of those people who was raised to include exercise as an important and healthy foundational part of their life, but I have never, ever been that person. My outlet was never getting my heart rate up and hitting the gym; it was smashing a big glass of red, or a pint of whiskey, and ignoring any healthy foundational anythings. Matter of fact, people who ran always creeped me out. What a strange thing to want to do. I'd only ever really thought of running as something you do towards ice cream vans or away from threats of terrorism, obviously at the same pace for both.

If I was a believer in God, perhaps I'd have pinned the 'you have to run' voice on Him, but being a person who has tripped on quite a few psychedelic drugs, I know how powerful the combination of drugs, lack of sleep and the human mind can be – apparently, even drugs as acceptable as caffeine.

Standing outside the house, I put my headphones in my ears and set of, running 2.4km round Phil's neighbourhood. In a Hollywood film, this scene would have a golden hue, the camera panning up from my trainers beating fast against the ground, my balled fists graciously swinging by my sides, up to my smiling mouth, my skin glistening and eyes shining. It would show me finding my pace and gliding across the sidewalk, waving at neighbours behind white picket fences pushing lawnmowers across their front yards. But this wasn't a Hollywood film. Do you remember the 'belly's gonna get ya' Reebok advert from the 1990s? It was more like that.

I arrived back at the house a fucking mess. I felt like I was going to die. I was beetroot red and dry heaving. I actually felt like I might faint. I had a stern word with myself:

'Never, ever, ever fucking do that again, you dickhead.' But once the sickness had subsided and the blood had stopped rushing around my body, I started to feel, well, really fucking good. I felt this sense of accomplishment that before then I'd only felt when I'd done something related to work, like securing a song on a big advert or playing a really successful show.

I had just run 2.4km. Matter of fact, forget this distance, I had just *run*. My friends were not even out of bed yet. I anticipated that when they did rise from their beds, they would be unable to keep their heads upright and I had just run around a Vegas suburb on a crisp and sunny January morning. Not only did I feel accomplished and a little bit high, I also felt like a right smug bastard. It was just wonderful.

I have no idea what happened that morning. Apparently, the desire to exercise happens to a lot of newly sober people. I don't think it was the Red Bull that gave me wings that morning. I have my suspicions that at six months sober, my body was starting to physically miss the highs from the drinking and the drugs. In my case, all night I'd been in places where I'd normally be experiencing a chemical high from something a little stronger than caffeine, and my body started to wonder where all the dopamine had gone. My brain was quite certain we should still be getting some, so it decided we would get the endorphins elsewhere. I'm glad it chose to run and not to skydive or race motorbikes, otherwise this book might never have happened.

Even though I had warned myself never to run again, the next day I found myself running. And the day after that. And the day after that. Something had clicked and I have no idea, even now, what that was. I can't say I ever *enjoyed* running. Maybe it's the feeling I get from running that I enjoy. Maybe it's the clarity it gives me, or the feeling of accomplishment. It is very, very rare that I wake up and think, 'I would love to run right now.' I think that's what a lot of people expect to feel after a few weeks of running – a burning desire to do it and a motivation that comes from that desire. I can only speak from my own experience but I still have to drag myself out of the house to run. A lot of my runs are spent checking my watch to see how far I have left, checking the time with the same enthusiasm I had for the end of an online speed awareness course I recently had to attend. Anyone I know who runs ultra distance or who has completed a marathon has told me that during the race, all they can think about is how they are never going to do it again and how fucking ridiculous it is that they are participating in such an event. Then they all say the same thing: afterwards, when they are wearing a shiny gold medal around their neck, having a big dinner with their family, endorphins coursing through their every fibre and a deep, vibrating feeling of accomplishment, not to mention a nod of comradery to anyone else wearing the same medal, they say: when can I do that again?

I ran my first 10km three weeks after that vomit-inducing 2.4km. That same all-or-nothing complex I'd struggled with my entire life had sunk its claws into something else, something more positive. I used an app to measure the distance of my first run and tried to go a little further each time I went out. I had, finally, found the first thing in my life that bought me a bit of peace. A challenge without being a competition. An accomplishment that wasn't work. A suitable silence. It sounds so silly to me now but I don't know how I lived without it before.

Fitness has become a huge part of my life and I've been asked a lot about how I got into it. Starting to run is my response. Stopping drinking and starting to run. But that's not to say everyone needs to get sober to start to do anything. It just made it easier for me. Without a hangover, I had a space on a Sunday morning which needed to be filled with something. Without that groggy the-morning-after-a-large-glass-of-red feeling on a Tuesday, I could find fifteen minutes to see how fast I could get around the block. Like anything worth having, my ability to run took time. Regardless of whether you drink or not, you have to push yourself to do anything that is hard. I had to let go of the idea of motivation and, as Nike say, just fucking do it. My advice to anyone who wants to start running? Don't stop. Go as slow as you want but don't you dare stop until you're done.

It's an awful place to say this but, as with anything in this life, it really is a marathon, not a sprint.

Dear Lucy,
Las Vegas? At six months sober? . . . Really? All or nothing, eh?

It's quite a ballsy move to go on holiday to the actual City of Sin when you are effectively trying to avoid sin, but, I have to say, I admire the gung-ho-throwing-yourself-in-the-deep-end-ness of it all.

To be fair to you, you exceeded your own expectations by quite a lot. I mean, you expected to stick out the sobriety thing, but the running?! No one saw that coming.

When you quit drinking the most common question people ask you is 'do you not get bored?' and you provided me with pretty solid response. You taught me that sober people can go to Vegas and party with their friends. You taught me that sober people can go to bottomless brunches and just abuse the small plates, leave more mimosas for the rest of them. You also taught me there is only so much orange juice a human can consume without prosecco, so do not try to keep up with the drinkers. But, most of all, you taught me that sober people can choose where they find their fun.

By waywardly getting on a flight to Nevada, you began your process of feeling out what worked for you as a non-drinker. You also realised that being in a club past a certain time often leads to an anti-climax. It's probably one of the reasons that lots of sober people say, 'Nothing good ever happens after 1 a.m..'

I'm proud of you for bowing out of a round of tequila on the casino floor.

I'm proud of you for saying no to coke when it was quite literally under your nose.

I'm so proud of your belief that you didn't need any of that stuff to have a good time, even before you knew that to be true.

You always blame the science of sobriety for the running, you were just missing the endorphins and the chemicals, but don't forget that underneath all that was you.

You are the reason you got up and ran.

Without YOUR brain willing you on and YOUR feet treading step-by-step, you'd have just stayed still.

PROCESS

Without your discipline you'd have answered that call for endorphins and chemicals with the same old substances you have done all your life.

Thank you for the recklessness.

Love,

Lucy x

Seems to be the Hardest Word

I didn't really understand the power of apologies until, in late 2021, I received one that changed how I felt about pretty much everything.

I never understood the part of religion that preached forgiveness: 'Forgive those who trespass against you'. Truthfully, I was always more of a 'trespassers will be shot (or at the very least prosecuted)' kind of gal. I used to believe that forgiveness was just a weak way out of an uncomfortable situation, probably because I had never truly forgiven anyone. I suppose that's because the first genuine apology I ever received, for something that desperately deserved one, was this one.

As an adult, I've always had this solid outer shell. I've always wanted to seem impossible to mess with because I have been messed around so many times, physically and emotionally. At the same time, underneath this front, I have always over-trusted people and had an open heart.

I have always had a deep belief that humans are innately good and are to be trusted. Ultimately, I broadly still believe that, despite the fact that I have given away too much trust far too soon and have learnt that, sometimes, people will instinctively abuse your trust and use it for their own gain. I know there are a minority of people out there that see trust as a weakness. They see trust as the soft underbelly of a person that, once exposed, is the cue to get in close and dig in their dagger of exploitation.

When I was fifteen, my friend and I spent an entire night camping with a boy and girl we'd just met. We danced around the fire, shared jokes and stories and sausages and cider and forged what felt like the beginnings of a blossoming friendship. The next morning, my friend and I went to go and buy us all some breakfast, only to return to an empty camp and empty bags. They stole everything, including the MP3 player I'd just got for my birthday. Some people see a moment of vulnerability as an opportunity to gain and they take what is not intended for them. I know that only too well.

The apology that changed my life was from Simon Cowell.

I wasn't expecting it, which probably added to its power. The power that forcibly cracked open my chest, reached down into my heart and poured light into it, light that I don't think had ever been there before. The power of this apology taught me about forgiveness: even if you aren't directly responsible for something, apologising for your part in it can, quite literally, change the course of someone's life.

★

In February 2020, Caroline Flack died. Caroline was a much-adored British TV presenter. She'd grown through her early twenties on our TV screens: a beautiful, funny, relatable girl-next-door, who always came across as incredibly real. That kind of *real* is uncommon in showbiz. Everything I'd ever seen of Caroline on the television was so joyously authentic and later, when I got to be on the screen with her, her emotion and integrity were so genuine. She was involved in the journey of the contestants and always offered a smile or a comforting conversation when the cameras were off. It's always lovely to meet someone like that. Someone radiant.

On 13th December, 2019, Caroline had a domestic altercation with her boyfriend and was arrested for common assault, something that was widely reported on, resulting in intense and incredibly divisive public commentary in the tabloids and across social media. I remember watching it unfold and thinking 'how the fuck is this happening?' and wondering where the hell all the people who were supposed to protect her were.

On 15th February, 2020, Caroline took her own life after learning that she had been charged with, and would go to trial for, the assault on her boyfriend.

Caroline's death moved me in a way that no other death has and it was her death that inspired me to start writing this book.

Since then, there has been plenty of commentary on the duty of care that should have been dedicated to her in her time of need. Fingers have been pointed in the direction of her management, the police and at TV, but also back towards the public and the media who were so keen to dissect the areas of her life that would have been private had they found themselves in the same situation. The hashtag #BeKind began trending across the world when the news of her death spread, with people taking to social media to encourage more kindness, and less bullying, commentary and brutality towards not only those in the public eye, but those out of it. It was a plea to everyone to join the movement of kindness in the wake of the tragic death of a young and talented woman.

Truthfully, it made me wince. The idea of the same people who gleefully took part in the communal rotation of the grindstone that wore Caroline down so harshly being overcome with sadness and grief made me feel ill. The same people who had secondary, nameless social media profiles that they used exclusively to bully online were instructing other people to #BeKind on their primary, identifiable accounts. The same red-top tabloids that smeared and belittled Caroline's name held frontpage vigils for her. ITV ended some of their most popular shows with a moment of memorial for her. To me, that seemed to resemble an afterthought. Where were her employers when her well-documented spiral began?

As the months went by, social media slowly started to adopt its old, low standard of compassion and the media began to turn its gaze back towards, and hooks into, Katie Price or whoever else's struggles would be perfect column fodder. I knew that the revolution wasn't coming. Nothing was going to change.

This was when I told myself that if my next album was in the top ten, I would have proved myself enough as a musician to tell my story without just being '*that girl*'. It's deeply sad that I even considered this: I should have been able to tell my story as soon as I was ready to, not when I thought my public image was prepped for it. However, my readiness and my album *Choices*, that charted not only in the top ten but in the top five, arrived at the same time.

I started writing this book. Except, back then, it wasn't a book at all. It was streams of consciousness. Paragraphs and paragraphs of anger had started flowing onto the page – questions about why I was left behind, how it had even happened in the first place. I realised that I wasn't writing a story, I was writing a letter. I saw that, in order to write this book, I needed answers. Answers that I'd never had.

Dominic Crossley, once again, helped me out. He listened and collated everything that I wanted to say, then, on 9th April, 2021, I sent this letter to each of the companies behind *The X Factor*: ITV, Fremantle, Syco and Sony.

Dear Sirs,
I am in the process of writing my memoir. This letter is so that you are aware of the account I am likely to give concerning my experience as a contestant on the television show The X Factor. *In the relevant chapter of my memoir, I propose to give an account of:*

- *My auditions and appearances on the show and my experience as a contestant.*
- *The fact that I was the victim of a serious criminal offence during the course of the show, when placed in a hotel away from all but one other contestant and the security they enjoyed.*
- *My view on the failure of a duty of care owed to me.*
- *The immediate aftermath of the offence including a) the medical care I received, b) the way my*

mother was notified and my feeling of isolation the day afterwards, c) my accommodation and the fact that a security guard was appointed to me (without being requested) and was told not to leave me unattended until the day of the final show.

- *The long-term aftermath during which you offered no support or consideration for my mental or physical health or the adverse consequences for my career. You may be aware, because I have spoken about it publicly, that I attempted suicide in 2014.*

- *My view of the lack of care towards reality TV contestants more generally, and that the commercial entities involved in their production and the exploitation of contestants prioritise their own commercial interests even in extreme circumstances such as my assault.*

This letter is to offer you an opportunity to respond to the above points and, if you consider it appropriate, apologise to me for what I have had to endure. Should you offer any such apology or explanation, it is likely that I will include it in my memoir.

In responding, please also notify me if you intend to refer to or rely upon any alleged obligation of confidentiality owed by me. As you will no doubt accept, I should not be prevented from giving a full and truthful account of my experience, but should you (or any third party you are connected with) wish to assert any such intention please notify me immediately so that it can be addressed. You will also be aware of the scale of the public interest that arises from the issues referred to.

Please note that this letter is confidential. It is written to notify you of my current intention in terms of publication but it is not to be construed as consent for you to disclose any of the above information or other sensitive information concerning me. It is entirely for me to decide the extent and timing of my personal account (and whether to publish it) and you should understand that any attempts to 'leak' this story or otherwise take steps in advance of publication other than providing a full and frank response to this letter would be wholly inappropriate. Nothing in this letter should be construed as a waiver of my rights or remedies, which remain fully reserved.

I await hearing from you.

Yours

Ms Lucy Spraggan

As you can tell, Dominic is a fucking bad-ass. My letter probably would have ended with a 'PS. Fuck you, you big wankers', which would almost certainly have taken the oomph out of it. Once the letters had been emailed over, it was a waiting game. I didn't know what was going to happen. I started panicking, late at night. I'd lie in bed and think about all the showbiz horror stories I'd heard about – theories on whistle blowers or apples that had upset the apple cart who had been found dead or involved in car accidents. I started to wonder how deep all that went. I knew that my story and, more so, the way I'd be treated afterwards, would have huge implications for the companies involved. The multi-million-pound companies that were involved, all with private shareholders and profiteers, would be affected by my voice. I was nearly two years sober at this point and whether or not I needed to, even if my suspicions were just paranoia, I still told my friends and family that if I was found dead behind the wheel of a car, or in a hotel room, with drugs and alcohol in my system, I did not put them there. Those things had nearly killed me many times before, but never again.

I waited.

I'd like to share with you the response that I got from ITV, nearly a decade since my last contact with them, that took them two months to send after receiving my letter.

11th June 2021
Dear Ms Spraggan,

Thank you for bearing with me while we consulted with Thames about your letter dated 9 April 2021, which I am now in a position to respond to more fully.

First, we are very sorry that your experience on The X Factor *was such an unhappy one and we acknowledge that what happened to you must have been devastating. It takes great courage and strength to speak out about a time that must be very difficult to revisit.*

I understand that Thames has written to you in relation to the specific issues you raise about your treatment while a participant on The X Factor. *As ITV did not have any direct dealings with you in respect of those matters, there is nothing further we can add.*

However, you also say that you believe that there

is a lack of duty of care generally towards reality TV participants, which is something that we do not agree with.

ITV is committed to having in place suitable processes to protect the mental health and welfare of programme participants, and we expect all producers of commissioned programmes to have in place appropriate procedures to look after the mental health of programme participants as well as their physical safety. Those processes and procedures will differ from programme to programme, and are constantly developed to ensure that the welfare of all participants in ITV programmes is appropriately safeguarded.

I can also reassure you that the welfare of participants is one of our highest priorities at ITV as reflected in our Duty of Care Charter and the detailed guidance we now have available for all producers to ensure that the welfare of participants is appropriately safeguarded on all our programmes.

Yours sincerely,
ITV

An 'unhappy experience'. That's what I'd had. I'd never heard being raped described as a happy or unhappy experience.

The welfare of participants is one of their 'highest priorities' too. I must have just slipped through the net in that case. Oh, and Caroline. And Sophie Gradon and Mike Thalassitis, two *Love Island* contestants who also committed suicide. And Steve Dymond, a guest on *The Jeremy Kyle Show*, who took his own life. And all of the reality TV contestants I know personally who have battled with their mental health since being on one of ITV's shows. They were apparently *all* safeguarded, just like me.

I had hopes for that letter. I thought that letter might hold the key to the beginning of my healing process. But instead, the message I took away from it – just as was made clear over the last decade – was that I didn't matter. And I never did.

I received responses from all four companies, each with a very different tone, none of which contained an apology. Truthfully, I expected the most aggressive response to be from Syco. I mean, the name of that company itself gives a vibe. I was more than shocked when my expectations of Syco, or more specifically Simon Cowell, were shattered, and in the tiny shards that were left, little sparks of hope started to glimmer through.

Syco is Simon Cowell's record company and I'm going to assume I don't need to formally introduce him to you. We all have our perceptions of him, don't we? The straight-talking, serious, ruthless TV judge. Simon had been working on America's Got Talent when I was on the show, so I'd never met him or come into contact with him before. Knowing Simon the way I do now, which I will get to very soon, I believe that perception is wrong. The general public consumed the idea that I was ill when I left the show because that is what was written in the newspapers. My experience taught me that so much of how the media presents those in the public eye is based on lies and misconceptions. I'm also very aware that despite our pasts, we are all capable of change. I made a choice to find out who Simon really was.

Against what I imagine every aide and lawyer advised, a

phone number flashed up on my screen; my iPhone told me the call was coming from Malibu. I knew who that was. His assistant had arranged a time with him to call me. I picked it up and a voice I recognised instantly, a voice I'd heard on the TV my entire life, spoke.

'Lucy, before you or I say anything else, I want to tell you that I am sorry.'

Like the ending of Disney's *Beauty and the Beast*, where true love suspends Beast and spins him in mid-air, transforming him back into the man he once was, 'I am sorry' immediately evoked something I didn't know was there. My eyes pricked. There was a pause between us.

'I have thought about you many, many times over the years, about what happened to you, about how I should've been there for you, about so many things. And I want you to know that I am truly, truly sorry.'

My story (or my life, as it's otherwise known) undoubtably has six, if not more, of the elements that the Godfather of Storytelling, Aristotle, deems necessary to qualify as a tragedy. To be a tragedy, a narrative arc needs plot, character, thought, diction, spectacle and song. Every story also needs a hero and in mine, there have been so many. In the beginning, you met the people who raised me, the people who held me up high and wanted the world to see me, who believed in me. In the middle, I was left to be my own hero. In the end, there was another hero I never, ever expected.

Aristotle has a theory about the Tragic Hero. They must be noble, capable and powerful – here's the multi-million-pound man, famous across the world. They must be flawed – he's the definition of a villain on our televisions, dark-eyed, dark-haired, shattering people's dreams with the hit of the big, red buzzer. And they must suffer a reversal in good fortune – in August 2020, Simon broke his back in a biking accident, rendering him unable to move and giving him what he told me was a new perspective on what it means to be powerless and to need help. 'A man does not become a hero until he can see the root of his own downfall,' said Aristotle.

'I should have reached out earlier, and I will do anything I can to help you,' said Simon.

His apology was honest, authentic and genuinely life-changing for me. Almost immediately after the phone call ended, I burst into tears of relief. The heaviness I had been carrying for nearly a decade thawed out and melted away in different directions. My anger dissipated like frightened mice, scrambling away from me through the cracks under the door, never to be seen again. It was the first time I felt how soothing the word 'sorry' can be. No one else had said it before. The 'sorry' that Simon chose to give me closed one of the most uncomfortable chapters of my life.

I didn't want anything else from Simon and that was hard for him to understand at first. He didn't quite grasp what he'd already given me. I explained how I had been treated on the show; I showed him the response from ITV; I sat with him for hours and hours and told him everything about the last decade, how I'd released six top-forty albums, toured the world, had a legion of wildly supportive fans, sobered up, trimmed down and, over everything else, survived. He was in shock: 'How did you do it?' he asked me. 'I just did,' I said.

As our friendship developed, Simon listened to my entire back catalogue of music and expressed a genuine interest and belief in my song writing. He asked if he could be involved in my career. At first, I thought he wanted to try to help give me back some of the future that had been snatched away from me in 2012, or maybe that he wanted to make things up to me. I accepted that with gratitude. Since then, it's become clear that Simon thinks I have real talent, and that is what he wants to champion. I want to be completely clear about the fact that Simon has never once asked me not to write this book. Every time we have spoken about it, he has told me that the most important thing is that I do whatever I need to do to feel better.

In late 2021, Simon knew I was in the middle of parting ways with the manager I'd struggled with for years and he suggested he try to get me managed by a bigger, more professional outfit. He had a relationship with YMU, one of the world's most recognisable management companies, who agreed to take me on under their 'showbiz' department, not the music department. This set the tone before the relationship even began. Initially, I wasn't aware of the deep-running ties that YMU had with ITV.

The very showbiz plan was for me to participate in *I'm a Celebrity... Get Me Out of Here!* to propel me back into the public eyeline. Should have been easy enough – I'd just had a number-five album and had a suitable level of notoriety; YMU managed Ant and Dec and, more so, I had Simon Cowell standing with me. But ITV did not want to play ball on this.

This was the very last opportunity I would give ITV to cut me a fucking break. I was willing to work alongside them even after they'd sent me that letter that made me feel microscopic. But, as I had suspected had been the case over the last ten years, they didn't want to give me a platform.

There were months where they told my management I was being considered but at the same time they were dancing around a definitive answer, so Simon called the talent manager and pulled rank. Weeks later, we read about the line-up for the show – I wasn't on it.

They'd gone against Simon, they'd decided against throwing me a line and, instead of respectfully letting either of us know about it, we found out from the tabloids. Simon was not only furious but shocked. He was seeing, first-hand, how ITV conducted themselves when it came to me. Days later, he pulled out of ITV's new talent show, *Walk the Line*.

All the while, in planning meetings at YMU, when I voiced my intention of finding a publisher for my book, I was told that I should be focusing far more on my music and to forget about the book for a while. I was not on board with that. It took me nearly a decade to arrive at a place where I felt strong enough to start turning the wheels of what would eventually be the release of this book, and every time I brought it up in front of YMU, I was stonewalled. In one meeting, one of the directors asked me, almost sarcastically, why I would want to release this book. It caught me off guard. Wasn't it clear? I'd lived in the shadow of what really happened to me for so long. I'd been swimming relentlessly against the tide in my career, struggling to keep my head above water. I'd had the script that I'd written for my life crumpled up and thrown in the bin and I'd fucking made it out the other side. I wanted to tell other people that they could make it out the other side too. I wanted to speak my truth. I wanted the public to understand me more.

Looking at me through their thick, round glasses, leaning their elbow on the long, glass table, resting their chin on their hand, the director asked me sceptically, 'Why do you want to talk about this?' They told me, in front of the four or five other people around the table, 'The public are very fickle, they won't remember you as much as you think they will. Things might get twisted. A book is a bad idea. It'd be better for you to go on a famous podcast and talk about it there, if you *have* to talk about it.'

Do you know who manages the famous podcast host they were referring to? YMU.

In January 2022, I unsurprisingly told YMU I no longer wanted to be managed by them. I was surprised that, after all this time, the message still wasn't clear: I am not a puppet and I never fucking will be.

Simon is a very important person to me now and we see each other quite a lot. He is an older male figure, a consistent kind that I've never had before. He looks out for me and calls me just to talk about life. He likes to make sure I'm OK and I do the same. I look up to him and he looks up to me too. I genuinely care about him a lot. I often think about the impact that fame had on me back in 2012 and then try to imagine a lifetime of that. It's inconceivable to me. I also can't imagine being involved in such a ferocious and perilous industry, where someone is always trying to collapse your empire.

One Sunday, just before Christmas 2022, I went down to Simon's house in the countryside and we all spent the day doing festive things. We had a roast and sat around the table just chatting away with Christmas songs playing in the background. In this weird twist of events, Simon, and his family, now feel like family to me.

Dear Lucy,

When you heard that Caroline had killed herself, you knew that the duty of care crisis had hit an all-time low. Now ITV, and all the involved production companies, would have to hold themselves accountable for the damage that has been done to so many people. People who have worked for, appeared on, been catapulted into fame by, presented or been involved in their shows. You were convinced that they'd reach out to you, that now they'd have to go back and save all of the other people. You believed that this was the catalyst that would start to turn the wheels of change. So, you waited.

And no one showed up.

I know that hurt.

When they did respond to your letter, it hurt even more. You read it once, sat down and had to steady yourself. Half a page; an 'unhappy experience'.

The hope had been for accountability, for recognition, for an apology. That letter was anything but that. It made it worse.

You were used to it, though. When you and Billy got drunk as young children, the adults rushed around and shouted at you instead of pausing, thinking and saying, 'We let you down. This was our fault. It should never have happened.'

Our experiences, along with Simon's apology, have

offered me a completely new perspective on the way I practice accountability. I am not ashamed to be wrong and I am not scared to apologise. I know the power of that now. I am ready to be accountable for myself and for others, especially for the young or vulnerable people in my life.

You realised early on that all the while you kept your right to anonymity, you were inadvertently protecting The X Factor *and the corporations behind it. You suspected, right from the beginning, that they didn't want your voice to get loud enough to tell your story.*

Right now, I give you all the permission you will ever need to say what you want. Be as loud as you need to be.

For years, you were part of the army of contestants that directed their anger and feelings of abandonment towards Simon Cowell, until, quite simply, he was the first person to treat you like a human being and you got to know a little more about how it all works.

You started to suspect that blaming the celebrity face of the show might be exactly what the companies behind it want you to do.

Ronald McDonald is the face of McDonald's. When you get food poisoning from McDonald's, you don't send a letter of complaint to the clown, do you? You send it to the McDonald's Corporation.

All of the contestants who had their lives turned upside down never blame the production companies. Perhaps they should start.

You became privy to the fact that there is a network in showbiz, a network of people who can build you up and break you down. Regardless of your status, they can give you a big red nose and make you the fall guy, too. It's all very clever. It's scary too.

Funny thing is, for you, if they give you nothing, they can't take anything away from you.

I am proud of you for getting through it all by yourself and, not just that, you had six top-forty albums in the process . . . That's powerful stuff.

Trust your instincts, kid. Don't let people make you feel small.

I'm very proud of you.

Love,

Lucy x

'But, how did you do it?'

I've been completely open with you about everything I've come up against in this life – it's all here for you to see. My most prized achievement is that I've survived, so far, quite a lot of trauma and pain. I am still sober and I work hard to maintain that every day. Yeah, I lost weight but my biggest accomplishment is maintaining a better relationship with my body now, rather than obsessing over my diet or exercise for fat loss. I'm far from perfect and, as a matter of fact, seeking perfection with my predisposition of being a *tad* extreme showed me that perfection doesn't exist. It's far rarer now but some days I am fucking miserable and I can still easily slip into depression and despair. That's part of who I am and making it through those days is the hardest thing I do. I can accept that I have achieved things that I never dreamed of but I still find it hard to praise myself for those achievements and I can still instinctively underplay them. I am incredibly grateful to be reminded of all those things by the people around me, in real life and online. Alongside the compliments and praise that I am so bloody humbled to receive, I am often asked this one question: 'How did you do it?'

I know that question means different things for the different people who ask it. For some, it's 'How did you lose the weight and keep it off?' For others, it's 'How did you stay sober? Do you not get cravings?' Or 'How did you recover from being suicidal? How do you manage your mental health?' For Simon Cowell, it was 'How did you create a career like the one you have without any help?'

It's an honour to be asked questions like that, it makes me feel like I have made some good decisions in this life, but I feel like a bit of a preacher when I try to answer them. In fact, I feel like writing a chapter called 'But, How Did You Do It?' and answering a question that *you* didn't even ask is a bit pompous, but I'll give it a go anyway.

I will say, though, my answer is not to the question 'how did you do it?' but 'how are you doing it?' because I am still very much *doing it*. Every day.

I wish I had a simple answer. Actually, the answer itself *is* simple. But implementing it really isn't. The honest response is: I try, every day, to love myself. I try, every day, to show myself the compassion and empathy that I show my friends. I try to be as dedicated to myself as I am dedicated to my work or my beliefs. Every day, I accept that anything worth having takes time and effort to get and that I need to actively pursue feeling better about myself or else I won't. I need to implement goals with intention and enforce my adherence to them. It's a long, long process.

★

Three months into discovering running, I started to run everywhere. I figured there wasn't really any reason to walk anymore. I swapped my entire casual wardrobe for luminous running jackets and Nike leggings. To me, running was another little gang I could be a part of. When I feel like I'm in a club or crew it gives me the sense of belonging that I crave so badly.

Before I was a runner, I was completely perplexed by them. I used to see them, admittedly at 6 or 7 a.m. in the morning when my night was just finishing, jogging down the road and think, 'What the fuck are you doing?' Now I have to supress the urge to lean out of my car window and shout unasked-for support at people running down the pavement. I want to tell other runners that their calves look great. When I run towards other runners, I smile this big, proud grin at them and sometimes offer a little wave – nod to our secret worldwide running gang. These gestures are reciprocated about 2 per cent of the time, which is a shame, but I do believe that someone out there feels the same. I am just so happy to see someone else out there on the road, or trail, who has unlocked the joy of running. It makes me happy to see anyone unlock the joy of enjoyment. Because it is enjoyment that makes us feel fulfilled. Without enjoyment, we are trudging towards nothing and the same goes for everything we do.

Some things take a little time to enjoy, like running. I told you, the first thing I thought after my first run was, 'Never, ever, ever fucking do that again, you dickhead,' but the feeling of accomplishment soon overwhelmed that. I wanted to do better in the future, despite the short-term discomfort. In 2021, I had the word 'RUN' tattooed just above my sock line on my right foot. Not just as a reminder to always put one foot in front of the other, but a reminder of what running has taught me. I want to be permanently committed to self-improvement and, more importantly, maintaining that improvement. I want my positive habits to be as permanent as the tattoo that will remain on my leg for the rest of my life.

You don't have to run anywhere, by the way. I understand that running isn't for everyone. Running became *my* initial outlet but it could have been anything. All you need to do is find out is what you love doing. And I mean, really love doing. Something that makes you feel untouchable, or talented, or just happy in that moment. Go to classes, learn an instrument, start knitting, take up wheelchair basketball, play World of Warcraft – it doesn't matter, just find it and keep doing it.

Who fucking knows why running caught my fancy but it opened up a whole world of pursuits for me and, through that, I have found what makes me truly happy. I found a range of different things I use to keep me grounded, emotionally aware and self-disciplined: cold water dipping and journaling to name a few – but they might be different for everyone. Anything which helps ground you in yourself will always create positive change.

One of the most fulfilling passions I have discovered is fighting. No, not like the kind of fights that I had been involved in throughout my life. No fence posts or karaoke bars. Not fights that start in pubs or in drunken arguments – fights that happen in gyms: boxing, kickboxing, Jiu Jitsu and wrestling. The kind of fights that require tactical thinking, discipline and knowledge. The feeling I get from exchanging kicks and punches in the ring with a willing participant, or having my limbs tied up in all kinds of shapes on the mat, brings me joy and it brings me empowerment.

For years after the assault, I never imagined that I would be able to get physically close to a man. I didn't even like being on public transport next to a man and the idea of being touched by a man I didn't know made me panic. But I have been introduced to a world that taught me how to trust men again, one in which I can grapple with them and enjoy the art of being thrown on the floor and trying to separate myself from their choke holds, as they try to get away from mine. It's put me on a level playing field. Both MMA and sobriety make me feel able to defend myself in most situations, or at least be the most prepared I can be if I ever run into trouble again. I also know that I can always run away.

Fighting helped me control my anger, that white-hot rage that followed me around for a lifetime. Physically moving my body helps me dispel unspent energy. Getting punched in the face taught me how to avoid getting punched in the face. I wish I'd got into this kind of fighting earlier because it would have been so beneficial to know the rules of engagement throughout my life. 'Protect yourself at all times,' the referee says as a fight begins.

★

It was late 2019, and I'd gone from being seemingly in-your-face loved-up and married to separated; from being almost completely physically inactive to running everywhere; from an uncontrollable booze hound to a one hundred per cent sober person. From an outside perspective, it was very clear that there was a massive shift happening in my life, but I didn't really acknowledge it at the time. That's kind of how life goes, isn't it? Habits are formed over time, both positive and negative ones, but they are formed quietly. To us, we are just doing us. And yet, it only takes one scroll down your preferred social media platform to know that we, as social media consumers, are obsessed with 'transformations'. We fixate on physical transformations, before and after pictures of weight loss or muscle gain, or people who have had cosmetic surgery.

Before my own 'transformation', when I'd see that someone had lost a lot of weight, done a photoshoot and uploaded it to their social media, I'd instinctively think something negative like, 'I'd rather have a fucking Mars Bar!' If I saw that someone had stopped drinking or one of my friends chose to have a break from drinking, 'boring bastard' would flash across my mind. I'd cringe at someone showing off their achievements. I was so intimidated by the dedication and commitment that it must have taken that person to have changed everything in the way that they did that I couldn't even begin to imagine myself able to do the same. Without me realising it, their achievements made me feel inadequate.

In the past, when I saw another musician win an award or have a hit song, it would cause a knee-jerk reaction from me and I'd think of something negative about their music or personality. When I saw someone sober at a wedding or a party having a great time, dancing and chatting away, I'd be confused about how they were doing that. How does one have a good time without alcohol? They *don't*. They can't be, because I certainly couldn't. 'Sad bastards.' There it was, the negative thought. They were doing something I didn't believe I had the capacity to do, so I made them out to be a bad or boring person. I had friendships where we mutually enabled and perpetuated that kind of negative thinking and speaking, keeping one another in that toxic cycle.

The way I thought was so detrimental to my own mind and mental health. I now realise that my negative thinking was born out of my lack of self-belief and feelings of inadequacy: I didn't believe I'd ever be able to enforce any of the changes I would have really liked to. Those feelings of inadequacy and intimidation, the lack of self-belief and a bit of self-loathing, are all indicative of a feeling I used to get about a lot of things other people had that I didn't: jealousy.

I don't make comparisons anymore. We all have something that someone else is jealous of. Now, when I think a jealous thought (which, of course, still happens), I know it comes from my fear of never being good enough. It took a lot of corrective work and self-talk, but the way I saw the world definitely shifted once I realised how much damage I was causing myself. Noticing and dissecting my negative thoughts literally changed my life. My metaphor for self-awareness is that I have a rolled-up newspaper ready to swing at any of my own thoughts that aren't productive, whether that be about myself or others. I bash the negative thoughts away and I replace them with something positive.

I'd love to say that I followed a set of steps to self-belief, or that there's an eight-week plan for self-compassion, but that's not the case. Self-compassion, self-worth, self-belief, self-anything are skills. As with any skill, I need to keep honing mine. We aren't born with these virtues; matter of fact, as we grow up, we can adopt bad habits from the people we're surrounded or parented by, habits that weaken our relationship with ourselves. We learn to punish our bodies instead of nourish them, or to abandon our emotions to make others comfortable. When it came to learning how to practice self-worth, I had to unpick a lot of my stitching and start again.

Someone once told me, 'You are not your thoughts.' As soon as I heard that, I realised that every single thought I have doesn't have to be acted on. That I can make choices. When a thought pops into my head, I don't need to rush to act on it. I can take a breath, make an assessment and, if I want to, I can tell that thought to fuck off. Day-to-day, I think this skillset is the most valuable I have in my arsenal. And as with the other skillsets, it takes practice.

Every day is filled with choices to make. I used to act on whatever that impulsive, negative voice told me. That voice is definitely made louder by alcohol and drugs. Both of those things suffocate our ability to tell that voice to fuck off. That's how I ended up doing so much cocaine. 'Buy another bag,' the voice would say, so I would. 'Have one more drink,' it encouraged, and I was out until the sunrise. I do things differently now. I used to have a back and forth with the voice, weighing up the pros and cons of going for a run or going out for a drink. I don't have that conversation with myself every day now, though I did for a long time. After putting not-listening-to-the-voice into practice for so long, it became second nature to make the right choice. I know now that a run will make me feel better, so instead of having to tell myself that again, my decision to go is because I am going. Do I nip into the pub for a glass of wine? No, because I do not drink anymore. I established my connection with those things, so instead of having to weigh up every situation as it happens, I have a ready-made answer. I am prepared.

If it's not something I have come up against before, I lay out all of the information in front of me, weigh it all up and do my best to make the right choice. To me, being able to hear and assess the voice inside my mind, without acting impulsively, is called discipline. It means that you can say yes or no to the things that the voice in your head – or another person's voice – tells you to do. Discipline overrides my need for motivation when it comes to things I'd rather I didn't do. I don't need to look for inspiration to do the things that make me uncomfortable because I use discipline instead.

I started therapy years ago, I even flirted with it during high school after I'd been appointed the school's resident counsellor to help with my unruly behaviour. It didn't work. I really didn't like the woman and even more so, I did not like her approach. I stopped going in the end, something I'd done with all of the many therapists I've worked with over the years. I'd tried CBT, talk therapy – God, I even tried hypnosis at one point – all to no avail. I was convinced that therapy just wasn't for me. It turns out, there isn't a one-size-fits-all approach to therapy. Some people are forever changed by the effects of CBT, some can only work with psychotherapists, some opting for EMT or they swear by hypnosis, but what has made the most difference to me is finding the right person (or app, or group) to provide that advice. I searched high and low for someone I 'clicked' with and in 2021, decades into my quest for effective therapy, I found Bev. I actually found her through BAPAM, a health and well-being charity for those in the Performing Arts.

She has been an incredible support to me and has taught me so much about how to manage my emotions. The most important tool that Bev introduced me to was journaling, something I do every single day. I write about my intentions, my feelings, the things that bother me, the things I love, that I am grateful for. It helps to frame my perspective and to make sure I really know how I feel about things.

'One man's trash is another man's treasure'. The best therapist in the world wouldn't suit everyone. Of course, being able to have therapy is a huge privilege and if you are in the position to look for a therapist, please don't give up when you're looking for the right one. There's someone out there for everyone. It might take a while but I promise it's worth it.

Bev has always warned me about the mythical demon that is the 'Fuck It Fairy'. The Fuck It Fairy will appear in many situations – you will have heard her before, perhaps when you're trying to be 'good' and there's a delicious slice of Victoria sponge cake thrust in front of you. 'Fuck it!' the fairy says, and you eat the cake. The Fuck It Fairy loves Dry January too, when you're trying desperately to stay on the wagon and your friend buys you a pint. 'Fuck it!' the fairy says, and you listen. Whenever I am presented with a situation and I hear the fairy whisper 'Fuck it!' into my ear, I know that I need to think more about what I'm about to commit to. If the Fuck It Fairy gets too strong, she could undo all of my hard work in one swift 'Fuck it!'. Look out for her.

When my last album came out, I got asked a question about longevity in the music industry. I genuinely laughed out loud. I laughed because I realised that longevity in any industry, or any part of life, comes from clinging to whatever it is you have chosen and refusing, against all adversity, to let go of it. Longevity is just another word for perseverance. I truly believe that if you keep going and keep going, regardless of what is thrown at you, you will get what you want. Actually, you might not get exactly what you want – I'd be lying if I said that – but you will eventually be rewarded for your persistence. And that will make you feel fulfilled. Longevity, perseverance, persistence, survival … they are all the same thing. I told you before, my morbid motto in life is 'don't kill yourself', which is the most basic version of longevity. It means I tell myself: I don't quit.

When PTSD slams back into my life – which it does from time to time, I am yet to be completely free of that – I use grounding techniques to get myself back into my surroundings and out of the episode. When I feel the physical effects beginning (increased heart rate, rapid breathing and like my conscious thought is fading away), I ground myself by looking around the room for a colour, a shape and a sound. Focusing on these things can help prevent the attack from taking me deeper into dissociation.

Though I talk a lot about the relationship that I have with myself, the relationship I have with my friends and loved ones is equally important. When I started to adjust the way I lived, many of my friendships expired – I've learnt that relationships do that. Though a few of them didn't expire and I started to meet other people on their own quest for fulfilment. I have an incredibly supportive set of friends and we are able to be transparent, open and honest with each other. We have a mutual agreement to always tell the truth and never to tell each other what we think the other *wants* to hear. I can tell them exactly how I feel and not fear any judgement – something that is vital for anyone who suffers with mental health issues, like me.

I am incredibly sensitive and it took me nearly thirty years to appreciate what a blessing that is. I care about a lot of things but more recently have been dedicated to prioritising what I care about. I have come to accept that not everyone is going to like me or understand me. Just like I won't like and understand everyone else I meet. Rather than focus on the opinions of people who don't like or know me, or try to change their perception of me, I try to focus on the opinions of people who really do matter to me and who are prevalent in my life: my friends, my family, the people I work with, the people who support me. I do care what those people think but now I can now confidently say, 'I don't care about what people that don't know me think about me.' I didn't grow a thicker skin, I just put a coat on.

When people ask me 'how did you do it?', it reminds me that I am not done. I'm nowhere near the finish line – I'm not even sure there is one. The question reminds me that everything I have done, and carry on doing, is part of my process.

The answer is: 'I am still doing it. And I hope I continue for the rest of my life.'

Dear Future Lucy,
I spent so much time thinking about the past that I nearly forgot to embrace the future version of us.
Writing this book has made me realise how much of a difference ten years can make to a human being. I spent so many years stuck in oblivion, unable to pull

myself back out of the dark. But once I saw a little crack of light and decided to move towards it, things started to change. I started to change. My personality and coping strategies have developed. My flaws, though I still have plenty of them, are unrecognisable from the Lucy I was a decade ago.

I hope you keep chasing the light.

I've made a lot of mistakes; things I wouldn't do if I could go back in time, but I can't, and that's the point, isn't it? I suppose they aren't mistakes; they're lessons. All of those things are part of who I am. Who we are. It's all part of the process.

I can't see into the future but I do know that in ten more years, you will be a whole other person. You'll have to accept that some things I've written in this book deviate from the way you feel as time moves on. You will cringe at yourself. I hope you have compassion for who I am now.

I hope that you keep surrounding yourself with people who love you, and who value you, and who tell you that they are proud of you. Even if you aren't related to them, they are your family.

I am excited to know what my siblings' children turn out like. I hope you are the kind of aunty they know they can turn to when they need anything. Please stay as close to them as you can and give them the extended family you didn't have.

I guess it's only you who will know if we're going to have kids, Future Lucy. I think I hope you do. For many years, I told myself I wouldn't, for fear of fucking them up, or losing my independence, or that my work wouldn't ever allow me to look after them. I think the experience in our early twenties made me associate having kids with extreme fear and inadequacy. If you do have kids, make sure they know how much of a privilege it is to be around them, support them in whatever they choose to do and always tell them how proud you are of them. It will go a long way. I think you'd make a great mum but you will, as every parent ever has, fuck up your kids, if you have them. It's the way the world works.

Who knows if you'll ever get married again. If you do, and if you pay the mortgage, please remember to put that in your name. Tenants in common, Future Lucy.

Steven is sitting right beside you as you write this final letter but he won't always be here. The worst part of having a dog is that one day, you are going to have to endure the pain of losing him, and I have no doubt it will be the hardest thing you ever have to do. He saved your life – not just in that car but every time you opened the front door and he ran towards you, his whole body shaking with excitement; when he lay down next to you when you cried; when he was the only reason you got out of bed and went outside on your worst days and all the times he sat silently beside you offering the kind of love and trust that no human being can. Please be as prepared as you can; love him every second of every day.

I hope you continue to embrace that being a black sheep doesn't feel so isolating once you find your flock. Weirdos, outcasts and people who think a little differently to the norm – they are our people. The people I hang around with are all black sheep. The rough little gym I go to is full of them. I hope as you travel, relocate and adventure, you always look for them.

Ben and I stopped speaking around 2019. After so long trying to be best friends and work colleagues at the same time, our relationship frayed and we didn't speak for years. It was this book that brought us back together when I reached out to him in 2022. He was always a good friend to you; I hope you guys become close again in the future.

My body has been SO good to me through years of abusing it. Please don't ever forget to maintain the relationship you have with it. Always run and always fight, inside and outside of the gym. I hope you get better at appreciating what your body can do over how it looks, because you deserve that. Eat to fulfil and to nourish it. Remember that every day could be your last and, once you're gone, there's no more cake. Eat it while you can.

As for the tattoos, I think you'll look quite cool as an old person. There are so many and you may as well collect more. Just don't get any neck tattoos, please.

I hope you stay sober. I've often wondered if you'll ever decide to drink again. I don't think you will but I hope that if you do, it'll be by choice and not by recklessness or for escapism. Maybe you'll change your stance on moderation but, until then, I hope you grow old sober as a judge.

A few weeks ago, someone asked me how I was and I said, 'I'm so busy, man!'

PROCESS

He turned his hands out, shrugged and said, 'That's the life you chose, though, isn't it?'

It isn't though, is it? Because we don't get to choose how life goes. I know that now.

All I can do is make the best guess at what to do next, do it with intention and thought, and always do it with kindness.

I don't know who you'll be in the future but I will always be eternally proud of you.

All of my love,

Lucy x

A Message to the Reader

I wanted to say, directly to you, thank you.

Thank you for taking the time to read this book and to hear about my story.

I have been considering how to do this for so many years and I never anticipated that I would legitimately write my own book. It is the hardest but most rewarding and healing thing I have ever done, and I am so grateful that I have been able to share it with you. I really hope that I have offered you a perspective on some views that differ from your own but also that you have found common ground with some of my experiences too.

To know that you're reading this part of the book gives me hope that you enjoyed it, but what I hope most is that you can take even the smallest part of it forward with you in life. When I set about writing this book, I was asked why I was doing it. There were so many reasons but the one that kept coming back was that if I could help anyone, even one person, with the contents of this book, it would be a million times worth it.

You've helped me by reading this. By you knowing more about me, I feel free from the shackles of the narrative I was given all those years ago. A lot of it wasn't pretty but sharing it with you makes it feel, I don't know . . . right. Like the record was set straight.

I hope that you weren't triggered or affected too deeply by this book's contents and I am sorry if it had you reliving anything uncomfortable from your own past. Over the last ten years, I have undeniably struggled to carry my own secrets and burdens and it's through this that I learnt that I am not strong enough to carry anyone else's trauma. So, because of that, I have a strong favour to ask of you.

If you ever see me about, on the street, in the gym, at a show, a book signing or a speaking event, please come and say hello. My favour is that I ask that you not to tell me about your own trauma or about similar things that have happened to you.

I will be leaving a lot of my pain in some of these chapters and then I will be closing the book.

As honoured as I am if you feel safe enough to share them with me, I know that hearing your equally heart-breaking stories will stretch the scars that I have spent so long trying to close.

If you are one of the incredibly strong people who has overcome a huge trauma in your life, and I bet you are, I want you to show me that by offering me a nod, or a fist bump, or a very simple 'I am with you'. I will tell you that I'm proud of you. Because I am.

I hope that request doesn't come across as self-absorbed;

I just want to continue my journey of self-preservation as much as possible and protect myself from any more harm.

Thank you again for giving me your time, it means more than the world to me.

All my love,

Lucy x

Acknowledgements

I'd like to give the most very sincere thank you to Jo Monroe: without your crash course in becoming an author and your steadfast advice, this book would never have taken the shape that it did. Thank you for telling me I didn't need a ghost-writer, you made me feel like I could actually do this. You also shared the most delicious sandwich and snacks with me across that table in London. I appreciate it all.

To my manager, Paul Humphreys: thank you for finding me at the point that you did, when I had just about fallen out of love with this industry. Your work, guidance and, more importantly, your support, is greater than you know. I am so grateful to have such a wonderful friend in you. Let's cling on for dear life for the next part of the story.

To Brenda Combs, thank you for just being so awesome, so organised and always dressed so bloody well.

To Sarah Hornsley, my fierce book agent, for helping me work out why I wanted to write this book and for finding it such a wonderful home.

339

PROCESS

To Susannah Otter, Sophie Nevrkla, Lucy Tirahan and the team at Bonnier for a beautifully (and unexpectedly) smooth editing process. I have been so very lucky to have such powerful women on board with me.

To Dominic Crossley, thank you for all of the times you have saved my day.

To Ciara for your care and selflessness, you made a world of difference.

To Ella, just for being you.

To Alba and Wilf for being the weirdest and most excellent niece and nephew, and for teaching me a new kind of love.

To Steven, my best friend, I know you can't read this, but I hope you know how many times you saved my life. Thank you for being beside me every step of the way.

To Josh, for always being there, through the rough and the smooth. My anchor.

To Evangeline, for all of the love and for reassuring me every time I felt overwhelmed.

To The Sprags, the fanbase that I ADORE. You literally rock my world. Always with you.

Thank you to James North, Jonny Petch, Tim Bates and the team at PFD.

Thank you to Steve Tilley, Steve Zapp, and Chris Rockliffe.

And lastly, thank you to every single person who has ever been kind to me – you make the world a better place.